THE NORTHERN IRELAND QUESTION
IN BRITISH POLITICS

CONTEMPORARY HISTORY IN CONTEXT SERIES
Published in association with the Institute of Contemporary British History
General Editor: Peter Catterall

Other titles include:

Harriet Jones and Michael David Kandiah (*editors*)
THE MYTH OF CONSENSUS?

Wolfgang Kaiser
USING EUROPE, ABUSING THE EUROPEANS: Britain and European Unity, 1945–63

Paul Sharp
THATCHER'S DIPLOMACY: An Assessment of her International Statesmanship and Contribution to British Foreign Policy

The Northern Ireland Question in British Politics

Edited by

Peter Catterall

Director, Institute of Contemporary British History, and
Visiting Lecturer in History, Queen Mary and Westfield College
University of London

and

Sean McDougall

Research Fellow, Institute of Contemporary British History

First published in Great Britain 1996 by
MACMILLAN PRESS LTD
Houndmills, Basingstoke, Hampshire RG21 6XS
and London
Companies and representatives
throughout the world

A catalogue record for this book is available
from the British Library.

ISBN 0–333–63866–2 hardcover
ISBN 0–333–63867–0 paperback

 First published in the United States of America 1996 by
ST. MARTIN'S PRESS, INC.,
Scholarly and Reference Division,
175 Fifth Avenue,
New York, N.Y. 10010

ISBN 0–312–12982–3

Library of Congress Cataloging-in-Publication Data
The Northern Ireland question in British politics / edited by Peter
Catterall and Sean McDougall.
p.   cm.
Includes bibliographical references and index.
ISBN 0–312–12982–3 (cloth)
1. Northern Ireland—Politics and government.   2. Great Britain–
–Foreign relations—Ireland.   3. Ireland—Foreign relations—Great
Britain.   4. Great Britain—Politics and government.   5. Irish
question.   I. Catterall, Peter, 1961–   .   II. McDougall, Sean.
DA990.U46N672   1996
941.6082—dc20   95–53126
                                                                            CIP

---

10   9   8   7   6   5   4   3   2   1
05   04   03   02   01   00   99   98   97   96

Printed in Great Britain by
Ipswich Book Co Ltd, Ipswich, Suffolk

Contents

List of Tables and Figures

Tables

Figures

A Note on Nomenclature

As anyone who has ever struggled to make a point in front of a 'mixed' Northern Irish audience will know, language has, to some extent, become a test of faith and allegiance. The subtleties of 'derry/Derry/Londonderry replicate themselves in every sphere of the vocabulary, such that (it seems) no scholarly work is now complete without a page setting out particular reasons for choosing to capitalise this and/or abbreviate that. Though the fashion can claim a lineage stretching back to the 1930s and the editorial policy of T. W. Moody and R. Dudley Edwards in the pages of *Irish Historical Studies*, scholars now seem to be divided into three distinct camps. One group, by far the largest, and represented here by J. J. Lee, attempt to assert their impartiality by using a plethora of rival and mostly inaccurate terms – 'Ulster', 'the province', 'the North' – 'as stylistic convenience dictates'.[1] This might be summed up as an attempt to appear objective by offending all sides in equal measure. A second, more recent and therefore smaller, group is typified by David Miller, the media sociologist. For him, even terms such as 'the United Kingdom' are problematic, as inevitably their usage tends to favour the *status quo* over the alternatives.[2] Terms such as 'Northern Ireland', then, cannot be said to be legitimate just because they have the force of law. The problem with this approach, however, is that it just forces scholars to choose between rival sets of nomenclature, delegitimising one without actually providing an alternative that can be said to be better. Furthermore, theory aside, abandonment of state or legal terms just makes it more difficult to describe present realities accurately, regardless of their legitimacy. Taken in conjunction with the capitalisation problem, then, it is no wonder that anxious academics soon find themselves conforming to a third pattern by making up rules as they go along. Thus 'British government' often sits next to 'Conservative Party' on the page: not something to lose sleep over, perhaps, until one contemplates the spectacle of 'Ulster unionist Party'. Quite apart from giving editors nightmares, the decision not to follow the rules almost inevitably leads to misunderstanding, as the phrase 'I'm for the union' shows.

In putting together this collection, then, sensitivities to nomenclature – and particularly the fact that many people who should simply do not care about it – have been appraised, and an editorial decision made to choose nomenclature and capitalisation with regard to the grammatical and punctuational rules of the English language rather than any political criteria. Terms such as 'unionist', 'government' and 'party' appear capitalised when they operate as proper nouns, i.e. when they describe an institution or recognised entity, even in abbreviation. When 'Unionist' appears capitalised and 'nationalist' not, it is because the views of a political party and a general community are being juxtaposed, not because one is being elevated above the other. Non English-language words have been italicised, as in *agent provocateur* and, though some might find it odd, *Sinn Féin* (who prefer its use in Irish to the English translation, 'Ourselves Alone'). 'Eire' has been eschewed in favour of 'Ireland' as it has no validity anywhere other than in a British court ('*Éire*', of course, is valid everywhere as the Irish-language name of the state).

As for 'derry/Derry/Londonderry . . . the temptation (as ever) was to refer to 'Stroke City', but in the end the editors chose to use Londonderry as the name of the county and the city, if only because the use of 'Derry City, County Londonderry' is still prescriptive rather than descriptive. This means that, as the correct term of reference for its local authority has been 'Derry City Council, Londonderry' since 1984, the authority has to be described using several different but successive titles, depending on which period is under consideration: lest the reader think this strange or inconsistent it is, however, worth pointing out that this is no more than what happens when Southern Ireland, the Irish Free State and Ireland are under discussion. We of course apologise for any lapses from this approach that have nevertheless survived proof-reading.

None of this, however, solves the vexed problem of what to call the region which is the focus for these essays. Here, the editorial decision was to use 'Northern Ireland', which, unlike any other term, is recognised in British, European and Irish law as the name of a delimited, precisely defined territory (which may or may not be legitimate). Lest it be argued that this disadvantages extra-legal nomenclature (!), the editors humbly point out that it is also recognised by every party to the dispute within the region, including loyalist and republican paramilitaries, though the latter are more concerned to have it removed from British statute books than to promote its use. In the meantime, as scholars have a duty to relate their subject-matter to the audience as accurately as possible, 'Northern Ireland' also has the merit of being less ambiguous than 'the North' and 'the province', and less partisan than 'the Six Counties' or 'Ulster'. In the absence of a term commanding even more widespread acceptance, it survives as the most accurate description of the *status quo* (which may or may not be valid), and on that basis the editors commend it to the academy.

NOTES

1. J. J. Lee, *Ireland, 1912–85* (Cambridge: Cambridge University Press, 1989), p. xxi.
2. D. Miller, *Don't Mention the War: Northern Ireland, Propaganda and the Media* (London: Pluto, 1994), p. 168.

Acknowledgements

The essays in this collection would never have been brought together if John Ramsden had not had the inspiration to organise a conference on this theme at Queen Mary and Westfield College, London, in March 1994. We would like to thank the Institute of Contemporary British History and the History Department at Queen Mary and Westfield College for supporting this conference. Thereafter, many individuals and bodies provided timely and helpful assistance. In particular, the editors wish to acknowledge the help provided by Gráinne Twomey, our commissioning editor at Macmillan. Malcolm Kendall and Alan Reed, of the University of Birmingham's Academic Computing Service, were extremely patient despite numerous requests for technical assistance. The editors also wish to thank the contributors, most of whom took part in the original conference, for their willingness to make changes in line with 'macro' requirements. Our thanks, too, to Christine Catterall for hosting the odd editorial conference and keeping Rebecca and Alexander occupied whilst their grave discussions took place.

Finally, grateful acknowledgement is given to successive British Governments for ensuring that this book found a place on the shelves. If it had not been for the failure of their efforts to isolate Northern Ireland over the last three-quarters of a century there would have been nothing to discuss.

PETER CATTERALL
SEAN McDOUGALL

Abbreviations

BBC	British Broadcasting Corporation
BLP	British Labour Party
CDU	Campaign for Democracy in Ulster
CSJNI	Campaign for Social Justice in Northern Ireland
DUP	Democratic Unionist Party
GOC	General Officer Commanding
IBA	Independent Broadcasting Authority
ICBH	Institute of Contemporary British History
ICJP	Irish Commission for Justice and Peace
ILP	Independent Labour Party
IrLP	Irish Labour Party
INLA	Irish National Liberation Army
IRA	Irish Republican Army
IRSP	Irish Republican Socialist Party
ITGWU	Irish Transport and General Workers' Union
ITUC	Irish Trade Union Congress
LP(NI)	Labour Party (Northern Ireland)
LRC	Labour Representation Committee
NICRA	Northern Ireland Civil Rights Association
NILP	Northern Ireland Labour Party
NIO	Northern Ireland Office
NRM	Northern Resistance Movement
OIRA	Official Irish Republican Army
PD	People's Democracy
PIRA	Provisional Irish Republican Army
PTA	Prevention of Terrorism Act
RUC	Royal Ulster Constabulary
SDLP	Social Democratic and Labour Party
TUC	Trade Union Congress
UDA	Ulster Defence Association
UDR	Ulster Defence Regiment
UIDA	Ulster Industry Development Association
USC	Ulster Special Constabulary
UTDA	Ulster Tourist Development Association
UUC	Ulster Unionist Council
UUP	Ulster Unionist Party
UUUC	United Ulster Unionist Council
UWC	Ulster Workers' Council

Notes on the Contributors

Brian Barton is currently Senior Research Fellow in the Politics Department, Queen's University, Belfast. His extensive publications on the history and politics of Northern Ireland include *Brookeborough: The Making of a Prime Minister* (1988) and *The Blitz: Belfast in the War Years* (1989). He is currently working on the second volume of his biography of Lord Brookeborough, to cover the years 1943–73

Dave Bloomfield is an affiliate of the Centre for International Affairs at Harvard University. He is the recipient of an award from the United States Institute for Peace for his research into the Brooke initiative. Originally from Belfast, he was previously a researcher in the Department of Peace Studies, University of Bradford.

D. George Boyce is Professor in the Department of Politics, University of Wales, Swansea. Among his most recent publications are *Political Thought in Ireland from the Seventeenth Century to the Present Day* (with R. Eccleshall and V. Geoghegan, 1994) and a third edition of *Nationalism in Ireland* with a chapter covering the most recent developments. He is at present working on a study of political ideas in eighteenth-century Ireland.

Peter Catterall is Director of the Institute of Contemporary British History, Visiting Lecturer in History at Queen Mary and Westfield College, London and Honorary Research Fellow of the Institute of Historical Research. He is editor or co-editor of *Contemporary Britain: An Annual Review*, *Contemporary British History* and *Modern History Review*. He is currently working on a study of the British Cabinet Committee system after 1945.

W. Harvey Cox has lectured in politics at Liverpool University since 1966, where he is now Deputy Director of the Institute of Irish Studies. He was born in Northern Ireland and was educated at the Royal Belfast Academical Institution, Trinity College, Dublin and the London School of Economics. The author of two books on urban politics in Britain, his articles on the Northern Ireland question have appeared in *Parliamentary Affairs*, *Government and Opposition*, *Parliamentary*

Brief and elsewhere, and he has broadcast frequently on the local radio network.

Terry Cradden is Head of the School of Commerce and International Business Studies at Magee College, University of Ulster. From a political science background, he is now an industrial relations specialist, and is author of *Trade Unionism, Socialism and Partition: The Labour Movement in Northern Ireland 1939–53* (1993).

James Goodman is a researcher in the Faculty of Social Sciences at the Open University, where he is working on the impact of the European Union on the conflict in Northern Ireland.

Maeve Lankford completed a PhD in the Department of Peace Studies, University of Bradford. From Cork in the Republic of Ireland, she is currently Equal Opportunities Administrator at the University of Bradford.

Sean McDougall is Research Fellow at the Institute of Contemporary British History, where he is cataloguing the papers of Lord Howe of Aberavon. He has recently completed his PhD thesis on 'State Propaganda in Northern Ireland 1921–56, and has broadcast on Northern Ireland issues on local radio.

Philip Norton is Professor of Politics and Director of the Centre for Legislative Studies at the University of Hull. His recent publications include *The British Polity* (3rd edn, 1994), *Does Parliament Matter?* (1993) and *Parliamentary Questions* (ed. with Mark Franklin 1993).

Brendan O'Duffy is Tutorial Fellow in Comparative Politics at the London School of Economics and Political Science. He has published articles on electoral systems and party competition, public perceptions of member states within the European Union and is currently finishing his PhD, entitled 'Violent Politics: A Theoretical and Empirical Analysis of Two Centuries of Political Violence in Ireland'.

Michael von Tangen Page is a researcher in penal policy regarding political violence in Western Europe. Originally from a historical background, he is now at the Department of Peace Studies, University of Bradford.

Peter Rose was a parliamentary lobby correspondent for nearly twenty years. He now teaches in the History Department, Queen Mary and Westfield College, where he is researching into the Labour Government's policy in Northern Ireland from 1964 to August 1969.

Howard Smith is Senior Lecturer in Broadcasting at the Institute of Communications Studies, University of Leeds. He was a radio and television producer at the BBC for more than twenty-five years. In 1972 he produced the first networked history of Ireland on British television.

1 Introduction: Northern Ireland in British Politics

Peter Catterall and Sean McDougall

In 1991 Peter Brooke, then Secretary of State for Northern Ireland, talked of trying to establish a three-stranded negotiation process on the future of Northern Ireland: between unionists and nationalists within Northern Ireland, between North and South on the island of Ireland and between the British and Irish Governments. This formulation reflected some of the many dimensions there are to the Northern Ireland question. There was, however, another dimension – one which Brooke chose to ignore and which has generally been under-explored in the voluminous literature on Northern Ireland. It is this fourth strand, that between the people of Northern Ireland and the Government of the United Kingdom, which is the focus of this study.

It is important here to underline the nature of our enquiry. In this collection, it is not our object to examine a British dimension to Northern Ireland politics. Our concern is instead the role of, one might almost say the intrusion of, Northern Ireland in British politics despite continued efforts on the part of successive Governments to keep it off the agenda. Unionists might protest that Northern Ireland is British and its affairs are therefore necessarily the very stuff of British politics. Yet, as far as most of the players in British politics are concerned, this is only true to a limited extent. British political parties, for instance, may have sister organisations in Northern Ireland. And the Unionists took the Tory whip in the Commons until the early 1970s. But, with the exception of the Conservatives (and, even then, only since 1989), British parties have been reluctant to take the integrationist step of establishing themselves across the Irish Sea. This is true even of the Liberal Democrats, led by 'Paddy' Ashdown, an Ulsterman. Labour, indeed, has faced the other way since the 1970s, pointing would-be supporters to the explicitly nationalist SDLP.

Nor has the mainland electorate shown a great deal more interest in Northern Ireland. Indeed, opinion polls during the Second World War demonstrated the considerable uncertainty in electors' minds as to whether Northern Ireland was actually part of the United Kingdom.[1] This lack of salience can also be illustrated by reference to general elections.

The object as far as possible, and maintained with decreasing success was to keep Northern Ireland *out* of British politics. Even after an election campaign in 1964, in which Harold Wilson had talked of attempting to improve civil rights for Catholics in Northern Ireland, this attitude persisted; and within five years, left to itself, Northern Ireland had reached its critical mass.

Despite this reluctance to intervene, British attitudes have often been assumed, especially by republicans, to be a key factor in the Northern Ireland problem. The PIRA campaign was indeed predicated upon this assumption: the stated objective of their terrorism was to win British withdrawal from Northern Ireland. Yet this massively over-simplifies the situation, and particularly the position of unionists. For Northern Ireland was at least as much the creation of unionists as of the British Government, and for its first fifty years it was they who ruled it. Unionists had demonstrated the unworkable (because it made no provision for the resistance to rule from Dublin of a large and territorially compact Protestant minority) nature of Gladstone's initial Home Rule proposals in 1886, *before* their cause was taken up by Gladstone's Conservative opponents. And it was mostly because the Irish question held the balance of power that it became the fissure between the two main political parties of the period: when it began to make stable government less rather than more likely it was swiftly dropped in favour of a remarkably stable, and thoroughly undemocratic, bipartisan approach.

Partition, the object of republican opprobrium, remained firmly off the agenda in the Edwardian period, except for a few Liberal Unionist politicians who favoured trying to solve Anglo-Irish tensions by subsuming them in a general federalisation of the United Kingdom – if not the empire.[6] There was still no special provision for the North in the Liberals' third Home Rule Bill in 1912. That Home Rule eventually involved the creation of a separate polity in Northern Ireland was thus a concession to the Unionists and their Conservative supporters in the changed circumstances of the 1915–22 Coalition Government (and concurrent events in the South), rather than a Government imposition.

This created not so much 'British' rule as unionist rule in Northern Ireland. Northern Ireland was 'British' because a local majority wanted it to be. The fledgling statelet faced the difficulty that a substantial minority within its borders did not recognise its legitimacy, and Unionists sought to contain the problem by discriminating against these 'enemies' of the constitution. As long as any Government of Northern Ireland was managing and containing the situation, however, British Governments were reluctant to intervene.[7] Instead, for most of the next

half century, the creation of Northern Ireland as a devolved polity helped
to quarantine Irish issues, which had so frequently distracted Parliament in the past.

British policy was founded upon the recognition that unionists could
not be coerced into a united Ireland, a recognition also accorded by
William Cosgrave, the first Prime Minister of the Irish Free State, in
1922. During and after the Second World War there was also gratitude, widespread even in the traditionally anti-partition Labour Party,
for the support of Northern Ireland in contrast to the neutrality of its
Southern neighbour. But it remained the case for most Governments
most of the time that unionists saw themselves as British, not that
British Governments saw themselves as unionist – at least not with
regard to Northern Ireland. The two did not share the same position,
nor have they ever done. As this book shows, Unionist anxieties about
the thrust of British policy are not new, even if they have become
more explicit since the 1985 Anglo-Irish Agreement.

So what was and is British policy? Its nature has become clearer as
British policy has been ever more publicly articulated in recent years,
culminating in the Downing Street Declaration of 15 December 1993.
The Declaration stated that the British Government has 'no selfish strategic or economic interest in Northern Ireland', reiterating Peter Brooke's
1990 comments. This was part of a strategy of persuading the PIRA to
lay down its arms by making it clear that it was not the British Government which stood in the way of its ambitions, and that the removal of
the British presence would not automatically guarantee a harmonious
united Ireland.

However, this is not to gainsay that a keen appreciation of the strategic importance of Ireland was a historic reason for the British presence there, not least in the passing of the 1800 Act of Union. Strategic
concerns also shaped British policy during and in the aftermath of the
Second World War, prompting them to maintain extra divisions in
Northern Ireland in case they should need to be rushed to the south in
the event of a German invasion. But, except in such emergencies, British
Governments have not tended to see Northern Ireland as a major strategic asset. Nor has it been an economic one; especially since the Second World War Northern Ireland has instead been a steady drain on
the British Exchequer.

Brooke's comments then, were statements of fact. Uncomfortable as
they may have been to unionists, with their overtones of British disengagement, they were also statements of what had long been true. Indeed, comments similar to Brooke's were made by Lloyd George at

the time of the setting up of Northern Ireland. Its place in the United Kingdom, reiterated in the 1949 Ireland Act and since, was guaranteed because this remained the will of the majority of its population. The sole role of the British, as Peter Brooke underlined, 'was to protect the validity of the ballot box'.[8] Withdrawal in such circumstances is not, then, the panacea assumed either by Northern republicans or, traditionally, citizens of the Republic; nor is it likely, given the attitudes of the majority, to provide a solution. The British, as Michael Lillis, a Dublin civil servant and one of the chief architects of the Anglo-Irish Agreement, stressed, neither could nor should exercise such an option.[9]

They are instead saddled with the unpleasant ultimate responsibility for the rule of law in a territory where no state form commands the allegiance of all communities. This responsibility is based upon the wish of the majority to remain part of the United Kingdom, and was exercised at first at arm's length through the majority itself in the form of the unionist state. The collapsing legitimacy of the unionist state (and the virtual collapse of the RUC) in the early 1970s meant, however, that subsequently it had to be discharged more directly. Faced with the choice of allowing a discredited state to take control of the military or of becoming involved, British Ministers, reluctant as always, chose to end Stormont and impose direct rule in Northern Ireland.[10]

This changed the circumstances in which British policy operated and brought the topic of Northern Ireland more clearly into the ambit of British politics. The thrust of policy remained, however, to externalise the problem from British politics. Integration, particularly, was in the politician's equivalent of the sphere of deviance. Thus, while this option found increasing favour within the UUP throughout the 1980s, Conservative Governments pressed consistently for devolution. That they still do so while opposing the same measure for Scotland is testimony to the fear which the region engenders in fans of stable government. Instead, there has been a repeated search for a replacement for the old Government of Northern Ireland, but one which has much greater legitimacy across the communities of Northern Ireland. Fourth-strand options, including integration and the continuance of direct rule (oddly enough, both communities' second preference at the time of writing) do not form part of this agenda.

So how can the British Government safeguard the peace while abandoning control of Northern Ireland's governance? Firstly, there has been an effort to build consensus in Northern Ireland itself by forcing the political representatives of the various communities to share power. This policy, of course, is based on the view that it is only through the building of such consensus that a wider solution to the inter-communal conflicts of Northern Ireland can emerge. A major obstacle to the creation of consensus, however, is that these communities feel loyalties to two different states (and some only to themselves). The second strand in policy has therefore been the involvement of the British *and* Irish Governments in the facilitation of the consensus-building process, with the intention of de-legitimising the entrenched positions of both the nationalist and unionist communities.

In particular, the aim is to marginalise terrorists by undermining their legitimacy and by making clear that the Northern Ireland problem has to be solved by agreement between its communities. This has meant that both Governments have had to abandon the inflexible positions of the past. The 1985 Anglo-Irish Agreement, for instance, sought to undermine the electoral success enjoyed by the PIRA's political wing in the wake of the mishandling by the British of the 1981 hunger strikes. The PIRA's legitimacy essentially rested on the notion that it was fighting to expel an occupying power. The Agreement demonstrated that it was not that simple: instead, the fact that Northern Ireland is in the United Kingdom as a result of the wishes of the majority of its people was made still more explicit. The difference from previous formulations was that under Article 1(c) it was also made clear that if the view of the majority changed the British Government would accept this. This publicly established for the first time that whilst the British were willing to retain Northern Ireland as long as it wanted them, they were also prepared to leave.

This shift in declaratory policy caused much offence to unionists, of course. To them the British were making great concessions to the nationalist position, not only through 1(c), but also through accepting the Republic's involvement in areas such as security and criminal justice. But there was nothing new in a British preparedness to contemplate such moves, nor their further development, including the North–South body with executive and co-ordinating powers envisaged in the 1995 Joint Framework Document. A Council of Ireland on which both North and South would be represented had been put forward in the 1920 Government of Ireland Act as a means of giving the South a semblance of the Irish unity it desired whilst acknowledging unionist sentiment. It was also central to the operation of the short-lived Sunningdale Agreement. Without acceptance of the Council idea, however, the British were simply left with the will of the majority in the unionist state, until Stormont's demise allowed a renewed search for cross-border agreement to occur.

But crucially, the Anglo-Irish Agreement has brought about a shift in the declaratory policy of the Republic too. The British *and* Irish Governments signed up for Article 1(c), despite the judicial niceties and the 'constitutional imperative' of Articles 2 and 3 of the Irish constitution. This marked a formal acceptance, for the first time, by an Irish Government of the unionist position. The cultural denial of the significance of unionists had always been most acute in *Fianna Fáil*, but with the Downing Street Declaration a *Fianna Fáil* Prime Minister publicly reached the same conclusion. More recently, a *Fine Gael* Prime Minister described the Joint Framework Document as a guarantee that there could never be a united Ireland without the consent of a majority in Northern Ireland. This belated legitimisation of partition, and more importantly, of the social and political bases of partition, marked a major shift in the Irish Government's declaratory policy, much greater than any shifts made by the British Government at the time. It is the kind of progressive thinking which helps to keep loyalist terrorism at bay. Indeed, it made it possible at last to make progress on the long-stalled objective of promoting North–South co-operation.

Such an arrangement is, of course, a fudge. As Robert Rhodes James said of the 1920 Act: 'It was a good example of Lloyd George's skill at apparently placating all sides; apart from the Ulstermen, it placated nobody'.[11] But in a situation where political objectives are so diametrically opposed such proposals, and successors down to the Joint Framework Document, mark an attempt to substitute a generally acceptable compromise. A united Ireland, given the unionist viewpoint, is impossible; an agreed Ireland remains, however, a possibility. As the Downing Street Declaration defined this policy:

> The role of the British Government will be to encourage, facilitate and enable the achievement of such agreement over a period through a process of dialogue and co-operation based on full respect for the rights and identities of both traditions in Ireland.

But this cannot be seen as a new departure: instead, it makes clear the *continuities* in British policy in Northern Ireland. It is the Irish, far more than the British, Government that has shifted its ground since 1985. The British position has always been based upon the consent of the majority in the North. The Republic has only recently caught up.

There have, of course, been changes in the nuances of British declaratory policy. Whilst the devolved government survived, Northern Ireland issues were indeed marginalised as much as possible in British politics. Direct rule changed that. As the only state which could now speak for Northern Ireland, declaratory policy has had to be increasingly articulated. But all this has done is to make publicly ever clearer what has always been implicit; that the status of Northern Ireland as part of the United Kingdom rests upon the wishes of the majority of its population. What the Anglo-Irish Agreement and subsequent declarations have made explicit is that this is now the only basis for this status. But they have also made clear that this status will only change if the view of the majority changes.

As John Hume told *Sinn Féin*'s leader, Gerry Adams, during their first series of talks, the problem was not that the United Kingdom was attacking or coercing the nationalist community, it was the legitimate opposition of the unionists to being themselves coerced.[12] Earlier in his career Adams, in contrast, had been a great articulator of the traditional republican view that it was the British who were the problem and who had to be forcibly ejected. Although he was the principal architect of the 'armalite and ballot box' strategy which added a political dimension to the republican campaign during and after the hunger strikes, he remained wedded to these old certainties.[13] The development of British declaratory policy in 1985 and after was, however, to undermine, and designed to undermine, such beliefs. Adams – who saw himself as the patient teacher of Irish history – was himself slow to learn, and it took several shifts in policy in the Republic before he began to question his diagnosis of the Northern Ireland problem. When the subsequent PIRA ceasefire announcement came on 31 August 1994 he claimed, as he had to, that the campaign had been worth it. Its main tangible achievement, however, had only been to make explicit in British policy what had always been implicit, what had been clear, if only he had listened, in his clandestine talks with the British Government in 1972.[14] Was it *really* worth so many deaths?

For it was not British policy that was the problem, nor was Britain's expulsion the solution. This could only be arrived at by agreement between the two communities of Northern Ireland itself, agreement which the two Governments have sought to foster since 1985 by explicitly distancing themselves from the communities' irreconcilable national claims. This is in keeping with long-term British policy. So far that policy has failed. If it should ever succeed, however, it will also fulfil another constant of British policy, which is to marginalise as far as possible the place of Northern Ireland in British politics.

NOTES

1. Pilot survey enclosed in letter from R. Clement Wilson to R. Gransden, 14 July 1943, Public Records Office for Northern Ireland: CAB 9F/123/ 17; see also 'English Ignorance of Ulster: Publicity Campaign Plea', *Irish News*, 13 May 1944.
2. Peter Catterall (ed.), *Contemporary Britain: An Annual Review 1992* (Oxford: Blackwell, 1992), p. 1.
3. Winston Churchill, *The World Crisis, Vol. 6: The Aftermath* (London: Thornton Butterworth, 1923), pp. 319–20.
4. See, for instance, Soskice (the Home Secretary) in the debate on the Race Relations Bill, 3 May 1965, *House of Commons Debates*, 5th ser., vol. 711, cols 941–2.
5. Reginald Maudling quoted in M. Hall, *Twenty Years: A Concise Chronology of Events in Northern Ireland, 1968–88* (Newtownabbey: Island, 1988), pp. 22–3.
6. See D. George Boyce (ed.), *The Crisis of British Unionism: The Domestic Political Papers of the Second Earl of Selborne, 1885–1922* (London: The Historians' Press, 1987), pp. xii–xiii.
7. The mere existence of the Northern Ireland state reinforced this reluctance, as Lord Callaghan emphasised at an Institute of Contemporary British History (ICBH) witness seminar on British policy in Northern Ireland 1964–70, held at the European Commission offices, London, 14 January 1992. Lord Callaghan also stressed that in his view it only became politically possible to intervene once a crisis situation had emerged, not least given all the other problems crowding in on the Wilson Government.
8. Quoted on 'Gerry Adams – the man we hate to love', *Panorama*, BBC1, 30 January 1995.
9. *Ibid.*
10. ICBH witness seminar, 'British Policy in Northern Ireland 1971–76', King's College, London, 11 February 1993.
11. Robert Rhodes James, *The British Revolution: British Politics 1880–1939* (London: Methuen, 1978), p. 430.
12. Quoted on 'Gerry Adams – the man we love to hate' (note 8).
13. See, for instance, *An Phoblacht/Republican News*, 17 November 1983.
14. Private information.

2 Northern Ireland: The Origins of the State
D. George Boyce

INTRODUCTION

It is unusual – probably unique – in the history of the British Isles to have the opportunity to observe the making of a new state from the ground upwards. The history of the British Isles is characterised by a slow, evolutionary process, in which continuity blends easily into change and in which sudden breaks seem almost absent. 1688 was seen as a special kind of revolution, one which Edmund Burke characterised as marked more by its links with the past than any break in the past; one that conserved as well as altered the constitutional arrangements of England.[1] If we move forward to 1707 and 1800 – key dates in the making of the United Kingdom – we find again that there is little fundamental alteration in the institutions of state: Scottish and Irish MPs were added to the already existing contingents at Westminster, and the show went on much as before. Scotland kept its kirk and law; the Castle was retained in Dublin to give some sense of continuity, and to act as a social centre for aspiring upwardly mobile people, including in the end Roman Catholics: even the anti-English Cardinal Cullen eventually succumbed to its lure.

But between 1914 and 1922 we have something like a new departure. We see the climactic years of the conflict of nationality in modern Ireland that had reached civil war proportions in 1912–14, that changed its pace and emphasis with the Easter rising of 1916, and culminated in the birth of two states of Ireland in the troubles of 1919–21. We are here concerned with the Northern state, but as always, we cannot ignore the Southern state, nor of course the aims of the United Kingdom Government which had its own perspectives to think about. The Northern Ireland state was the product of this three-cornered conflict. But should we go further back in our search for origins?

A PLACE APART?

We have a choice here; we can take the long view, and characterise
the state as the culmination of a process: from plantation to partition.
The origins of the state might be seen to lie in the plantation of Ulster
in the reign of James VI and I in the early seventeenth century. This
act might be seen as establishing a distinct community in Ireland, a
Protestant or British community, with a destiny of its own, one characterised in a pamphlet written in the late 1960s advertising the Scotch
Irish Historical Foundation as follows:

> These people launched the great Plantation of Ulster which was to
> make the north of Ireland predominantly Scotch Irish and to lead in
> the twentieth century to the emergence of the state of Northern Ireland.[2]

This long view has its advantages. It is of great importance that we
acknowledge the distinctive regional history of the North, a regionalism defined not only by its geographical barriers, its special links with
Scotland, the presence of a large Protestant population – not only by
its key role in the wars of the seventeenth century, the United Irish
rebellion in the late eighteenth century, and its unionism of the late
nineteenth century – but also by the significance of the industrialisa-
tion of the North East, the growth of the city of Belfast, the making of
an urban working class. These all gave its politics a distinctly regional
flavour, and its social structure a sharp differentiation from the rest of
Ireland – which extended even to its rural society, where Ulster cus-
tom, or tenant right, was peculiar to the North (and much demanded
by tenant farmers of the South).[3]

    Yet scholars have rightly reminded us that Ulster politics, though
regional, were not simply a prologue to the unionist–nationalist dichotomy of 1886 onwards. There was Ulster Liberalism, forged by
informal, but important links between Catholics, and Presbyterian and
Methodist dissenters. There was the cross-cutting impact of the land
question, when Presbyterian and Catholic tenant farmers found a common interest in demanding that their rights be secured in hard times.
And there was the wider view: the unionist struggle was, initially, one
to defeat Home Rule for *all* Ireland: a project that did not seem ill-
conceived, given the Conservative/Unionist strength in the House of
Lords, in the constituencies and, after the General Election of June
1886, in the Commons. And when the Home Rule tide receded, as it
did between 1886 and 1891, and after 1894, then again the varied
objectives of the unionist people were exposed – there was no solid,

unchanging Protestant community, except in time of threatened calamity. Even when that time returned in 1912, some unionists were slow to become involved in the formation of the Ulster Volunteer Force (UVF), a force raised to defeat the conspiracy of Asquith and the Home Rulers, and it was not until the spring of 1914 that the Protestants could be seen as a whole people in rebellion against Home Rule.

So the idea of a community, totally united and historically destined, requires qualification at least. Even Andrew Bonar Law, certainly the British politician most in empathy with the Ulster Unionists, saw his primary aim as that of wringing a General Election from Asquith's Government, rather than securing the partition of Ireland. Indeed his Party did not want the partition of Ireland, and Law believed that any scheme of partition – of county option, clean cuts or whatever, would not be acceptable to Redmond, and so must flounder; and Home Rule flounder with it.

But the Ulster dimension was changing. We can note the foundation of the Ulster Unionist Council in 1905 – a body composed of local Unionist associations, the Orange Lodges, MPs, peers and other ex-officio members. We can see the significance of the Ulster Unionist decision in 1911 to set up a 'provisional government' in the event of the Home Rule Bill becoming law, and to draw up a constitution for their government. The signing of the Ulster Covenant, although it pledged Ulster Unionists to defeat Home Rule for the whole of Ireland, was signed on *Ulster* Day. We can note too the growing disillusionment with the politics of Westminster, a growing awareness of the roots of unionism in Ulster, and the power of provincialism.[4] Yet we must also note that the unionists, for all their talk of a provisional government, had no long-term plans to constitute themselves as a separate state – indeed, it is impossible to see how they could have done so, for the means to govern were mostly more shadow than substance. Nor did the Liberals, in their search for a way out of the impasse, seek to create a separate state in the North. Whatever the nature of exclusion, it would be just that – the retaining for some time of certain areas under direct rule. There was talk of a federal reorganisation of the United Kingdom, of some kind of 'Home Rule all round', but this was never a serious option before 1914, or even 1916. These schemes were too radical for the British constitutional way, or were not acceptable by the Home Rulers, or were not demanded by the Ulster Unionists.

THE LLOYD GEORGE SETTLEMENT

It is useful to link these pre-war Home Rule issues with the attempted Lloyd George settlement of 1916, a much neglected episode (because it failed). The last offer that the Liberals made on Ireland, in the summer of 1914, was to exclude those Ulster counties which wished to opt out of the operation of the Home Rule Act for a period of time, but with direct rule from Westminster, and an arrangement whereby Dublin Castle would continue to oversee the administration of the excluded areas.[5] After the Easter Rising Lloyd George proposed the exclusion of six counties, under direct rule, with the whole question of the role of the excluded area to be settled at some future date. Meanwhile, Lloyd George assured Sir Edward Carson that 'we must make it clear that at the end of the provisional period Ulster does not, whether she wills it or not, merge in the rest of Ireland'. Making it clear was what Lloyd George was of course anxious not to do. But it is important to note nationalist ambiguity also. When Asquith was asked about the eventual intention with regard to the excluded counties, he replied: 'They could not be included without a Bill.' And yet this did not elicit from the Irish Nationalists a demand for a specific guarantee that partition would not be permanent. A letter from Captain W. H. Owen, Lloyd George's 'scout' in Dublin, helps explain the enigma. Owen had discussed the matter with Joseph Devlin (leader of the Nationalists in the excluded area, and therefore a man to whom partition was of vital importance):

> I asked him whether he thought it advisable that any fresh statement of the proposal should be made in the House of Commons before Friday. He said 'no' because Sir Edward Carson might think it his duty to place a fresh interpretation upon them, and so lead the Ulster Nationalists to believe that their exclusion was in fact permanent. This would prevent their accepting the proposals on Friday [i.e. at a meeting of the Ulster Nationalists in Belfast on 23 June to discuss the Lloyd George plan]. *As to the apparent difference of opinion between Mr Redmond and Sir Edward Carson whether exclusion is permanent or temporary, he thinks that this is more apparent than real, that it actually represents two legitimate views of the same proposal, and may easily be cleared up afterwards.*[6]

Redmond needed his parliament; the Ulster question could be left to another day. By 1916, therefore, some elements of an Ulster settlement had emerged – a six-county area (accepted by the Ulster Unionists and the Irish Nationalists); direct rule from London (accepted by both); a provisional period (accepted by both) but with a final resolution still in dispute.

But let us think of the ideas that lay behind these political moves. Lloyd George, when he took up the issue again in 1917, referred in March to the existence of two nations in Ireland; there was in the North-East corner, he said, a population 'as alien in blood, in religious faith, in traditions, in outlook – as alien from the rest of Ireland in this respect as the inhabitants of Fife or Aberdeen.'[7] Yet Ulster Unionists themselves did not like to deploy the two nations theory. Sir James Craig liked to refer to Ulster Unionists' 'friends' in Canada, 'our friends in the empire'. This was not unlike Joseph Chamberlain's concept of the British as an imperial nation. Ulster was for unionists an 'imperial province', not in the sense that it was a colony, but in the opposite sense – that it was part of a wider British community, in the United Kingdom, in the Empire.[8] It was not the property of the British Government to dispose of as it wished, but it was a permanent and enduring part of the wider imperial nation, of which Britain, and not merely England, formed a part. Ulster Unionists presented themselves as modern, progressive, industrial, as distinct from rural, backward Ireland. Ulster Unionists were therefore British and imperial; nationalist Ireland was non-British and marginal to the destiny of the United Kingdom, a drag on the wheels, a brake on its manifest destiny.

And yet they ended up with a state. I want to explain this, but also explore some less discussed aspects of this – notably the period when the Ulster Unionists were trying to establish their state in the teeth of opposition, not only from nationalists, but in the face of a lukewarm British Government; for such an exploration helps explain the subsequent history of Northern Ireland.

THE BRITISH PERSPECTIVE

Between 1916 and 1918 British Governments were struggling to reestablish their authority in Ireland, and trying to keep events under control. The Irish convention of 1917–18 is the exception, when the Government handed the job over to Irishmen of various persuasions to see if they could find common ground themselves (they could not). The Government had, of course, other problems, not least the winning of the war. And its last efforts in the spring of 1918 to combine military conscription in Ireland with Home Rule, and make that compatible with a federal United Kingdom, has all the marks of desperation. Yet return to the issue they must, if only because after the peace treaties were signed, then the long standing Home Rule Act which received the royal assent in September 1914 must come into operation, and yet clearly the Irish situation had moved well beyond this. How far it had moved depended not only on the political mood in Great Britain and Ireland, but on the new post-war world, with its slogan, the rights of small nations.

It was against this background that the Government considered the options that lay before it in 1919. The protagonists now stood in a very different relationship to each other than they did in 1886 or even 1914. Ulster's unionists, for their part, had a chequered history in the battle over Home Rule. They were in 1886 a minority community, dismissed by Gladstone as rather like the Scottish Highlanders, certainly a community, but not that different from the rest of the nation, and rightfully belonging to it as part of one unit. By 1914 they had established their claim to be considered a very distinct minority, yet this claim was based on their view that they were not an Irish minority, but a part of a British *majority*, and they demanded that their citizens' rights to remain part of this majority be respected. After 1916 they were in a more favourable position, since 1916 was a blow aimed at the British war effort. Yet by 1917 they were being seen as something of an obstacle to the settlement that the war effort needed. It was not hard for the British press to cry that 'Ulster blocks the way'. However, they had the advantage of having the support in 1918 of the Conservative constituencies for their safeguarding, as a Central Office survey revealed.[9] In the December 1918 General Election Lloyd George proclaimed that 'in accordance with the pledge which has been given by me in the past' he would 'support no settlement which would involve the forcible coercion of Ulster'.[10]

But this must be set against the angry reaction in Great Britain to Sir Edward Carson's threat in July 1919 that if any attempt were made to take away the rights of the Ulster people he would call out the UVF. One Conservative MP called his loyalty 'the loyalty of Shylock'. Lloyd George confided to C.P. Scott that Carson had alienated a good deal of Conservative sympathy.[11] We can see again that unease between Ulster Unionists and the Conservative Party that Law had managed to conceal, but never quite banish, in his pre-war leadership of the Party.

This, however, is not the main point. It is vital to stress the key changes that had overtaken British politics since 1914. There had been a notion then that politicians should get together and apply a problem-solving method to intractable questions like Ireland, and not only Ireland. The party system then was too strong to allow this, if ever it was a serious proposal. But by 1918 the facts of political life and the mood were different. The war had seen the making of coalition politics and its continuation in the General Election of 1918. By 1919 a non-partisan approach to Ireland was an idea whose time had come, though the Conservative predominance in the coalition meant that any settlement plan had to be one that satisfied the Tory rank and file. But this was largely a new Tory rank and file, impatient to put behind them the wilderness years of their party between 1906 and 1915, and anxious that the old rage of party should not stand between the Party and the needs of modernization.

PLANNING PARTITION

And so we have the spectacle of unionist stalwarts, Law and Walter Long, sitting in the Cabinet's Irish Committee and acknowledging that a balance must be struck between unionism and nationalism. A special Ulster Committee in a Dublin parliament was rejected because such an arrangement 'would block and stultify the work of the Irish Government and parliament' without enabling the Ulster committee to 'develop Ulster itself'. The Cabinet Committee also rejected any kind of artificial over-representation of unionist areas because this would not survive 'public and parliamentary criticism in view of the great advance of democratic sentiment and practice since 1914'. County option was deemed to be unworkable. A plebiscite was rejected too, for this would only inflame passions further and partition Ireland more in spirit. But the simple exclusion of Ulster, or part of it, with direct rule from Westminster, was rejected, since this would mean the retention of British authority in Ireland, and 'if it is retained anywhere in Ireland the opponents of Great Britain will be able to say either that Great Britain is ruling nationalist majorities against their will, or that it is giving active support to Ulster in its refusal to unite with the rest of Ireland'. The committee recommended the establishment of two parliaments in Ireland, each with powers of Home Rule similar to those of the 1914 Act, but with a Council of Ireland to consider matters of common concern, whose powers might be enlarged with the agreement of the two parliaments. Ulster had the right to self-determination, but not to the extent that she could determine herself to remain an integral part of the United Kingdom.[12]

Once this proposal was approved, the area to be placed under the Northern parliament became a matter of vital concern. If the Government was sincere in its desire to minimise the partitionist implications of its decision, then a nine-county state would be the appropriate area. And, here again, the Committee, with Law and Long present, did recommend that the state consist of the whole province of Ulster, since this would indeed facilitate the reunification of Ireland. This recommendation was accepted, subject to what the Ulster Unionists might have to say about it, when seen, as proposed, by members of the Government.[13]

The second issue on which the Ulster Unionists must be consulted was an equally vital one: the transfer of powers from the Westminster Parliament to the Home Rule Parliament. Long's committee was anxious that the two parliaments be encouraged to make proper use of the Council of Ireland in order to move closer to the desired aim of a union of the whole of Ireland under a single legislature. Therefore, it recommended withholding certain services which would be transferred if and when the two Irish Home Rule entities achieved the desired objective – a single legislature. Long originally proposed holding back services which it would be undesirable to partition: agriculture, technical education, old age pensions, unemployment insurance, health insurance, labour exchanges. The Council of Ireland would advise the British Government on the administration of these services for one year, at the end of which they would be partitioned and transferred, unless both Irish Governments in the meantime requested their transfer to the Council of Ireland. This was regarded as a powerful incentive to Irish unity. But Sir James Craig pressed strongly for a reassessment of this policy. The Committee, then, from December 1919 began to change its tack, acknowledging that it was impressed with the argument that not enough powers had been transferred to the two parliaments, and so these services were partitioned.[14]

Craig and his fellow Unionists did not vote for the Government of Ireland Act; nevertheless, they knew what they wanted: six counties and an early transfer of services. Hugh T. Barrie wrote to the editor of the *Spectator*, St Loe Strachey, as early as April 1918, that:

> Privately, we fully share your view of preference for the six counties exclusion, rather than the whole province exclusion, but tactically we preferred to claim the whole province during the Convention proceedings. We shall be very content a little later, if we can get exclusion for the six counties.[15]

This was long before the idea of a six-county state emerged; but the Unionists knew what area they thought they could control, and when they were presented with the Government of Ireland Act in 1920, they were determined not to accept territory that would prove beyond their capacity to govern. The Government's eventual decision to opt for six counties was not merely a concession to the Unionists; it must be seen against the predicament in the rest of Ireland, where the war of the Irish Republican Army (IRA) and the Black and Tans was spreading. The Government could not hope for much from nationalist Ireland by way of a response to its policy; therefore it did not make sense to open a second front against the Ulster Unionists over the question of area. And, as Lloyd George put it to his secretary, Philip Kerr, it would 'take Ulster out of the Irish question which it had blocked for a generation'. To have created a nine-county Northern Ireland, Lloyd George told Philip Kerr, would have 'reproduced on a small scale the same difficulty which Ireland as a whole had presented to us on a great scale. It would have given her a disturbed and irreconcilable minority only to be ruled by force.' And to have arrived at a more exact delineation, dividing Tyrone and Fermanagh, would have required a religious census which was highly undesirable.[16] Or, as the Cabinet put it more bluntly, it 'would be difficult for the government to force through a scheme which was unacceptable both to their friends and to their critics.'[17]

Craig possessed another advantage over the Nationalists. *Sinn Féin* had absented itself from Westminster after the 1918 election. This was in accordance with Arthur Griffith's 'Hungarian policy'; but it was to prove a costly choice. Craig and his Unionists were on the spot, and able to negotiate some important concessions which reduced the pan-Irish aspects of Government policy. In February 1920 they demanded, and got, a separate judiciary. In September 1920 Craig argued strongly for the formation of a local volunteer force, based on the pre-war UVF, to counteract the IRA offensive on the province, an idea which appealed to Churchill and Lloyd George, but was resisted by the General Officer Commanding Ireland, General Macready, and even Sir Henry Wilson, who feared that such a move would mean 'taking sides', 'civil war and savage reprisals'.[18]

Dublin Castle was, of course, still responsible for the administration of the six-county area that would constitute the new state. Yet it was showing itself slow moving, and Unionists feared that it was drifting, not getting to grips with the situation. Craig, in September 1920, asked the Government to appoint a Royal Irish Constabulary Commissioner for the six-county area exclusively; he also pressed for the creation of a new civil authority in Belfast, with powers vested in an Under-Secretary who would be directly responsible to the Irish Chief Secretary and thus by-pass Dublin Castle. The new authority would work for the transfer of powers under the Government of Ireland Act to the new Northern Ireland Government and administration. The British Government did not want to be seen to be acting at Craig's behest, and even Law warned of the dangers of seeming to act at Craig's dictation.[19] Yet it did move some way towards what Craig wanted, appointing an Assistant Under-Secretary (still technically subordinate to the Dublin Castle Joint Under-Secretaries) and raising a constabulary for all Ireland, consisting of any 'well disposed persons'. Moreover, the new Under-Secretary proved to be a man who played a key role in the establishment of the Northern Ireland state: Sir Ernest Clark, a forgotten man amidst the formidable figures of Craig and Carson. Clark was an experienced administrator with a South African background, and South Africa was, after all, a successful self-governing experiment. Clark recorded how Craig made his wishes clear. 'Now you are coming to Ulster you must write this one word across your heart, and he tapped out with his finger in my chest ULSTER.'[20] He has been described as midwife to the new State of Northern Ireland. Yet it must be noted that the Government had positioned in Dublin Castle administrators who were sympathetic to Irish nationalism, though not of course Irish separatism;[21] and so this was a kind of *quid pro quo*, and perfectly consistent with the general tenor of the Government's Irish policy: to be as even-handed in Ireland as far as political realities, and the immediate aims of the British state, permitted.

NORTHERN FEARS

Yet there was a doubt at the heart of the assertion that partition would facilitate unity. Ulster Unionists at least had no illusions about the prospects for unity, Craig warning the House of Commons that unity would not come in the lifetime of any man in the House.[22] But the Unionists were not yet secure, for the British Government did have its own perspective, its own needs, and these were to get an Irish settlement that would end the damaging war with the IRA in the South, and bind Ireland firmly to the empire. The Government's desire to keep alive the dualism of its policy was seen in its decision in May 1921 to hold elections for the Northern and Southern Parliaments simultaneously.[23] The failure of these elections to produce a Southern Irish

Parliament did not mean that Ulster Unionists were clear of all Southern entanglements, for they could not be clear of these while the Government was searching for a settlement with the nationalists of the rest of
Ireland. Thus from July 1921, when the British Government began its
search for a comprehensive Irish settlement on the basis of dominion
status plus safeguards, Ulster Unionists were once more drawn into
the complexities of Anglo-Irish relations, or, as they would have put
it, Ulster was again to be held to blame for everything that went wrong
in Ireland, and in England as well.

Here, then, was tension, and not only the tension that resulted from
Sir James Craig's determination not to be drawn into the complex
negotiations at Downing Street. He, under Sir Ernest Clark's guid-
ance, was pressing ahead with the administrative foundations of the
Northern Ireland state, ranging from mundane matters such as office
equipment, pens and pencils, to the various departments that were needed
to run the country and the recruitment of the civil service (including a
'proportion' of Roman Catholics).[24] But the Treaty negotiations, though
they followed the establishment of the Northern Ireland Government
and Parliament, necessarily influenced their development, in the sense
that the transferring of full powers to that Government was, in British
eyes, subordinate to the need to get a satisfactory settlement with *Sinn
Féin*. The British had to try and convince *Sinn Féin* that the Northern
state was not yet a *fait accompli* – and this could best be done by
withholding the services that were to be transferred to the new state,
using the pretext to Craig that the Government of Ireland Act stated
that these were to be transferred simultaneously to both parts of Ireland. Without these services, let alone the control of law and order,
the Northern Parliament would, one official told the Northern Ireland
Cabinet on 12 August 1921, turn into a farce, 'nothing more than a
debating society'.[25] Craig warned the Government on 16 September
1921 that failure to transfer the services would be a 'breach of faith'.[26]
Still the Government delayed, for it was now moving closer towards
face to face negotiations with *Sinn Féin* plenipotentiaries. And since
Lloyd George told his Cabinet on 7 September 1921 that men would
die for throne and empire, but not for Tyrone and Fermanagh, then the
apprehensions of the Northern Ireland statelet can be appreciated.[27]

The Northern Ireland Government's fears were increased when, after
the truce between the British Government and *Sinn Féin*, the IRA virtually ceased its activities in the South, but were able therefore to step
up the pressure in the North, which now suffered serious outbreaks of
disorder.[28] Lloyd George's tactics were these: he held out the possibility

that partition was by no means permanent, for after all, the Northern
Ireland state was as not yet possessed of significant powers of government and administration. This would keep *Sinn Féin* in the talks, and
prevent their 'making the break' on Ulster. Yet Lloyd George knew
that Ulster was the problem which might wreck a settlement, leaving
the Irish free from blame. In the earliest exchanges on the Ulster issue,
Lloyd George defended the Government's decision to take a six county
unit on the grounds that this was the outcome of the fact that no-one
from the nationalist side came forward with whom the Government
could negotiate. But he made the admission that, as he put it:

> If you wish it to be made clear that we are impartial, that we shall
> not stand in the way of legitimate persuasion by you to induce the
> others to come in to a confederation by offering advantages to N.E.
> Ulster, we are prepared to do so.
> Mr Churchill: Smuts is at this moment offering Rhodesia induce-
> ments to come into the Union, customs etc.
> The P.M.: We stand neutral.[29]

Lloyd George endeavoured to turn his disadvantage into an advantage
– getting certain pledges that if he, Lloyd George, were to put pressure on Ulster to come into an Irish settlement, then Arthur Griffith
would not let him down. Lloyd George would then propose that Craig
accept Dublin or London rule, with a boundary commission.[30] But Lloyd
George also used the transfer of services as a means of putting pressure
on Craig in November 1921 to enter the negotiations. On 5 November
1921 Craig met Lloyd George in Downing Street to demand the transfer
of powers. This he got; then Lloyd George asked Craig to come into a
united Ireland, a request which Craig seems temporarily to have believed
to be unavoidable, though the evidence is not conclusive.[31] In the end
Craig refused, perhaps stiffened by his Cabinet. On 9 November the
King made two Orders in Council, one of them transferring services to
Northern Ireland on the appointed days: 22 November, 1 December,
1 January and 1 February. But this was coupled with a formal request,
made on 10 November, that Craig, while retaining his existing powers,
should do so under an all-Ireland parliament instead of under Westminster. The question of the area which would remain under Belfast's
jurisdiction would be left for discussion, but the creation of a national
parliament 'would clearly further an amicable settlement of this problem'.[32] Craig refused, declaring that if Ulster were to be expelled from
the United Kingdom then it must be with the status of a British Dominion,
thus retaining her role in the Empire which Ulstermen had built up,
and to which they were proud to belong.

THE EAST-WEST GULF?

This chapter is not concerned with the last dramatic moves by which Lloyd George induced the Irish to sign a treaty on 6 December 1921, his use of Griffith's promise not to 'break' on Ulster, a promise made when Lloyd George was having his problems with the Conservatives, or at least with those opposed to a treaty with *Sinn Féin*. But the Ulster episode is instructive in revealing the new mood in Britain towards the Ulster Unionists – one which Bonar Law summed up as 'apathy, even moral apathy ... The man in the street and the man in the House of Commons too, is thinking only of getting peace on any terms'.[33] And the story was not yet over, for after the treaty was signed, the British Government was anxious to do all it could to support the provisional Government of the Irish Free State, to ensure that in drafting its constitution it complied with the Treaty, and to ensure also that those factions who opposed the Treaty would not be able to unite with those who supported it on the issue of Ulster. Ulster was still the weak point in the Government's armour; and the weakest point of the weak point was the issue of law and order. Here the Northern Ireland Government found itself deeply at odds with the British Government, for as early as September 1921 Sir Wilfrid Spender, the secretary to the Northern Ireland Cabinet, remarked that 'nothing can be more disastrous to any community than to allow the rank and file to imagine that Civil Authority has broken down. The people cannot understand why, having elected a Parliament, and the Government having been set up, that government is not functioning.'[34] Northern Ireland was given control of the Special Constabulary in November 1921, but the British Government was anxious about the impact upon its image of 'Orange pogroms'. The Northern Ireland Government found that the British military was reluctant to act under the Restoration of Order in Ireland Act. The seriousness of the law and order predicament cannot be doubted: between 6 December 1921 and 31 May 1922, 236 people were killed, and 346 wounded, with Roman Catholics suffering the worst casualties. When in May 1922 the IRA invaded the 'Pettigo triangle', a strip of land on the border with Donegal, they were ejected by the military, but Lloyd George warned again that the key point for the British was the Crown and Empire, not the 'swamps of Lough Erne'. 'Now I understand we are marching against some rotten barracks at Belleek garrisoned by a friendly blacksmith and a handful of his associates', he wrote to Winston Churchill in June 1922, pointing out that the 'friendly blacksmith', McKeown, was a strong Treaty supporter whose death 'would be a disaster to the cause of reconciliation with the Irish race'.

'We have already done everything that Ulster can possibly expect to secure its security'.[35]

The British Government indeed found itself in a dilemma in dealing with the new state that it had created in 1919–21. It did not want too direct a role in the restoration of law and order, hence its refusal to use the army more than sparingly. It had therefore to finance the Ulster Special Constabulary (USC); yet it always pleaded with Craig that he must maintain a wholly impartial law and order policy. Yet the USC was plainly a Protestant force, whose presence would be welcomed by few nationalists in the North. The failure of the British to protect the border, or even want to, in February 1922 meant that Craig found himself obliged to use what he called the 'best members' of the USC to defend the border of his state, while deploying what he (rather alarmingly) called the 'less excellent' parts of the force in the disturbed areas of Belfast.[36] Craig had to restore order, yet he had also to ensure that his actions would not earn the censure of the British Government and public opinion. Meanwhile disorder escalated. Michael Collins' intervention in the North, and his determination to press the British Government on the law and order issue, further heightened nationalist hopes and unionist fears. The Unionists could not admit that their forces were in any way a contributory factor in the violence in 1922, and so the gap between the State and the Northern Ireland nationalists widened. The Unionists' anxiety about the intentions of the British Government, and its desire to appease the Free State, made it impossible for the Unionist Government to do other than appease its own people – for the unionist people were anxious that their own state would not let them down and truckle with the British Government, and thus also the Irish Free State. The Northern Ireland Home Affairs Secretary, Dawson Bates, soon became a byword for discourtesy bordering on contempt for the Roman Catholic community, and even Craig, well-meaning though he was, had to keep in touch with the grass roots, lest his state suffer from the actions not only of its enemies, but of its supporters as well.[37] After peace was clearly winning at the expense of disorder in August 1922, the Free State Government chose to ignore Northern Ireland, which reciprocated, and the British Government, relieved of the burden of Ireland, felt satisfied that it had gained what it wanted from the treaty: an Irish Dominion with safeguards. And thus it could distance itself from the Northern Ireland state.

CONCLUSION

The last acts of the play followed on quite naturally: the Northern Ireland state's poor relations with the Irish Free State; its decision to abolish proportional representation for local, and then parliamentary elections as a means of retaining unionist solidarity; the mutual suspicions between Northern Ireland and the British Government; the boundary commission of 1925 that proposed making only minor transfers of territory, and ended with all sides accepting that it was best to leave well enough alone altogether. 'Ulster', said Sir James Craig, 'and Czechoslovakia are born to trouble as the sparks fly upwards'.[38] This trouble can be seen as the outcome of a long-gestating conflict of nationality, stretching back as far as the seventeenth century; or from 1886; or it can be dated from the era of 1912 to 1922, when the Home Rule crisis reached a violent climax. The character of the area itself influenced the conflict, with its mixed population, its religious divisions; and the smallness of its size: as the Northern Ireland Government pointed out in 1922, 'Ulster was in a different position from Great Britain, inasmuch as in a comparatively small country such as Northern Ireland every action of the Government was scrutinised by the whole population'.[39] But it is important to trace the final circumstances in which the state of Northern Ireland was created, launched, and secured. This explains why unionists, though they appear to have made off with the spoils of victory, remained doubtful and embittered by an experience that, in theory, should have left them confident and secure behind their one-party, self-governing state, open perhaps to cross border cooperation and reconciliation with the Roman Catholic minority. It also explains of course why that minority felt (rightly) that in this conflict it had been the loser.

For the state that the British created in 1921, while based on the British constitutional style of a two-chamber parliament, mass democracy, free elections and the rule of law, diverged in important respects from the Westminster model. It did so, not only because it was a one-party state, with a mainly Protestant police force and civil service. It also had embedded in it a vital structural flaw; the authority of the state was based on the unionist perception – a very real perception – that the minority withheld its allegiance to the state. Unionists believed that the Northern Ireland state could not easily (as the British state could) incorporate opposition of any kind into its theoretic structure. The authority basis of the Northern Ireland state precluded 'normal' political activity (a possible change of government), and 'normal'

institutions (agencies of state open to all); it also made it hard to interpret opposition of any kind as anything other than an attack on the
authority, and therefore the legitimacy, of the state. Thus, when the
Roman Catholics demanded rights to rather finite resources (e.g. jobs
in a state with very high unemployment) or political rights (the abolition of plural voting in local elections) they were perceived as seeking
rights without conceding prior allegiance to the state. In this view, the
Roman Catholic nationalist was seen as a manifestation of David Hume's
'rational knave', operating under the guise of feigned compliance, while
all the time looking for an opportunity to gain an inadmissible advantage without losing the benefits of his seeming compliance[40] or, as
unionists bluntly put it, 'not loyal to the Crown, but loyal to the half-
crown'. Moreover, a Unionist Government that seemed prone to re-
treat from its political obligation to defend the unionist state would
itself incur the hostility of large sections of its own people.

But the Northern Ireland state suffered from another – or rather a
parallel – flaw, in its relations with Great Britain. To the British Government of 1919–21, Ulster Unionists themselves often appeared as 'rational knaves', operating under a feigned compliance, while all the
time looking for the inadmissible advantage. As Lloyd George put it
(echoing the unionist attitude to nationalists), Sir James Craig's demand
in November 1921 for dominion status (as a counter-move to the British
pressure on Ulster Unionists to accept an all-Ireland system) was simply
because Craig wanted 'a six bob tax as against three bob'.[41]

This introduced a rancour into British–Ulster relations which cannot
be ascribed merely to the policy choices of this or that government,
but were inherent in the overall structure of the British–Ulster relationship. It is apposite to cite, and amend, the late John Whyte's often
quoted observation that 'it is because Protestant distrusts Protestant,
not just because Protestant distrusts Catholic, that the Ulster conflict
is so intense'.[42] The amendment is: and because Protestant distrusts
the British state that the Ulster conflict as so intense, and to a large
extent, why it still is.

NOTES

1. Edmund Burke, *Reflections on the Revolution in France* (London: Dodsey, 1790), *passim*.
2. Quoted in D. G. Boyce, 'Ulster: Some Consequences of Devolution', *Planet* (Carmarthen), No. 13 (August–September 1972), pp. 8–9.
3. Brian M. Walker, *Ulster Politics: The Formative Years*, 1868–1886 (Belfast: Institute of Irish Studies, 1989), pp. 1–10.
4. Alvin Jackson, 'Irish Unionism, 1905–21', in Peter Collins (ed.), *Nationalism versus Unionism: Conflict in Ireland, 1885–1921* (Belfast: Institute of Irish Studies, 1994), pp. 35–46.
5. Paul Bew, 'The Easter Rising: Lost Leaders and Lost Opportunity', *Irish Review*, No. 11 (Winter 1991–2), pp. 10–11.
6. D. G. Boyce, 'British Opinion, Ireland and the War, 1916–1918', *Historical Journal*, Vol. xvii, No. 3 (1974), pp. 575–93, 581.
7. *House of Commons Debates*, 5th ser., Vol. 91, col. 459 (7 March 1917).
8. A. T. Q. Stewart, *The Ulster Crisis* (London: Faber, 1967), pp. 55–6.
9. Sir George Younger to J. C. C. Davidson, 3 May 1918, House of Lords Record Office (hereinafter HLRO): Bonar Law Papers, 83/3/11.
10. D. G. Boyce, *Englishmen and Irish Troubles: British Opinion and the Making of Irish Policy, 1918–22* (London: Cape, 1972), p. 106.
11. *Ibid.*, p. 107; C. F. Scott's Diary, 12–14 August 1919, British Library, Add. Ms. 50, 905, fol. 203.
12. Boyce, *Englishmen and Irish Troubles*, pp. 108–9; Public Record Office, London (hereinafter PRO): Cabinet Committee on Ireland, first report, 4 November 1919, C.P. 56, CAB 27/68; Richard Murphy, 'Walter Long and the Making of the Government of Ireland Act, 1919–20', *Irish Historical Studies*, Vol. XXV, No. 97 (May 1986), pp. 82–96.
13. Boyce, *Englishmen and Irish Troubles*, pp. 109–10; PRO, 'Notes of a meeting held in Bonar Law's room, 17 Feb. 1920', CAB 23/68; Cabinet Conclusions, 24 Feb. 1920, CAB 23/20.
14. John McColgan, *British Policy and the Irish Administration, 1920–22* (London: Allen & Unwin, 1983), pp. 38–40.
15. Barrie to Strachey, 17 April 1918, HLRO, Strachey Papers, S 21/2/10.
16. C. P. Scott's Diary, 15–17 March 1920, Add. Ms. 50, 906, fols 1–2.
17. Boyce, *Englishmen and Irish Troubles*, p. 110; see also C. P. Scott's Diary, 30 Nov.–1 Dec. 1919, Add. Ms. 50, 905, fol. 215, and 20–23 Dec. 1919, Add. Ms. 50, 905, fols 217–18.
18. Imperial War Museum, Sir Henry Wilson's Diary, 26 July 1920.
19. John McColgan, *op.cit.*, pp. 26–7. Bryan A. Follis, *A State under Siege: The Establishment of Northern Ireland, 1921–25* (Oxford: Clarendon Press, 1994), Chapter 2.
20. McColgan, *op.cit.*, pp. 30–31; Follis, *op.cit.*, pp. 6–8.
21. Notably Sir Mark Sturgis, Assistant Under-Secretary, who was appointed to open channels of communication with *Sinn Féin*, and who candidly admitted that the problem of Ireland was that, while the Irish were incapable of governing themselves, neither the English, nor for that matter the Welsh, had the ability to govern them either (PRO: Diary of Sir Mark Sturgis, 3 August 1920, PRO 30/59).

22. Boyce, *Englishmen and Irish Troubles*, p. 110.
23. In March 1921 Lord Birkenhead told a deputation of eminent persons who were deeply concerned about the state of Ireland that Ulster might prove to be a 'working model' for the rest of Ireland (PRO: C.P. 2807, CAB 24/122); Boyce, *Englishmen and Irish Troubles*, p. 133.
24. McColgan, *op.cit.*, p. 56.
25. *Ibid.*, p. 63.
26. *Ibid.*, p. 64; Follis, *op.cit.*, pp. 61–2.
27. Michael Laffan, *The Partition of Ireland, 1911–1925* (Dublin: Dublin Historical Association, 1983), p. 78.
28. Patrick Buckland, *The Factory of Grievances: Devolved Government in Northern Ireland, 1921–39* (Dublin: Gill & Macmillan, 1979), pp. 194–205.
29. Keith Middlemas (ed.), *Thomas Jones: Whitehall Diary, Vol. III, Ireland, 1918–25* (London: Oxford University Press, 1971), p. 131.
30. Laffan, *op.cit.*, pp. 83–4.
31. Middlemas, *op.cit.*, p. 160.
32. Laffan, *op.cit*, p. 84. In October 1921 Lloyd George outlined his Ulster options to C. P. Scott, declaring that the policy of placing the six counties under a 'common assembly for the whole of Ireland which should administer the large additional powers now to be conceded – trade and finance, police etc.' was 'by far the easiest' solution (C. P. Scott Papers, 28–29 October 1921, British Library, Add. Ms. 50, 906, fols 90–91).
33. Bonar Law to J. P. Croal, 12 Nov. 1921, HLRO, Bonar Law Papers, 107/1/83.
34. Buckland, *op.cit*, p. 187.
35. Lloyd George to Winston Churchill, 8 June 1922, HLRO, Lloyd George Papers, F 10/3/3.
36. Buckland, *op.cit.*, p. 201.
37. *Ibid.*, p. 203.
38. Middlemas, *op.cit.*, p. 186.
39. Buckland, *op.cit.*, p. 215.
40. Rex Martin, *A System of Rights* (Oxford: Clarendon Press, 1993), p. 216.
41. Laffan, *op.cit.*, pp. 84–5.
42. Quoted in Buckland, *op.cit.*, p. 278.

3 The Projection of Northern Ireland to Great Britain and Abroad, 1921–39[1]

Sean McDougall

> It will interest you to know that Lord Rothermere has promised . . .
> to place the *Daily Mail* and his other chain of papers entirely at our
> disposal to urge the public across the Channel to make this their
> venue for the holiday season . . . Our idea is that we can get at a
> large section of the population by starting this movement as each
> tourist on his return will be an agent for the Ulster cause.
>
> James Craig, Prime Minister of Northern Ireland, 30 January 1933.[2]

INTRODUCTION

Propaganda has always had a role in Irish history: from the twelfth
century, when the *Leabhar Gabhaela* (*Book of Invasions*)[3] was written, through to the nineteenth, when two varieties of Irishman fought
their Home Rule battles, the projection of inclusive and exclusive images was of central importance to the island's political elite. Yet a
glance at the current body of research implies that, just as the age of
mass communications seemed certain to produce an exponential growth
in the importance of propaganda, unionists somehow lost their ability
to define, articulate and justify their beliefs. In other words partition,
symbolically presented as the cutting of Ireland's throat, seems to have
cost unionism its vocal cords.

This matter has more to do with the selective nature of inquiry in
Irish historiography than with any failings on the part of unionism.
While much work has been done on the monster rallies and techno-
logical splendour which characterised unionism's Home Rule phase
(most notably by Patrick Buckland, John Harbinson and Alvin Jackson),[4]
little if anything has been made of the half century when Ulster Unionists
had control of state as well as party machinery. Instead, scholars have
tended to assume that the absence of published research can be equated

with lack of activity by unionists. Liz Curtis gives blunt expression to this penchant in *Northern Ireland: The Propaganda War*, describing the period 1921–68 simply as 'the silent years'.[5] But probably the comments of Arthur Aughey are more notable, as he is the scholar who has argued most strongly for the consideration rather than dismissal of unionism as a belief system. In a recent article, focusing on unionism's apparent reluctance to articulate beliefs, he remarked (italics added):

> Unionism has been noted for its inarticulateness. This has little to do with the rhetorical skills of unionist politicians. It has to do with the ability of unionists to convey to others in an intelligible, defensible and coherent manner what they believe. Unionist may speak cogently unto unionist but, as Brainer has observed, 'problems grow when unionists try to explain to others how they want to live'. *Because unionist politicians have failed in the past 'to explain to others' or even give their politics a second thought* it has been quite easy for opponents to fix upon unionism the label of an ideology of sectarian supremacism or to dismiss it as nothing but the flotsam and jetsam of Britain's imperial past.[6]

Clearly, unionists had lost the propaganda war – as fought in the public sphere – by 1972; but it should be recognised that the assertion that it was ever thus is in reality nothing more than an unproven assumption. There is a great deal of evidence to suggest that the Stormont years were not 'silent years' at all: indeed, it can be argued that from beginnings, in the period 1921–39, which were themselves characterised by a finesse belying current understanding, the Unionist ability to disseminate their views actually increased in each decade until the late 1950s. Rather than becoming a mute and inflexible monolith, unionism retained multi-faceted and bi-lingual abilities long into its period in hegemony. Government and Party drip-fed the local electorate propaganda demonising nationalism and the Irish Free State; mainland newspapers were monitored for inaccuracies and hostile comment, which were promptly and courteously dealt with; Commonwealth businessmen were told of the region's importance as part of the British economy; and American journalists were treated to low-profile, high-cost social events designed to leave them on friendly terms with the Unionist administration. The perception that unionists were and are bad communicators, then, is one based on dialogue within Ireland and between communities; yet unionists would respond that discussion of that kind only ever led to a demand to end partition. This was certainly the case in the period 1921–39.

UNOFFICIAL PROPAGANDA, 1921–25

As George Boyce has shown in the previous chapter, unionists faced a strong impetus to batten down the hatches in 1921, for they were subjected to unprecedented levels of verbal and physical assault designed to bring about the collapse of the state. Nor was this just an Irish nationalist attack: the British Government, after all, had put the border under review and granted very limited powers to the state in the expectation that it would be a short-lived affair. Nevertheless, the new state survived long enough to watch its Southern counterpart descend into civil war, which led in turn to a decline in the volume of propaganda levelled against Northern Ireland.[7] The British Government also turned its back on the region, content to have expelled the Irish question from the chamber after forty years and implying strongly that silence would in future be a virtue for unionists, provoking no response and thus safeguarding the Union. Still, there was a certain merit in using the Irish civil war as a means to juxtapose the two new states – if only for the benefit of the unionist electorate – and it initially appears curious that the Northern Ireland Government maintained such a magnanimous silence on this issue (as indeed it did on everything). It would be churlish, however, to assume that the state simply had nothing to say: more precisely, the unionist desire to put as much distance between North and South – to create partition of mind as well as of land – was frustrated by the peculiarities of the administrative system which brought the state into existence.

The problem, as Phil Taylor has pointed out in his study of interwar overseas diplomacy, was that propaganda was seen as an 'un-English' activity by Whitehall's mandarins, used only by lesser states (including, supposedly, the United States, Germany and most of the western world).[8] In Northern Ireland, one consequence of this ostrich-like attitude was that the new Government felt compelled to maintain an official silence in the face of hostile propaganda, despite the precariousness of its position, as any departure from the practice (which would in any case have contravened the Government of Ireland Act) would have been presented by its enemies as proof that the region was not, after all, as British as it claimed to be. Honour may also have had its say: Unionists, after all, may have agreed with Westminster's leading lights when they suggested that it was improper for the state to shape opinion against the wishes of any section of the electorate. Yet as anticipated by Sean MacEntee, the Belfast-born republican, in the debates on the Anglo-Irish Treaty, both Governments in Ireland felt an acute pressure to distance themselves ideologically, physically and culturally from their twin.[9] The dilemma for Unionists, then, was in reconciling 'Step by Step', the policy of conformity to British practices, with defence of the state.

One source of strength was the Ulster Unionist Council (UUC) Propaganda Committee. Initially, its members tried to establish the idea that, far from encircling a pogrom-zone, the border represented a line separating peaceful British and anarchist Irish. The polemical *Month Of* series of posters, for instance, provided a day-by-day catalogue of atrocities in the Southern territory for the consumption of the unionist electorate.[10] Posters depicting Royal Irish Constabulary officers and family moving North to escape the attacks complimented reprints of press articles such as 1923's *Free State Under Home Rule, Dark Record of Tragedy and Crime, Financial Embarrassments Contrast with Peaceful Ulster* and the more considered *Government of Northern Ireland: Its First Three Years*, which detailed seventy-six acts passed since partition and boasted that 'The Government has so thoroughly re-established law and order that in every part of the area peace and security and confidence prevail'.[11] Furthermore, the Committee almost certainly continued to exercise its pre-partition responsibility for the overseeing of delegations to Great Britain and the United States, supplying news and features free to the American press, ensuring world-wide distribution of leaflets and commissioning sketches of Parliament from leading lobbyists.[12] Links with the mainland press might have been facilitated by the historical associations binding various media figures with links to the Unionist hierarchy – Henderson, for instance, owner of the *Belfast Newsletter*, had long been on the board of directors at Reuter's – and it also seems likely that the Propaganda Committee made some use of parliamentary connections as well, particularly in the case of mainland editors and owners who combined their tasks with service in one of the Houses of Parliament.

The Irish Government saw the work of the propaganda committee as 'extraordinarily elaborate'.[13] The UUC Annual Report states that in November 1922 a delegation was sent to England to canvass over five hundred parliamentary candidates,[14] but Free State intelligence makes clear that they also planned to address over six hundred public meetings and had prepared a press campaign of huge proportions.[15] Evidently, the Irish Government viewed the recruitment of the *Manchester Guardian* to its cause as a response to Unionist successes,[16] hinting that the cultivation of personal links at editorial and proprietorial level were high on the Unionist agenda. Other intelligence suggested that there was a need for leaflets and pamphlets and the canvassing of parliamentary candidates, again in response to the Unionist effort, so it may be inferred that such efforts were perceived to have had an effect.[17] It is ironic, then, to note that the delegation in question returned in the face of complete apathy on the part of the English electorate: to them, the Irish question was last year's problem; and now that it had been 'solved', it was displaced by unemployment.

Though the Northern Ireland Government appeared to greet each attack on its existence with stoic indifference, it too was engaging in propaganda – albeit indirectly. The vehicle for its propaganda was a private company entitled the Ulster Association for Peace With Honour. This body, established in 1922 with capital of £10,000 per annum (£180,000 in 1990 terms) existed to create:

> support for the Prime Minister in the stand which he, as head of the Northern Government, was making against the attacks upon the integrity of the Constitution assured to Ulster by the Act of the Imperial Parliament, to support by financial and personal effort such measures as might be considered requisite to defeat the propaganda attacking Ulster, and to take immediate action to reveal to the people of Great Britain the real nature of the insidious attacks upon the constitutional rights and liberties of the people of Ulster as British citizens.[18]

The Ulster Association, unlike Party and press, spoke as the voice of Government – if not actually a part of it – as the *Annual Report* for 1922–3 made clear:

> The closest liaison has been established with the Prime Minister's Secretariat and the various Governmental Departments, on whose behalf the Association has become the medium of circulating official information to the Press.[19]

The report continues by identifying Craig as the Association's President and states that its propaganda strategy was settled at a meeting attended by him. Special thanks were given to Robert Baird, Trevor Henderson and Samuel Cunningham, respectively proprietors of the unionist *Belfast Telegraph*, *Belfast Newsletter* and *Northern Whig* newspapers and members all of the UUC Standing Committee. Their willingness to publish pro-Union material, not solely a matter of commercial self-interest, has been well documented by Dennis Kennedy, who has shown that it was of crucial importance in forming images of the Irish Free State and thus bolstering unionist sentiment.[20]

In its first year in existence, the Association met 134 times, and thereafter met three times weekly.[21] Each of the Cabinet ministries sent representatives as observers and 'readily' supplied information which formed the core of a continuous stream of press releases. Occasionally, Ministers provided complete articles for distribution in the United States of America. So much, in fact, did the Association integrate itself into the Government fold that journalists called at its London office for information whenever Northern Ireland Ministers visited the capital and went through it when a personal interview with Prime Minister Craig was required. Ulster Association material was distributed to every daily newspaper in Great Britain and every unionist newspaper in Northern Ireland. Among its many successes was a weekly 'Letter from Ulster' which was carried by between fifty and sixty mainland tabloids, which the Association augmented by providing tailored articles unique to specialised journals and up to 20,000 trade maps highlighting Northern Ireland's economic importance and geographical proximity to the mainland (the latter being produced with assistance from the Ministry of Commerce). The Association was also the body responsible for publicising the visit of the otherwise abortive UUC delegation to Great Britain for the General Election of late 1922. Its success was palpable: in the first year of its existence, the Association was able to secure publication of over 60,000 column inches of information on Northern Ireland, all of which were likely to create a positive impression of unionism and the Union for the interested.

Newspaper and journal reports represented half of the strategy for the maximum dissemination of pro-Union material. Additionally, the Association distributed large quantities of pamphlets produced by various bodies, sometimes to specific interest groups. For instance, 3,088 Scottish ministers were sent a copy of *The Church of Rome and Irish Unrest*, while the London Orange Council were credited with distributing 'large quantities' of similar material.[22] The distribution list, reproduced below, covered over 7,000 institutions, many of which had many thousands of members. The crude reference to the Orange Order in the United States, Australia and Canada, for instance, masks respective membership figures of 3,000, 40,000 and 300,000 (in this latter case out of a population of 4–5 million).[23]

All information produced by the Association was sent to the following:

House of Lords	310 clubs and hotels in
House of Commons	Great Britain
British embassies and	495 clubs and hotels in the
legations abroad	United States

Foreign embassies in London	412 clubs and hotels in
Chambers of commerce and	Canada and Newfoundland
Rotary clubs	649 clubs and hotels in
British universities	Australia, New Zealand and
Colonial governors	Tasmania
Conservative Associations in	600 members
England	763 on a general list
Scottish churches	Orange Lodges in the United
840 British libraries	States, Australia and Canada

The list shows a Protestant and middle-class bias, which reflects the Ulster Unionist strategy of appealing only to those likely to be sympathetic or able to influence events.

In Dublin, the activities of the Ulster Association did not go unnoticed. As the author of the *Irish Independent*'s London letter saw it in 1923, the Ulster Association and the Government's propaganda machinery were one and the same:

> Some steps should surely be taken to teach the authorities of the Government of 'Northern' Ireland the necessity of precision of expression in referring to the territory under its restricted jurisdiction. The organisation which rejoices in the grandiloquent title of the 'Ulster Association for Peace with Honour' has circulated to the Press some propagandist matter in the course of which the association itself six times describes the North-East corner as 'Ulster' and once as 'the Province'.[24]

The assumption that the Government of Northern Ireland was responsible for material issued by the Ulster Association demonstrates the level of acceptance which that body achieved. However, it is also interesting to note that the author was concerned at the appropriation of the term 'Ulster' as a name for the state. Belfast, Dublin and London all opened files on the nomenclature of the region, knowing full well that the name of the state would associate or differentiate it from the Southern one in the minds of the British public – hence, the *Irish Independent* referred to 'the North-East corner' while unionists promoted 'Ulster' whenever possible. On the day after the letter appeared, the Law Officer of the Executive Committee in Dublin was instructed 'to draft a letter of protest to the British Government on the subject'.[25] Clearly, then, Unionist propaganda was not without significance at this time.

SEMI-OFFICIAL PROPAGANDA, 1925–38

With the ratification of the border in 1925 and the establishment of the Empire Marketing Board a year later, the need for unofficial and political propaganda receded somewhat. In order to make the most of the opportunities offered by the Empire Marketing Board, the Northern Ireland Government formed the Ulster Tourist Development Association and the Ulster Industry Development Association (UTDA and UIDA), which received state funding at £500 and £750 per annum respectively, later to rise to £4,000. As semi-autonomous bodies with more interest in the tourist and industrial potential of Northern Ireland than its Government, both organisations produced only a small amount of material at this time which was of sufficient relevance to warrant preservation in the Government archives. However, some interesting facts do emerge. In the first year of its existence, for instance, it appears that the UTDA's publicity was produced by the remnants of the Ulster Association for Peace with Honour's London publicity branch, which had been hived off in 1926 after the Government recognised that the need for political propaganda had receded.[26] This level of control over what was supposed to be a limited company is, to say the least, surprising. Furthermore, correspondence begun in 1931 demonstrates that the Government recognised the popular appeal of film propaganda featuring elected dignitaries. In August of that year, the Secretary of the UTDA (C. W. S. Magill) wrote to Charles Blackmore, the Cabinet Secretary, asking if the Government would be willing to be filmed by representatives of British Movietone News, the Gaumont Company Ltd, Paramount Sound News and British Pictorial Productions Ltd.[27] Magill pointed out that Ramsay MacDonald had accepted a similar offer in 1929 and, thus assured as to precedent, the Government considered the potential of the idea. A four-point plan was drafted, and when the cameras arrived they recorded a commentary focusing in turn on Northern Ireland's links with the United States, the region's economic prosperity, the local Government's attitude to the economic crisis, and finally the border, which was presented as a line defining the area safe for tourists.[28] Generally a positive message, it clearly demonstrated that Unionists understood how commercial and political messages could be intertwined to great effect. Perhaps that is why Craig supported grants of £45,000 to the linen industry for promotions run between 1927 and 1930. With time, this became their central philosophy regarding propaganda.

Yet slowly but surely the mainland public's awareness of Northern Ireland was being allowed to drift. While voters in Belfast and surrounding areas were subject to a near-continual barrage of pro- and anti-partition propaganda (mostly in newspapers with commercial interests in preserving their political niches, but supplemented by periodic poster and pamphlet campaigns) their mainland counterparts were not targeted by the Party after 1925. From March 1922, when the Speaker of the House of Commons ruled that discussion of Northern Ireland's internal affairs lay outside the competence of the House, mainland newspapers, long used to covering Westminster's daily debates, had lost interest in the region; but now the effect of the Party's withdrawal was to ensure that the vast body of British electors were left in ignorance of the constitutional relationship with Northern Ireland. By 1932, ten years after the UUC delegation had returned from Great Britain dismayed at public indifference to the Irish question, the Union could be described as safe, but only because the voters who chose the national Government were completely apathetic about it as an issue.

In this context it was thus most unfortunate for the Northern Ireland Government that Eamon de Valera, the Irish *Taoiseach*, should have chosen that year to put the Irish question firmly before the British voter. In June, as part of his campaign to establish Irish independence on more than a purely nominal level, de Valera moved to abolish the oath of allegiance to the Crown which all Irish TDs were obliged to swear as members of a Commonwealth parliament. Very shortly afterwards he also announced that henceforth the Irish Government would refuse to pay land annuities owed to the British Exchequer. In July, Westminster responded by passing the Irish Free State (Special Duties) Act, which imposed a 20 per cent duty on around two–thirds of all Free State goods exported to the United Kingdom. Suddenly, Unionist silence, designed to keep Northern Ireland within the United Kingdom, was shown instead to have contributed to widespread public belief that it was instead part of a united Ireland. British shop-keepers, confronted with Irish manoeuvring and without evidence to the contrary, tended to assume that customs were payable on Irish goods whether their point of departure was Belfast or Dublin, and, as they cancelled contracts on all Irish goods, their mistaken assumption inevitably brought many local businessmen to the verge of bankruptcy.[29] Northern Ireland's other main trading region – the Irish Free State – had by its actions succeeded in curtailing almost all North–South trade, with serious consequences for the economy in Londonderry and the border regions. Thus, having produced an Imperial Contribution[30] of £545,000 for the year 1930–31 (a year before duties were imposed), the economy shrank to the point where in 1934–5 it was able to produce a surplus of just £10,000.

Suggested responses sent in by worried businessmen included sending the unemployed over to mainland Britain, there to walk the streets
wearing placards proclaiming Northern Ireland's constitutional position.[31] However, the Unionist response showed greater subtlety. Draw-
ing upon informal connections, Craigavon and Robert Baird (proprietor
of the *Belfast Telegraph* and 'a powerful ally')[32] persuaded mainland
press barons to inform their readers that no customs were due on goods
from Northern Ireland and that it was highly suitable as a holiday
venue. In June, an English contact wrote to Craigavon to report on the
success of his meetings with Lord Rothermere:

> For your own *private information* only I had a favourable oppor-
> tunity last night to speak to Lord Rothermere on the subject of the
> *Daily Mail* and his other journals giving Ulster a helping hand in
> respect of:
> (1) the establishment of fresh industries.
> (2) the advantages of travel in our area.
> You are aware that his mother was born in County Down and in
> spite of the vagaries in which he indulges from time to time, he
> possesses highly sentimental feelings for Ulster. He himself had no
> hesitation in saying that by careful organisation he could influence
> at least another 100,000 visitors to our shores.[33]

The campaign was launched early in July with an article penned by
the successful Ulster playwright St John Ervine. In fact, the initial
intention had been to begin earlier, but plans were scuppered when it
was announced that Dublin would be holding the Eucharistic conference.[34] Aimed at tourists, it offered two main benefits: first, there was
the prospect of increased revenue as visitors disposed of surplus income; second, and just as important to Craigavon, was the promise
that each would leave 'as an agent for the Ulster cause'.[35] Certainly,
the commercial benefit was tangible: the tourist figures, as Craigavon
recounted in August of that year, broke not only their previous records
but also their heightened expectations.[36] Moreover, there is a profound
irony in the fact that the additional income which these tourists spent
while learning about the region may have prevented the balance sheet
from dipping beneath its £10,000 nadir into the red. Propaganda thus
begot propaganda, for in later years Unionists boasted that Northern
Ireland had never made a loss; and in the meantime they were spared
another onslaught on the viability of their state.

OFFICIAL PROPAGANDA, 1938–39

The use of friendly articles as a means to educate may have been effective but it was reliant on an entirely *ad hoc* system within the Civil Service. As the media explosion continued unabated, the merits of establishing a permanent Government body to deal with the press were occasionally reconsidered, though on each of the three occasions on which it was considered in the period 1932–37 it was rejected on financial and policy grounds. Despite the huge diseconomies of scale, Northern Ireland ministries were expected, from 1935, to respond on their own initiative to errors in the press,[37] though the only reason for doing so would appear to be that such was the practice in the large departments in Whitehall.

However, there were long term problems with this approach. Primarily, de Valera's on-going plans to establish an independent and unified Ireland did not augur well for peaceful coexistence. At the same time, the Unionist Party's relative ability to campaign outside Northern Ireland was going into swift decline, partly in consequence of the growing tendency of its supporters to view Stormont as their parliament rather than Westminster. When, in 1937, de Valera produced a new constitution renaming the state 'Ireland' and claiming sovereignty over the whole island, Unionists had little available by way of response. A year later, Irish diplomats used propaganda with remarkable effect to secure the return of three naval ports which Britain had retained for defensive purposes since 1921. In consequence Unionists at last took the decision to introduce a state propaganda machine in the hope of forestalling catastrophe.

It is worth retracing the process by which Unionists came to take this final step as it demonstrates the degree to which Government and Party cooperated in defence of the state. The first indication that change was afoot came in January of 1938, when Hungerford wrote to Craigavon to announce that he would shortly be writing to all known 'Ulstermen' in England with regard to the increase in anti-partitionist propaganda.[38] His hope was that by persuading many of them to monitor their local press for examples of hostile news the Party could more effectively organise to respond to it, and ultimately, the plan envisaged a core of sympathisers in Great Britain who would agree to sign letters of response issued by Party headquarters. While the plan began well, it quickly became clear that the Party could no longer cope with such a task, and thus in May, a week after writing to the Government asking that departments provide him with relevant material, Hungerford wrote again to argue that the Government had a duty to respond to what he called 'non-political' matters, amongst them the treatment of the minority, gerrymandering and Civil Service appointments.[39] This time the Government did not disagree; and in August it rented space at 21 Cockspur Street in London, there to open its first trade bureau, the Ulster Office. While Ulster Office employees were forbidden to engage in matters of political controversy,[40] approved activities allowed the Ulster Agent and his assistants to monitor the press for inaccurate comments relating to the social services, unemployment, Civil Service statistics and many of the issues which Hungerford identified in his letter as grist to the nationalist mill. The methods by which inaccuracy was challenged, ranging from prompt, courteous and factual letters of response to relaxed lunches for individual newspaper editors, were also likely to generate a wave of sympathy for the Government in a manner which could not otherwise be achieved.

Though the Office was ostensibly there to promote trade, some of the leading figures of the day clearly recognised its potential to transmit political propaganda. As a memorandum written by Sir Roland Nugent, Chairman of the Ulster Development Council and former President of the Federation of British Industries, made clear, commercial advertising could serve secondary purposes:

> Successful publicity is the result of innumerable minor activities skilfully combined to build up in the Press and Public an attitude of mind favourable to your purposes whatever these may be . . . In our own case we must decide what ideas and beliefs concerning Ulster we wish to implant in the British consciousness, satisfy ourselves that these ideas are of such a nature that it is psychologically possible to get them into the British mind and then see to it that all our publicity work, whatever its immediate object, whether attracting new industries or what not, is consistent with the major objective and if possible helps towards it.[41]

For a Unionist Government the pressing need was to establish and legitimise the state's position within the United Kingdom – this was the 'major objective' to which the 'immediate object' was subordinated. Of course, the Government could always claim that political inaccuracy affected economic competitiveness, but there remains the suspicion that it also saw the political benefits attached. When one Minister proposed that the regional Government emulate Whitehall by creating a single press office he stated: 'I do not think that political news, especially of a constitutional nature, should be entirely excluded'

– though he did add that it would be best to avoid politically contentious material.[42] After authorisation was given to employ a press officer,
in December 1938,[43] an advert was placed in local newspapers stating
that 'the officer appointed must be fully conversant with the general
constitutional position and the social and economic problems of Northern
Ireland'.[44] In May 1939 the Government appointed Frank Adams, a
Yorkshireman and former editor of the liberal-unionist *Northern Whig*,
to the position, his tasks listed in a confidential memorandum of the
same month as involving the supply of information to the press officer
in the Ulster Office (so that he could distribute them to the British
press and overseas press agencies), the preparation of a weekly bull-
etin for distribution throughout the British provincial press, and assisting in campaigns initiated by the independent publicity organisations
to attract new industries.[45] However, on the matter of political propaganda, the Government now had this to say:

> In carrying out these functions, the Press Officer would issue news
> material based strictly on facts. While he would not deal with Party
> politics, he would not be precluded from dealing with constitutional
> questions such as the position of Northern Ireland within the United
> Kingdom, or the jurisdiction of the Parliament of Northern Ireland
> in placing on the Statute Book the Civil Authorities (Special Powers)
> Act.[46]

This, of course, is not to say that civil servants would be passing an
opinion on the merits of detention without trial. In practice, though, it
meant that the Government produced material stressing that no customs were payable on Northern Ireland goods – because they were
British – and that the region was an excellent choice as a holiday
venue – because its currency was the British pound – and merely avoided
passing judgement on the desirability of the fact. The political consequences, of course, were tangible, not least because such publicity saved
the Party an otherwise necessary expense.

But was it a joint effort? There is no conclusive evidence, but points
made later in the memorandum on the duties of the press officer do
hint darkly at collusion. First is the suggestion that 'if the Government
desires to secure the acceptance of news circulated free from Northern
Ireland, such news must bear the stamp of authority and must be based
on facts. It must, moreover, be free of any suggestion of political propaganda'.[47] Though this is perfectly sensible, the use of the word 'suggestion' has to be seen in the light of an earlier point, in which the author
advocated 'the closest liaison' with the Party Propaganda Committee

on the constitutional question, and the later claim that 'one of the first steps to which the Ulster Unionist Council Committee should turn its attention should be the need for unity in the home sphere'.[48] In responding to anti-partitionist propaganda in Great Britain and elsewhere, then, the Government thus appears to have reached a point where it was willing to co-ordinate its efforts with a party, the one to raise awareness of the constitutional position by concentrating on trade and industrial links, the other to do so by issuing political publicity and attempting to undermine the opposition. The goodwill which existed between the two groups at the time is underlined by the willingness of the Government, in appointing its new press officer, to place onto the short-list the name of a candidate suggested by the Propaganda Committee, though he had not applied, was deemed too old and was not personally interested in doing the job.[49]

CONCLUSION

The opening of the Ulster Office marked the culmination of seventeen years of gradual movement, but the occasion was not significant in itself – it was, after all, just another continuation of a trend which had its roots in the heady days of Home Rule. Unionists had learned long before partition that it is the opinions of the influential and undecided that count, not those of committed Irish nationalists on both sides of the border, so they continued to produce literature aimed at a variety of overseas audiences, be they mainland electors, Canadian businessmen or important politicians, in an attempt to minimise the prospect of external factors forcing the British Government to change its policy on Northern Ireland. The Ulster Office in London just facilitated this by easing access to international media outlets and expediting the swift throughput of material produced in Belfast for distribution by the Ministry (later Central Office) of Information. To a certain extent it also formalised the means by which we can observe a vibrant, articulate and committed force at work – despite the presumptions of academics to date.

By locating in London, Unionists confirmed a second trend, which would be self-evident were it not forgotten so often. Except when responding to Irish nationalist accusation (as they have had to do for the last twenty-five years), unionists looked East rather than South for their inspiration. As a philosophy with the preservation of the Union at its core, it took British administrative practices as its model and produced propaganda designed to complement positively that of other

British regions. One dilemma for historians, therefore, is to understand the extent to which the dismissal of unionism as 'inarticulate' – which in turn fuels jibes at the injustice of their cause – is in reality based on a failure to give unionism its hinterland or is retrospectively influenced by events since 1969. Viewed through a wide-angle lens, early accusations that unionism could not defend its beliefs emerge as examples of gagging by Whitehall rather than any particular unwillingness, and the 'silent years' suddenly appear to be nothing more than neglected ones.

This third trend towards isolation of Northern Ireland within the United Kingdom is perhaps the most worrying. Certainly, no-one could deny that the experience of devolution and the Troubles means that Northern Ireland is different, but in many respects it bears comparison with other regions of the United Kingdom and Ireland. As such there is no reason to leave it out both of social and cultural histories of Britain, as Arthur Marwick has, and of Ireland, as Terence Brown has.[50] Nor does conflict explain why the standard histories of Northern Ireland have focused almost exclusively on political questions without regard to wider social and economic themes – the eradication of rickets, for instance, or the arrival of television, both of which make Northern Ireland appear more rather than less British. It seems fair to ask why so much of this evidence – as with unionist propaganda – has been left untouched by researchers who then write with certainty about matters as yet unproved. The very claim that 'in the past, unionists have failed 'to explain to others' has always been readily testable simply by working through the accumulated papers of the Ulster Office – which was, after all, set up for that very purpose. The suspicion must be that academics have grown used to seeing Irish history as an extension of contemporary politics and that this is best served by the maintenance of an 'us and them' culture in Ireland – one which makes no mention of outside influences. Such is a history which facilitates snarling references to unemployed shipyard fitters as 'a *Herrenvolk*' (Master race) – J. J. Lee's comments being based on visits to German archives but not, oddly enough, the Public Records Office for Northern Ireland.[51] Moreover, such history is inherently politicised: as Maurice Goldring recently observed, the commitment to Irish unification is matched by an unwillingness to examine the alternatives;[52] and in a climate which sees unification as inevitable one consequence is that the section of the island's people who have always seen their destiny met by the continuation of the Union – not by the frustration of Irish nationalist destiny – are denied a past which normalises the association with Great Britain. They deserve better. As the former leader of the Ulster Unionist

Party, James Molyneaux, made clear, theirs is a history best seen as part of the 'totality of relations within these islands', and regardless of the consequence it should be acknowledged. To do otherwise, after all, would be to risk aiding the process of unification by denial of alternatives; to risk making *Gastarbeiter* of the *Herrenvolk*.[53]

NOTES

1. I am grateful to the officers of the Ulster Unionist Council and to the Deputy Keeper of Records at the Public Records Office for Northern Ireland for permission to quote from archives.
2. Craigavon to McKee, 30 January 1933, Public Records Office for Northern Ireland (hereinafter PRONI): CAB 9F/123/7.
3. For an interesting discussion of the propagandist value of this, the first Irish history book, see H. Morgan, 'Milesians, Ulstermen and Fenians', *Linen Hall Review* (December 1991), pp. 14–16.
4. P. Buckland, *Irish Unionism II: Ulster Unionism* (Dublin: Gill & Macmillan, 1973); J. F. Harbinson, *The Ulster Unionist Party* (Belfast: Blackstaff, 1973); A. Jackson, *The Ulster Party* (Oxford: Clarendon, 1989).
5. L. Curtis, *Northern Ireland: the Propaganda War* (London: Pluto, 1984), p. 18.
6. A. Aughey, 'Unionism and Self-Determination,' in B. Barton and P. J. Roche (eds), *The Northern Ireland Question: Myth and Reality* (Aldershot: Avebury, 1991), p. 1.
7. G. Walker, 'Propaganda and Conservative Nationalism During the Irish Civil War, 1922–23', *Eire-Ireland* (Winter 1987), pp. 93–117.
8. P. M. Taylor, *The Projection of Britain: British Overseas Publicity and Propaganda, 1919–39* (Cambridge: Cambridge University Press, 1981), p. 13.
9. Speaking in the *Dáil* debates on the Anglo-Irish Treaty, MacEntee said:

   . . . the provisions of this Treaty mean this: that in the North of Ireland certain people differing somewhat from us in tradition, and differing in religion, which are very vital elements in nationality, are going to be driven, in order to maintain their separate identity, to demarcate themselves from us, while we, in order to preserve ourselves against the encroachment of English culture, are going to be driven to demarcate ourselves so far as ever we can from them.

   Quoted in A. C. Hepburn, *The Conflict of Nationality in Modern Ireland* (London: Edward Arnold, 1980), p. 125.
10. PRONI: D 1327/20/4/142.
11. *Ibid.*
12. UUC *Annual Report*, 1919; Dawson Bates to various journals, 2 June 1919; both in PRONI: D1327/20/2/5.
13. Assistant Legal Advisor, 'Very Urgent. Memorandum to each Minister.

The North-East and the Coming British Election,' n. d. [1922], Irish National Archives (hereinafter INA): S8892.

14. UUC *Annual Report*, 1922, PRONI: D1327/20/2/6. In 1914, 1,250 delegates were involved in an operation to canvass 116 constituencies. The scale of this subsequent effort may well have matched it. See UUC *Annual Report*, 1914, PRONI: D1327/20/2/1.
15. Assistant Legal Advisor, *op. cit.*
16. *Ibid*; 'The North East and the British Elections', 30 October 22, INA: S8892.
17. *Ibid.*
18. Ulster Association for Peace With Honour, *Annual Report*, 1922–23, PRONI: CAB 6/93.
19. *Ibid.*
20. D. Kennedy, *The Widening Gulf: Northern Attitudes to the Independent Irish State, 1919–49* (Belfast: Blackstaff, 1988).
21. Information in this paragraph is taken from the Ulster Association *Annual Report*, 1922–23. Mary Harris also reviewed this report while the research for this chapter was being completed: it is referred to, in surprisingly similar language to that used here, in *The Catholic Church and the Foundation of the Northern Irish State* (Cork: Cork University Press, 1993), p. 128.
22. *Ibid.*
23. T. Gray, *The Orange Order* (London: Bodley Head, 1972), pp. 262–4.
24. 'Our London Letter', *Irish Independent*, 15 Jan. 1923, in 'Six Counties: Use of Names "Ulster" and "Northern Ireland"', INA: S1957A.
25. 'Meeting of the Executive Council, 16 Jan. 1923. Improper Use of the Title "Ulster" for the Six County Area', INA: S1957A.
26. Memorandum from Milne Barbour to Cabinet, 25 Jan. 1927, PRONI: CAB 9F/87/1.
27. Magill to Blackmore, 13 Aug. 1931, PRONI: CAB 9F/114/1.
28. 'Interview between the Prime Minister and the Cabinet and the Representatives of the Various Film Corporations, Friday, 21st instant, at 3 p.m. at Parliament Buildings', PRONI: CAB 9F/114/1.
29. The situation had begun to affect Ulster businessmen even before the imposition of tariffs. See Dunn to Craigavon, 7 May 1932, PRONI: CAB 9F/123/1.
30. This was defined by the Colwyn Committee in 1923 as follows:

the extent to which the total revenue exceeds the actual and necessary expenditure in Northern Ireland shall be taken as the basic sum for determining the contribution . . . In determining the necessary expenditure there shall be eliminated:-
(a) All expenditure on every service in existence in both Northern Ireland and Great Britain incurred in providing Northern Ireland with a higher average standard of service than exists in Great Britain.
(b) Such expenditure . . . as is in excess of the strict necessities of the case in Northern Ireland.
(c) All expenditure undertaken by the Government of Northern Ireland on services which do not exist in Great Britain.

Quoted in J. I. Cook, 'Financial Relations Between the Exchequer of the United Kingdom and Northern Ireland,' in F. W. Newark (ed.), *Devolution of Government: The Experiment in Northern Ireland* (London: George Allen & Unwin for the Institute of Public Administration, 1953), p. 39.
31. Dunn to Craigavon, *op. cit.*
32. Comment written on *ibid.* Baird, of course, had the additional worry that many British industries would respond to the economic war by withdrawing advertising from the *Belfast Telegraph.*
33. Letter to Pollock, 7 June 1932, PRONI: CAB 9F/123/7.
34. Rothermere to Craigavon, 20 June 1932, PRONI: CAB 9F/123/7.
35. Craigavon to McKee, *op. cit.* (note 2). Of itself, this does seem Machiavellian in its callousness. However, it is also quite redolent of the views of Lord Derby, expressed in 1929 while Chairman of the Travel Association, that:

> The visitor who comes over here reads our newspapers, shares our recreations, talks with our people and makes friends with many of whom he keeps in touch afterwards . . . Such a person recognises the common interests of nations . . . In fact, he becomes an ambassador of this country.

Quoted in F. Donaldson, *The British Council: The First Fifty Years* (London: Jonathan Cape, 1984), p. 16.
36. Craigavon to Rothermere, 1 Aug. 1934, PRONI: CAB 9F/123/7.
37. Cabinet Conclusions, 16 Jan. 1935, PRONI: CAB 9F/123/1.
38. Hungerford to Craigavon, 27 Jan. 1938, PRONI: CAB 9F/123/9.
39. Hungerford to Blackmore, 28 May 1938, PRONI: CAB 9F/123/9.
40. Cooke-Collis to Gransden, 12 July 1939, PRONI: CAB 9F/123/10.
41. *Ibid.*
42. Milne Barbour to Craigavon, 27 Oct. 1938, PRONI: CAB 9F/123/2.
43. Andrews to Milne Barbour, 5 Dec. 1938, PRONI: CAB 9F/123/2.
44. *Belfast Newsletter*, 22 Dec. 1938.
45. Memorandum entitled 'Organisation of Publicity in Northern Ireland,' January 1939, PRONI: CAB 9F/123/10.
46. *Ibid.*
47. *Ibid.*
48. *Ibid.*
49. Memorandum entitled 'Government Publicity Office: Note of a discussion in the Prime Minister's Room on Tuesday, 18th April, 1939', PRONI: CAB 9F/123/2.
50. Marwick refers to Northern Ireland 'only where events there affected society on mainland Britain' while Brown's declared interest is in 'establishing the main outlines of the social history of independent Ireland since the Treaty of 1921.' See A. Marwick, *British Society since 1945* (Harmondsworth: Penguin, 1982), p. 11; T. Brown, *Ireland: A Social and Cultural History 1922–79* (London: Fontana, 1981), p. 15.
51. J. J. Lee, *Ireland, 1912–85: Politics and Society* (Cambridge: Cambridge University Press, 1989), p. 4.
52. M. Goldring, *Belfast: From Loyalty to Rebellion* (London: Lawrence & Wishart, 1991), p. 15.
53. Literally, 'guest-workers' of the 'master-race'

4 The Impact of World War II on Northern Ireland and on Belfast–London Relations

Brian Barton

ONLY HALF IN THE WAR: NORTHERN IRELAND, 1939–40

On 4 September 1939, the day following the United Kingdom's entry into war, Lord Craigavon, Prime Minister of Northern Ireland, promised a tense and expectant Commons at Stormont that there would be 'no slackening in [Northern Ireland's] loyalty. There is no falling off in our determination to place the whole of our resources at the command of the [Imperial] government ... Anything we can do here to facilitate them, ... they have only just got to let us know'.[1] In fact from the earliest stages of the conflict a stark contrast rapidly emerged between Northern Ireland's wartime experience and that found elsewhere in the United Kingdom. In the former, attitudes, patterns of behaviour and the overall pace of life were uniquely static and unchanging.

Of course, a measure of disruption could not entirely be avoided – rationing, travel restrictions, censorship, a progressive narrowing of cultural life, burgeoning military camps etc. Nevertheless, during the spring of 1940, a Belfast diarist was justified in describing the region as 'probably the pleasantest place in Europe'. She added: 'We are unbombed, we have no conscription, ... and life is reasonably normal'.[2] The perpetuation of 'normality' extended to other, less desirable, peacetime characteristics. Initially Northern Ireland's industrial capacity was seriously underutilized. Thus in December 1940 its level of unemployment was similar to that experienced by Great Britain in 1932, the worst year of the Depression. An official report to this effect prompted Churchill to initiate an immediate, full-scale, Imperial Government investigation as to its causes.

In addition, informed British visitors were shocked by the different atmosphere which they detected in Northern Ireland compared with

47

Great Britain. The slackness in public attitudes prompted one experienced observer to speculate that if anyone were to behave in London or Liverpool as they were continuing to do in Belfast, they would at once be noticeable and might even cause a riot.[3] There is no lack of evidence to corroborate these impressions, including the low level of military enlistment in Northern Ireland, the recurrence of disruptive labour disputes, the inferior output of its largest munitions factories compared with firms in Great Britain and its pervasive apathy towards civil defence. These features may be related to such factors as Northern Ireland's relative remoteness from the theatre of conflict and from Westminster, its internal sectional divisions and the absence of conscription. A further vital consideration was the ineffectiveness of the Stormont Government. The problems and issues which the war generated contributed ultimately to the overthrow of a Unionist administration, arguably the most dramatic event in the early political history of Northern Ireland. In 1938, Sir Wilfrid Spender, Head of the Northern Ireland Civil Service, wrote a devastating indictment of the collective incompetence of Craigavon and his colleagues in his diary. He concluded dejectedly that if the present loose conduct of affairs continued, it would do irreparable harm to the unionist cause and even pose a threat to the survival of democracy in Northern Ireland.[4]

When war began twelve months later, the composition of the Stormont Cabinet was unchanged. Against his own inclination Craigavon had been persuaded to remain in office, and he led his colleagues in increasingly dictatorial and whimsical fashion, straining the proper functioning of the cabinet system to breaking point. His most characteristic response to the increasing gravity and volume of attacks on his Government was either to make extravagant claims regarding the success of its policies or attempt to silence critics through concessions only justified by political expediency, such as grants, subsidies and the creation of a new department, the Ministry of Public Security. But they fell short of what was most stridently sought – a change in the composition of the Cabinet itself. Criticism of the Government focused mainly on its failure to reduce unemployment or make adequate provision for civil defence and its equivocation over matters such as education, electricity and transport. The marked deterioration in the strategic position of the Western Allies by mid-1940 and the formation of Churchill's administration at Westminster made the ineptitude of Craig and his colleagues seem even more indefensible. These considerations prompted Spender to predict in 1940 that the Imperial Government would before long be forced to impose martial law in Northern Ireland.[5]

Apart from Sir Basil Brooke's success in raising local food output, decisive Government measures were restricted almost exclusively to security matters, where Ministers displayed their customary zeal. However, in the spring of 1940 their actions were marginalised by a new development which was far more grave than the threat posed either by terrorism or invasion and potentially more divisive. From April onwards, Stormont Ministers and officials watched the on-going Anglo-Irish trade talks with growing apprehension. They feared that constitutional issues would be raised, with de Valera, the Irish *Taoiseach*, possibly offering, or being asked to trade, Irish neutrality for an end to partition. From late May, against the background of the Dunkirk evacuation and the fall of France, Craig came under more intense pressure from Westminster than at any time since 1921. Initially he was asked to make suggestions as to how the *Taoiseach* might be drawn into discussions about the defence of Ireland; later, he was invited to attend open-ended negotiations with the Southern leader in London. His response was as inflexible as it had been twenty years before; his priority remained the preservation of Northern Ireland within the United Kingdom. He refused to participate in an inter-governmental conference before the South had abandoned its neutrality or if constitutional matters were to be considered.

By mid-June, however, there were, perhaps surprisingly, indications that a split was emerging inside the Stormont Cabinet. Both Brooke and John MacDermott (Minister of Public Security) were apparently prepared to accept a change in Northern Ireland's constitutional status if, in response, Ireland proved willing to enter the war on the Allied side. In their view, loyalty to King and empire and the defeat of the Axis powers transcended their commitment to the maintenance of the Union. To their immense relief the crisis passed without the issue being put to the test, as de Valera adamantly refused to abandon Irish neutrality.[6]

THE ANDREWS PREMIERSHIP

On 24 November 1940 Craigavon died peacefully at his home. Next day, the Governor, Lord Abercorn, asked John Andrews, the Minister of Labour, to form a government. Both Brooke and Spender urged upon the latter the political necessity of making far-reaching Cabinet changes. Unwisely, he rejected this advice. He appointed just one new minister: Lord Glentoran, the Chief Whip, became Minister of Agriculture. From the outset it seemed unlikely that his newly formed administration, composed still of the 'old guard', would be capable of responding adequately to the pressures of war and so assuage the frustration and disillusionment increasingly evident within the Party.

Andrews was unfortunate to have become Prime Minister in almost his seventieth year, when his health had begun to fail and in the context of total war. In background, personality and experience he was ill-equipped to provide the leadership necessary. Inevitably, his appeal was lessened by his close identification with Craigavon's increasingly unpopular administration; in his choice of Cabinet he did nothing to reduce the negative force of this inheritance. From its inception the new Government appeared vulnerable. In March 1941 it lost its first by-election (in Craigavon's old seat). Over the course of the next two years backbench criticism tended to rise and the Cabinet suffered from diminishing morale and growing fractiousness.[7]

Andrews' premiership began inauspiciously with the German air-raids of April to May 1941. Due in part to earlier ministerial neglect and prevarication, Northern Ireland's defences were hopelessly inadequate and the public psychologically unprepared for aerial bombardment. In the course of four attacks on Belfast 1,100 people died, 56,000 houses were damaged and twenty million pounds damage was caused to property (at 1941 values). Fear and panic reached epidemic proportions; perhaps as many as 220,000 fled from the city. The collapse in morale prompted MacDermott to predict attacks on the parliamentary buildings at Stormont by an irate and frightened populace.

The blitz exacerbated the Government's problems. The region's experience of the raids helped focus interest on the conscription issue. MacDermott advocated it as a means of restoring communal discipline. Lord Abercorn also advised Andrews to 'strike when people's feelings are hot'. Meanwhile, quite independently, on 12 May 1941, Ernest Bevin, suggested to the Imperial War Cabinet that its application to Northern Ireland should be given further consideration in view of Britain's deteriorating strategic position. During the resulting negotiations, Stormont Ministers were unequivocally enthusiastic.

Nonetheless, on 27 May, British Ministers decided against extension. This was due to accumulating evidence of opposition from Ireland, the United States and Canada and, crucially, from within Northern Ireland itself. The nationalist anti-conscription campaign, culminating in a mass rally on Sunday, 25 May, so impressed Andrews that on his own initiative he contacted the Home Office and indicated that resistance would be greater than anticipated. Almost immediately the British Government issued a statement which concluded that its application would be 'more trouble than it was worth'.[8] The preceding policy vacillations on the part of the Stormont administration can only have served to reduce its credibility at Westminster and confirm doubts as to the quality of its leadership.

After a second by-election defeat in November 1941, Andrews expressed concern that in a general election his Government would cease to have a majority. Consciousness of his vulnerability reinforced his cautious instincts and more determined efforts were made to avoid contentious policies or unpopular legislation. Nonetheless, some politically hazardous issues required his attention; amongst these were the much-publicized activities of the Unionist-controlled Belfast corporation. A Home Affairs enquiry in June 1941 indicated that it had been guilty of wide-ranging corruption and the abuse of patronage. The Ministry recommended that as a compromise measure city administrators should be appointed who would act as an executive in the borough but be guided by the elected council. The subsequent legislation deepened divisions within the Government and alienated those who had opposed taking any action whilst failing to satisfy others who had favoured much stiffer governmental retribution.[9]

The Government's handling of industrial unrest also aroused serious doubts about its competence. In part public censure was directed at the official machinery for resolving trade disputes, which even MacDermott thought clumsy and slow. A much more damaging criticism was that the Northern Ireland Cabinet was spineless in its handling of labour and that this had contributed to a deterioration in industrial discipline. The worst strike of Andrews' premiership occurred in October 1942 and affected 10,000 men in Belfast's major strategic industries. It prompted Churchill to express his 'shock at what is happening' and Westminster officials to criticise the 'deplorable weakness' displayed by Stormont departments. By November 1942 MacDermott therefore once more advocated conscription to improve discipline. Soon afterwards Churchill likewise reopened this issue and similarly justified its introduction on the grounds of Northern Ireland's poor productivity and low level of recruitment. Andrews again rejected this response. Meanwhile, the Government's method of dealing with labour disputes remained unchanged; so too did the tensions within the Cabinet and the criticism of its performance which these circumstances engendered.[10]

There was, of course, a more positive aspect to the Government's policies. After taking office, Andrews became noticeably more enthusiastic about raising expenditure on social services, setting aside resources for post-war reconstruction and asserting more forcefully his independence of Treasury control. He expressed these opinions more stridently as he became more aware of the political weakness of his administration and of the changing aspirations of the Northern Ireland electorate. As elsewhere, war stimulated expectations of social improvement, a development associated with increased taxation, the province's huge imperial contribution, the publication of the Beveridge report and greater popular consciousness of the inadequacy of local welfare provision compared with Great Britain and of the extent of poverty in Belfast, so starkly revealed by the recent German air-raids. By mid-1942 influential elements within the unionist movement were urging upon the Premier the need to react positively by formulating plans for the post-war years; they thought this essential for the future of the province as well as the Party.

The tangible outcome was meagre and contentious. On 30 July 1942 the Prime Minister made a detailed statement at Stormont on post-war policy, which contained ambitious future plans for social services, transport, local government and industry. It immediately prompted an angry response from Kingsley Wood, the Chancellor of the Exchequer, and from Treasury officials, baffled by its timing, concerned by its content and irritated by the total absence of any preliminary consultation. In subsequent correspondence with Wood, Andrews deduced that he had gained extended financial powers for his Government from before. But this was self-delusion: his interpretation was not shared either by the Treasury or by his own Ministry of Finance officials. In the meantime, the governmental machinery for post-war reconstruction established at Stormont by Andrews had degenerated into a hopeless muddle of competing committees. His subsequent claim that he would apply foresight, energy and courage to resolve Northern Ireland's post-war problems lacked credibility.[11] Overall, there seemed no shortage of evidence to confirm the collective incompetence of the 'old guard' and obvious legitimacy in MacDermott's observation that Northern Ireland was 'only half in the war'.[12] Though responsibility for some of the province's unenviable features lay at Westminster rather than at Stormont, a growing and influential sector of local opinion attributed them to the failings of Andrews and his colleagues.

The extent of parliamentary disaffection was starkly revealed on 9–10 January 1943 when Unionist backbenchers held a secret meeting at which they formulated their demands. They called for a change of leadership and the appointment of younger Ministers. Their action was as much a symptom as a cause of political crisis. There was at the

time a widespread recognition amongst senior Party members, junior
Ministers and civil servants that the public had lost confidence in the
Government.

Surprisingly, given his Government's consistently submissive record,
Andrews' response was to resist the malcontents and to defend resol-
utely both himself and his Ministers. To strengthen his position with
the Parliamentary Party, he sought to rally the support of local Unionist associations and prepared an appeal to the annual meeting of the
Ulster Unionist Council (UUC). It seemed likely that he would then
proceed to purge critical junior Ministers from his front bench and
probably replace them with older men, so risking a potentially ter-
minal split in the Party. In fact, Andrews did receive UUC support, at
a meeting of 750 delegates held on 16 April 1943, and possibly then
believed that the crisis would pass. But his critics forced him to call a
further Parliamentary Party meeting on 28 April. When the thirty-three
Unionist MPs assembled, Andrews repeated his defence of his colleagues and insisted that he must be free to appoint his own Ministers.
No formal vote was taken, but it was far from certain that he enjoyed
the support of a majority of those present. It was evident that, if he
continued as leader, six junior Ministers would leave the Government
and the Party would be irretrievably divided. Shocked and saddened,
he reluctantly decided to resign.

Andrews' unwillingness to make the Cabinet changes urged upon
him stemmed not only from loyalty to long-serving colleagues and the
context of war but also political weakness; he refused to replace Ministers whose inadequacies he recognised. His obduracy also owed something to the confrontational manner in which the issue of Government
restructuring had been raised initially by his backbenchers. In any case
he regarded Cabinet appointments as the prerogative of the Prime
Minister. His overall response to the crisis suggests as well a measure
of miscalculation; specifically, his assumption that he could silence
his critics by a resolute stand and his inability to appreciate the true
nature of the pressures which had ultimately forced his resignation.

SIR BASIL BROOKE AS WARTIME LEADER

On 1 May 1943 Lord Abercorn asked Brooke to form a government; it
is unlikely that any other member would have commanded a majority
in the House. Nonetheless, it is improbable that he had been nominated
by Andrews who was firmly convinced that Sir Basil had conspired

against his leadership. Brooke dismissed such allegations as being without foundation. It is clear that the final outcome was not the product of his manipulative skills or unsated appetite for power; rather the region's administration collapsed in 1943 through the accumulating weight of its own incompetence; the balance was finally tipped by Craigavon's death and the mounting strains of war.[13]

In the context of war Brooke had much to offer the unionist movement, particularly his military experience and useful contacts in Britain. His Ministers were little known and, by Stormont standards, young. Most had administrative experience. For the first time a non-Unionist (Harry Midgley, Northern Ireland Labour Party) became a Minister so as to broaden the Government's representation in Northern Ireland; also Westminster officials had long advocated that the Stormont Cabinet should be composed on a more national basis. Its agreed policy priorities were to maintain the constitution, bring greater drive to the war effort and devise plans for the post-war years.

The change of Government and, more particularly, the manner in which it had occurred, caused enduring tensions inside the Party. There was considerable sympathy felt for the 'old guard' in the UUC and within sections of the unionist press. Most of the ex-Ministers felt embittered by recent events: some shared the late premier's conviction that they had been manipulated from office by backstairs intrigue. Andrews invariably attacked less popular aspects of Brooke's policy and, on occasion, briefed disaffected MPs on points of criticism which they might raise. In March 1944 his querulous behaviour attracted a strongly worded, though ineffective, public rebuke from Lord Londonderry. Amongst backbenchers, old loyalties and frustrated ambitions helped ensure that the new administration's initial control over the House was at best uncertain. These circumstances fuelled speculation regarding Brooke's prospects as Prime Minister. In December 1943 Spender recorded rumours then current in local business circles, that Glentoran would replace him inside three months.[14]

Like Craigavon and Andrews, Brooke sought to avoid making controversial decisions in wartime when a general election was impracticable and disunity might disrupt the war effort. Nonetheless, as Premier, he showed greater enterprise and activity than his predecessors. In addition, a number of divisive issues arose – some self-imposed and the others inherited or related to the war – all requiring his immediate response. Amongst these was his decision, in February 1944, to ask his Minister of Education, Rev. Robert Corkey, to resign. Sir Basil was satisfied that Corkey had neglected his duties. Corkey protested that his dismissal was due to disagreements on matters of principle. Specifically, he alleged that Brooke was not committed to the compulsory provision of religious instruction in state schools. He also claimed that an anti-Presbyterian bias operated in the administration of his own ministry, connived in by Brooke. The effect of his allegations was to impose a severe additional strain on Party loyalty; he received strong sectional support, having in Spender's opinion introduced a sectarian point of view. The far-reaching nature of the proposed educational legislation raised a number of sensitive and complex issues – that these required three more years to resolve was due in part to the bitterness aroused by Corkey's dismissal.[15]

From its inception, the Government was obliged to focus attention on another, similarly delicate matter. Its members experienced persistent pressure from councillors, Party officials and a number of local associations to restore to the formerly discredited Belfast Corporation those powers transferred to administrators in 1942. They were sympathetic in their response but also concerned to prevent a recurrence of the corruption which had previously disfigured the administration of the borough. In 1943 and 1944 measures partially restoring Corporation functions roused such controversy amongst councillors and backbenchers that they were abandoned. The issue was finally resolved when, in the spring of 1945, the Government relented and introduced legislation which in essence restored its original functions. It was by then widely felt that the council had been sufficiently punished for past misdeeds, whilst Government members hoped that their action would help heal party divisions.[16]

The most widespread criticism of the Government's performance centred on its allegedly inadequate response to the province's acute housing shortage. By 1943 Ministers considered that this had become the major focus of contemporary public interest, surpassing unemployment, and concluded that even in wartime it was politically necessary to do something, An official enquiry, in July 1944, estimated that 100,000 new houses were required to meet immediate needs: the figure had been significantly inflated by the effects of the recent blitz. Even so, the obstacles blocking an effective Cabinet riposte proved to be virtually insurmountable. To expedite progress the Cabinet established a Housing Trust, a corporate body, empowered to secure in coordination with local authorities the provision of housing accommodation for workers. The associated legislation once more elicited a hostile response from Unionist backbenchers who claimed that such centralisation was unwarranted and expressed concern regarding the future roles of private enterprise and local government in meeting housing needs.[17]

Overall, Brooke responded with ability, confidence and imagination to the immediate political problems which he faced. He had anticipated strong opposition to his Government, at least initially. Throughout his premiership he was constantly aware of fissiparous tendencies within the unionist movement. At any time, he regarded unionist unity as tenuous and dependent on the 'border question', without which he believed 'various opinions would make themselves felt'. More than Andrews, he recognised the necessity of boosting party morale. From the outset, he therefore invited a succession of leading British politicians to address meetings in Northern Ireland. He regarded publicity as a priority. He himself continually briefed journalists and at his first Cabinet exhorted his colleagues to do likewise.[18]

Shortly before Andrews' Government collapsed, Sir Basil had advised him that the Parliamentary Party was the only thing that mattered; and as Prime Minister he employed a variety of tactics to sustain its support. He sought to improve consultative procedures between Ministers and backbenchers. Thus meetings were held more regularly at which, not infrequently, Sir Basil intervened to appeal for unity and, on occasion, indicated his willingness to resign. In addition, he set in motion a process of Party reorganisation using the British Conservative Party as his model. The holding of an annual Unionist conference and appointment of a paid Party chairman were amongst the earliest innovations which resulted.[19]

He also strove continuously with success to reduce the level of bitterness between himself and the politically active remnants of the 'old guard'. Thus, in March 1944, he proposed as a conciliatory gesture that Andrews be re-elected President of the Ulster Unionist Council, a post which he himself aspired to. No doubt partly in reciprocation, Andrews proposed and Glentoran seconded Brooke's nomination as Party leader at a Standing Committee meeting held in March 1945. It was a response which Brooke valued. He had earlier complained that he had 'no status' and had become leader merely by virtue of being Prime Minister.[20]

Meanwhile Brooke and his colleagues began to devise plans for the post-war years in response to those pressures from within the Party which had helped precipitate Andrews' fall. As Premier, he stated his firm intention to keep pace with the rest of the United Kingdom in health and social services and initiated a series of investigations aimed at quantifying the comparative backwardness of Northern Ireland's welfare provision.[21] The impending increase in Government spending required a re-examination of the financial relationship between Stormont and Westminster. Local officials regarded the winter of 1943 as an opportune moment to initiate negotiations, aimed at ensuring that their departments had sufficient funds both to maintain parity in social services and to recover any proven leeway relative to British standards. Spender observed that there had been a general loosening in the recent budgetary policy of the Imperial Government, relations with Treasury officials were friendly, the Chancellor was sympathetic and the socialist members of the coalition were appreciative of Ulster's efforts. By early 1944, the basis for a future reinsurance agreement had been laid.[22]

The substantial expansion of governmental responsibility envisaged in these wartime plans helped precipitate a reallocation of functions between the Stormont departments. Implementation of the changes, in 1944–45, was complicated by the political context. Ministers were reluctant to relinquish functions which they had quite recently acquired, fearing that the electorate would conclude that they were unable to cope with the work done by their predecessors. Also Unionist back-benchers blocked Brooke's choice of Midgley as Minister of Health considering that he might 'do harm' there at a time when major National Health Service legislation was imminent.[23]

The economy represented the Government's other major area of attempted post-war planning. As at Westminster, Northern Ireland Ministers were committed to a policy aimed at full employment after hostilities had ended. As the flow of military contracts diminished they shared a deepening apprehension at the approaching spectre of peacetime recession and were convinced that no Government could survive if the number of jobless locally remained substantially above other regions of the United Kingdom. In response to these anxieties, a post-war reconstruction committee was established in September 1943. Six months later, a minister was appointed with responsibility for planning. Further legislation was prepared with the objective of attracting new industry to Northern Ireland in the post-war period. Meanwhile, Brooke and his colleagues constantly pressed imperial departments for further orders and investment and eagerly awaited their dismantling of wartime controls.[24]

An interesting consequence of Brooke's commitment to parity of social services with Britain and concern with regard to post-war economic prospects was his associated enthusiasm for conscription. In early 1945, he became aware of the Imperial Government's intention to extend compulsory service beyond the period of hostilities and he immediately requested that it be applied to Northern Ireland then as well. He justified its extension partly on grounds of principle; it would be a potent affirmation of Northern Ireland's constitutional status. He anticipated Westminster's previous response that it would be more trouble than it was worth by stressing that, after the war, larger numbers would be available for military service than in 1941 and that any disruption which might result from its application would have less grave consequences in peacetime. However, he also emphasised that if conscription was not applied it would be more difficult for Britain to help the province either by contributing to the cost of its social services or of assisting it to achieve full employment. Such was Brooke's enthusiasm for its introduction that he favoured establishing contact with the Catholic hierarchy in order to explore whether more generous grants to voluntary schools would lessen hostility to its adoption.[25]

British Ministers dismissed these arguments. They considered that to extend conscription to Northern Ireland for economic reasons would be 'indefensible' and that to apply it after hostilities had ended would be to invite universal condemnation; in 1941 military necessity had enhanced its legitimacy. Moreover, they believed that Brooke would be exposed to ridicule if he were to introduce military service at a time when it involved no risk to the conscripts. One further factor helped to determine Westminster's response – the conviction that Brooke's request was not in the best interests either of Northern Ireland or of the Union. One official observed: 'Nothing should be done to provoke rebellion . . . by a large minority who can always look for support from across the border.'[26]

Certainly within Northern Ireland there is little indication of any wartime shift in traditional political perspectives or relationships. It is clear that Unionist suspicion of the minority did not diminish during the conflict. A recurring theme of the resolutions then being discussed by the Party's Standing Committee was concern at Catholics 'getting in all over the province', whether purchasing houses or farms or finding employment in the Civil Service, Post Office or local industry. The context of war could in itself be used to justify illiberal policies. During its final stages, Spender received representations that houses should be erected 'in certain places on political grounds'. Though he had in the past forthrightly condemned sectarian discrimination he considered that there was 'some justification for the claim because protestants have been more willing to join the forces and volunteer for work in England than catholics and are therefore entitled to preferential treatment'. Occasionally, he reflected on the 'lack of any contribution' made by the minority to the war effort. Unionists certainly tended to regard them as a sort of fifth column: instinctively pro-German and anti-British; ever-willing to aid and abet the enemy; a community whose grievances were not as great as they protested.[27]

Though aspects of the Northern Ireland Government's policy were influenced by these narrow presumptions and prejudices, it was by no means invariably determined by them. On occasion, Ministers attempted positively to counteract discriminatory forces. Thus, for instance, the Housing Trust, from its inception in 1945, had a statutory obligation to allocate houses fairly. Its first chairman stated with apparent confidence that there was 'never any opportunity for undue influence to be used', mainly, he explained, because it selected tenants on the basis of an objective and undisclosed points system. Authoritative research has generally exonerated it of discriminatory practices. Similarly, when the Cabinet began to consider the scale of future Government grants to voluntary schools, in mid-1944, Brooke spoke strongly in favour of generous treatment, advising colleagues that the children must be the first consideration and he was supported by Hall-Thompson, the new Minister for Education. When Stormont Ministers decided to introduce family allowances on the same basis as at Westminster, they were aware that the minority would benefit disproportionately from their proposed scheme.[28]

The introduction of family allowances touched a sensitive nerve in the unionist mentality. Stormont Ministers had hopes, if not expectations, that social welfare measures combined with economic growth might in the long term deflect the minority from its aspiration to Irish unity. Indeed, in Brooke's opinion, expressed in 1944, the 'only chance for the political future of Ulster' was if it became 'so prosperous that the traditional political alliances [were] broken down'. In the meantime he and his Cabinet regarded the relatively high Catholic birthrate with the most acute concern. Sir Basil recorded a wartime discussion with John MacDermott on this issue; both reached the depressing conclusion that there was no immediate 'solution' to the problem of the 'increasing disloyal population'.[29]

The Government did, however, respond indirectly to the perceived threat by closely regulating the flow of Southern labour into Northern Ireland through a system of residence permits. Much thought was given to the possibility of differentiating Southern 'loyalists' (those who favoured partition) from the rest and facilitating their permanent settlement but no practicable scheme could be devised. Mounting anxiety that Westminster might refuse to sanction the continued monitoring of Irish migration after the war prompted the Unionist leadership to consider whether the 1920 act ought to be amended. Some favoured dominion status.[30]

Overall, as the war drew to a close the Unionist leadership faced the future with acute unease which was given additional impetus by the unexpected course of events during the summer of 1945. As hostilities in Europe drew to a close, Brooke noted privately: 'I find I have no feelings of elation only thankfulness that others will not have to endure the losses that we have suffered. One realizes also the vast and difficult problems which lie ahead'. No doubt with these thoughts in mind, he consulted his cabinet colleagues, during the euphoria of VE Day (8 May 1945), and 'decided to go to the country at once'.[31] When the results were declared two months later, the Unionist Party emerged with over half of the votes cast, thirty-three seats and an overall majority of fourteen in the new Parliament.

This was widely regarded within the movement as a setback and a Party enquiry was convened to determine its causes. Its most ominous feature was the challenge provided by labour groups, campaigning on social and economic issues. Collectively they had attracted the support of over one-third of those who had voted. Their efforts had been assisted by defective Unionist organisation and, in Brooke's publicly stated opinion, 'exaggerated fears of unemployment'; privately he shared the fears. Over two years earlier the *Newsletter* had detected an ominous swing to the left amongst local working people and a receding awareness of constitutional issues. During 1941–42, it was concern at the political advance of the local Labour Party which had prompted the Unionist leadership to resume party political activity. This had been suspended following the outbreak of hostilities, so that the energies of the membership could be single-mindedly devoted to the successful prosecution of the war.[32]

From a unionist perspective the one encouraging development in wartime was the awareness that relations between Westminster and Stormont had become closer. This was not primarily due to any outstanding commitment shown or sacrifice made by the people of Northern Ireland in the course of the conflict. In 1940, when Britain had faced defeat, Craigavon's priority had remained the preservation of the Union. Voluntary recruitment levels locally remained a source of disappointment to Northern Ireland Ministers, yet in 1941, on Andrews' advice, conscription was not applied. Local munitions industries performed only moderately well throughout. Rather it was Northern Ireland's strategic position which helped ensure that its contribution to the war effort was a significant one. Its importance derived from Germany's military

domination of Western Europe, combined with Ireland's undeviating policy of neutrality. As VE Day approached, Brooke expressed the 'hope that you [i.e. Britain] now realize that we are necessary to you'.[33]
His wish was vindicated. Herbert Morrison (the Home Secretary) had said of Northern Ireland in July 1943: 'Her strategic position alone ensures that her contribution is a crucial one'. Two months earlier, Churchill had also stressed the region's strategic role when writing to Andrews, who had just resigned as premier. He added that but for the loyalty of Northern Ireland, 'we should have been confronted with slavery and death . . . During your premiership the bonds of affection between Great Britain and the people of Northern Ireland have been tempered by fire and are now I believe unbreakable'.[34] These changing perceptions in Britain were to find tangible expression in the declaratory clause of the Ireland Act, agreed to by Attlee in 1949.

THE ATTLEE GOVERNMENT: ATTITUDES TOWARDS IRELAND

Nevertheless, four years earlier, the Labour Party's unexpected and historic electoral victory, in July 1945, had caused the Unionist leadership deep consternation. Brooke was concerned that the new imperial administration might 'try to force Northern Ireland into the Free State' and also feared that his own Government might be 'compelled to adopt very strong socialist measures'. He could foresee 'possible chaos,' even constitutional crisis if he, his Cabinet, or his Party found these unacceptable.[35] Unionist unease appeared to be fully justified. In its inaugural King's speech the Labour Government committed itself to a series of far-reaching reforms, whilst historically the Party had been consistently sympathetic to the principle of Irish unification. The return of a socialist Government immediately heightened nationalist expectations. Amongst at least a hundred Labour backbenchers there was a broad feeling that Northern Ireland did not conform to British standards of democracy. The anxieties which they articulated in Parliament were shared at governmental level. In April 1946, Chuter Ede, the Home Secretary, characterized the Northern Ireland leadership as being 'remnants of the old ascendancy class, very frightened of the catholics and the general world trend to the left'.[36]
Potentially the most serious clash occurred in January 1946, when the Stormont Cabinet indicated its intention not to introduce 'one man, one vote' into local government elections and the Home Office considered

withholding the Royal Assent from the relevant legislation. But the tension between the two Governments could easily be overstated; the causes of friction were generally resolved to the satisfaction of the Unionist leadership. For example,on the issue of 'one man one vote', the Labour Government considered that the substance of the legislation lay entirely within the competence of the Northern Ireland Parliament and that the effect of the 1920 Act would be nullified if Stormont Ministers were required to exercise their powers in accordance with the views of their colleagues at Westminster.[37] These considerations broadly determined the Labour Cabinet's perception of inter-governmental relations throughout these years. Indeed, the Unionist Cabinet came to regard the socialist leaders as punctilious in refusing to be drawn into any discussion on matters falling within its jurisdiction. There are in addition numerous examples of Labour Ministers being supportive, even generous, in their dealings with the Stormont Government. For example, in late 1945, the Treasury ratified a virtual trebling of pre-war expenditure on the Ulster Special Constabulary and generous interim reinsurance agreements were negotiated in 1946 and 1949.[38]

Overall Irish issues were accorded a low priority by the Labour Cabinet. Matters relating to Northern Ireland in particular were very rarely discussed and Government members used their influence to keep discussion of its affairs at Westminster to a minimum. Generally Attlee and his colleagues were sensitive to the opinions of the Stormont leadership and sympathetic to its requirements. Most recognised and respected the fact that a majority in the region favoured the preservation of the Union. Their reluctance to interfere reflected a desire not to become enmeshed in Irish politics, the urgency of the other problems they faced and the impact of war. Thus Herbert Morrison was not alone in his deep admiration for the aggressive loyalty towards the crown shown by most of Northern Ireland's population and he remained keenly appreciative of its vital strategic role in wartime. He was himself convinced that the widespread sentiments of gratitude which this elicited had permanently modified public attitudes in Great Britain towards the Irish question; his colleagues certainly acted upon this assumption. Lord Addison (Dominions Office) considered that it would be folly for Great Britain in the future to 'throw away that safeguard [i.e. Northern Ireland] unless on terms that will secure its continued availability'.[39] Moreover the cooperative response of Stormont Ministers towards Britain both during and after the war compared favourably with Ireland's neutrality and the potentially destabilising impact of its subsequent anti-partition campaign.

Regarding the island's long-term political prospects, the Labour Cabinet broadly considered it to be inevitable that North and South should enter into some kind of closer relationship and ultimately unite. But this remained an unspoken assumption; British Ministers considered it prudent to maintain a strict silence on the issue in public and so avoid controversy, whilst encouraging quiet, inter-governmental cooperation on matters of common concern. On one point of principle they were agreed, that Northern unionists should not be coerced into a united Ireland. In this context a statement made by Ramsay MacDonald, at Westminster in 1937, was often quoted in memoranda. He had commented: 'the position of this government is that any change made in the relationship between the two governments in Ireland would require the consent of both'.[40]

STORMONT–WESTMINSTER RELATIONS, 1945–48

Notwithstanding the generally supportive attitude of the Labour leadership, Stormont Ministers inevitably faced specific and complex problems when they sought to implement the far-reaching measures emanating from Westminster during the immediate post-war years. Both for reasons of principle and of political calculation they experienced least difficulty in applying those socialist reforms which sought to achieve a more equitable distribution of wealth. The tradition of parity in social services between Great Britain and Northern Ireland stretched back to 1926. It was assumed that to abandon it would likely result in a loss of votes to local left-wing groups, whilst to preserve it helped widen the gap in welfare provision between North and South, so providing a potent additional argument in support of the Union. Moreover the Labour Government proved more willing than its predecessors to contribute towards the proportionately higher cost of extending such measures to Northern Ireland. Thus Northern Ireland Ministers embarked with some enthusiasm on a post-war programme of reforms which included the Northern Ireland Health Service Act, National Assistance and National Insurance legislation and made provision for the introduction of family allowances. These were chiefly distinguished from the equivalent Westminster measures in their inclusion of a carefully modulated residence qualification to deter an anticipated influx of Irish citizens into Northern Ireland.[41]

It was elements of socialist policy other than this programme of social reform which caused Stormont Ministers greatest anxiety. A number shared an enduring fear that a major constitutional collision between the two Governments would eventually occur. It was anticipated that this would be caused not by blatant intervention from Westminster in the region's transferred powers or by any overt attempt to coerce unionists into a united Ireland but rather by the economic policies being adopted by Attlee and his colleagues. Several were concerned that the socialist Cabinet would impose an ever-expanding list of controls and regulations on Northern Ireland's economy and push forward with successive measures of nationalisation. Brooke observed that whilst he could 'defend particular bills, . . . controls seep into the whole fabric of our lives'.[42] Some local Cabinet members were anxious that they would ultimately find the application of these insidious policies unacceptable for reasons of principle. They also considered that they had no mandate for any far-reaching economic programme and that if one was imposed from Westminster, owing to differences in economic and social structure between Great Britain and Northern Ireland, it would be injurious as well as intolerable. Moreover, they also feared that the consequent expansion of central Government powers would undermine the residual authority of Stormont. To avert the risk of serious confrontation they favoured pre-emptive negotiations with the Labour leadership directed towards achieving increased independence for Northern Ireland, perhaps dominion status.

This however raised major difficulties. On a purely political level it was arguably perverse for an avowedly unionist administration to seek to dilute the Union. A more fundamental problem was the region's constant and growing economic and financial dependence on Britain. For this reason, though there was much internal Party discussion of constitutional change the essential features of the Government's policy remained as before. It sought to cooperate closely with British Ministers whilst at the same time, exercising a moderating influence on socialist policy at least in its application to Northern Ireland. In November 1947, Brooke told his colleagues that there was no practical alternative to inter-governmental cooperation and suggested that they should not look for obstacles that might never arise. He stated publicly: 'We are working well with the present government and have no valid reason for altering the constitution'.[43]

THE IRELAND BILL, 1948–49

During the winter of 1948–49, the relationship between the Unionist and Labour Governments was severely tested. This was as a consequence of the decision taken by John A. Costello, *Taoiseach* in the Irish coalition Government, to repeal the External Relations Act and thereby sever the last constitutional connection between Ireland and the Commonwealth. This not only produced a crisis in Dublin's relations with Westminster, it also had a profound impact on Stormont's relations with both. With typical opportunism, Brooke capitalised on the gradual inflammation in North–South political tensions by holding a parliamentary election, in early February 1949, on the single issue: 'whether we are King's men or not'. The Unionist leadership could later legitimately claim a victory; the Party's total vote rose to 12 per cent higher than in 1945 and the representation of the various labour groups collapsed. They were the foremost casualty of the contest.[44]

Meanwhile, Stormont Ministers sought to influence the terms of the Ireland Bill which was introduced by the Imperial Government in response to Ireland's secession from the Commonwealth. On 14 December 1948 they forwarded their list of proposals to London with the intention of exploiting a 'favourable moment in history'[45] in order to strengthen their political position. When the negotiations began three weeks later Sir Basil argued that, amidst the uncertainty generated by Ireland's repeal legislation, the Northern Ireland electorate required reassurance. His Government's most far-reaching request therefore was that statutory force be given to two unsolicited declarations made in the Commons by Attlee, on 28 October and 25 November 1948. The Labour leader had then stated: 'no change will be made in the constitutional status of Northern Ireland without Northern Ireland's free consent'.[46]

Attlee acceded to this proposal without hesitation. In part this reflected his genuine desire to ease the anxieties of Ulster's unionist community; moreover, he believed that such a guarantee would be popular with the British electorate. Principally, however, he and most of his colleagues supported it because they were firmly convinced that it conformed to Britain's immediate strategic interests. These perceptions had been influenced by both the recent experience of war and the imminent change in Ireland's constitutional status. Thus the Imperial Government's official working party concluded, in January 1949, that it had become a 'matter of first class strategic importance for this country that the North should continue to form part of His Majesty's dominions. So far as can be foreseen it will never be to Great Britain's advantage that Northern Ireland should form part of a territory outside His Majesty's jurisdiction. Indeed it seems unlikely that Great Britain would ever be able to agree to this even if the people of Northern Ireland desired it'.[47] During Cabinet discussion Lord Longford (Frank

Pakenham) alone opposed the inclusion of a declaratory clause. It was no doubt due to sympathy with the profound reservations which he expressed regarding the impartiality of Unionist administration that Ministers agreed it would be 'inadvisable' to add significantly to the powers of the Northern Ireland Parliament.[48]

Subsequently Brooke succeeded in extracting Labour Government agreement to just one further proposal of substance. He had requested that in order to qualify for the Westminster franchise in Northern Ireland all persons should have had a period of six months residence in the area. He argued that the change was essential in order to counteract the threat of large numbers of Irish citizens entering into Northern Ireland and claiming the right to vote. Labour Ministers were reluctant but they finally acquiesced to a three, rather than six, months qualification being included in the bill. Crucially Attlee himself had been persuaded that there was a genuine risk of Southern Irishmen crossing the border in a coordinated effort to outvote unionists, as a stratagem in their anti-partition campaign.[49] The Ireland Bill became the focus of virulent nationalist criticism which concentrated exclusively on the guarantee to Northern Ireland and ignored those sections of the measure which would maintain the rights of Irish citizens and help sustain trade. In Ireland, the declaratory clause was regarded as evidence of an alarming and fundamental shift in Imperial Government policy, whereas for most Labour Ministers it merely expressed what had always been their essential, if hitherto rarely publicised, position on the partition issue.[50] Stormont Ministers were predictably delighted with the second reading debate and in particular, the robust speeches made in defence of the measure by Attlee, Morrison and Ede. Most of all they were gratified by the measure itself, which in Brooke's view 'placed the fate of Ulster in our own hands'. Retrospectively, he observed: 'it was hard negotiating but I must confess the socialist government played the game'.[51]

The mood within the Labour Cabinet was notably less euphoric – its members less unanimous in their view of the legislation. Already, in March 1949, Philip Noel-Baker had indicated his uneasiness about its terms and argued that British Ministers should thoroughly reappraise their approach to Anglo-Irish relations. He asserted that 'to continue partition and thereby alienate the natural sympathy of the Irish people would be a short-sighted policy . . . Great Britain realises that the present situation cannot last and that sooner or later there will be a united Ireland'.[52] In Cabinet, on the day following the second reading debate, some Ministers expressed doubts about the wisdom of entrusting to the Northern Ireland Parliament the power to veto Irish unity as its

membership might not fairly represent the wishes of the local population. It was suggested that, after the Ireland Bill had been passed, the
United Kingdom Government might take steps to satisfy itself that
Stormont was so constituted as to reflect adequately the views of the
electorate. However, after due consideration it was agreed that the issues
concerned 'lay wholly within the jurisdiction of the Northern Ireland
government'.[53]

Meanwhile, despite the declaratory clause, inside the Unionist Party
the internal debate over dominion status had continued virtually unabated. In late 1949, Brooke privately professed his despair at its intensity and at the consequent threat to unity. He suggested that it was
caused by 'frustration due to a [Labour] government' and by backbench
MPs feeling 'safe' after the Ireland Act and therefore more 'prepared
to risk a certain amount of independence'.[54] He was much relieved
when the Conservative Party returned to office in 1951. But satisfactory inter-governmental relations could not be assumed even after the
Labour Party's defeat. In 1946 the Stormont Cabinet had noted the
observable drift to the left in British politics and it was suggested that
future Tory Ministers might well adopt policies which the Northern
Ireland electorate would find unacceptable.[55] There was, in addition,
by 1950–51 a widespread feeling amongst unionists that they were
'being taken for granted by the conservatives'. It was claimed, for
example, that during the Ireland Bill debates 'no word [was] put in for
Ulster's defence'[56] by opposition MPs and Conservative leaders were
regarded as loathe to visit Northern Ireland. Brooke's impression after
earlier private conversations with Churchill was that he was 'in favour
of Irish unity' though 'not by force and only with our consent.' Rather
tactlessly, the ageing leader had then requested that he 'be excused
from coming over [to Ulster] because he said he reserved himself for
countries where he could do some good'.[57]

Both Labour and Conservative politicians tended to assume that the
most likely cause of change in Ulster politics in the longer term was
the apparent certainty of a future shift in the demographic balance
between the two communities there. Even Morrison observed: 'One
must keep one's eye on the point in time at which, owing to the higher
birth rate, the catholics may overtake the protestant population.' Brooke
records the Home Secretary advising him that: 'our population would
in the end defeat us'. Brooke replied that 'it would not affect the situation in our lifetime'.[58] Nonetheless, he certainly regarded such matters
as legitimate cause for continuing unionist anxiety.

NOTES

1. *Northern Ireland Parliamentary Debates (Commons)*, vol. 22, col. 1902, 4 September 1939.
2. B. Barton, *The Blitz, Belfast in the War Years* (Belfast: Blackstaff, 1989), pp. 43–4; also Tom Harrisson Mass Observation Archive, Diary MO 5462, entry for 7 March 1940 (University of Sussex).
3. Tom Harrisson, Mass Observation Report, FR 1309, 12 June 1942, University of Sussex.
4. Personal memorandum in Sir Wilfred Spender diaries, Public Records Office for Northern Ireland (hereinafter PRONI): D715, 2 August 1938.
5. *Ibid.*, 16 December 1940.
6. See B. Barton, *Brookeborough* (Belfast: Institute for Irish Studies, 1988) pp. 160–63; also John Bowman, *De Valera and the Ulster Question; 1917–73* (Oxford: Clarendon, 1982), pp. 220–38.
7. B. Barton, *Brookeborough, op.cit.*, pp. 168–70, 195–6.
8. *Ibid.*, pp. 197–9.
9. *Ibid.*, pp. 201–2.
10. *Ibid.*, pp. 202–4.
11. *Ibid*, pp. 204–7; also R. J. Lawrence, *The Government of Northern Ireland* (Oxford: Clarendon, 1965), pp. 63–73.
12. Cabinet Conclusions, PRONI: CAB 4/473, 15 May 1941.
13. See Barton, *Brookeborough, op.cit.*, pp. 211–16, for more detailed analysis.
14. See Spender diaries, *op.cit.* (n.4), mid December 1943; also B. Barton, *Brookeborough, op.cit.*, pp. 226–9.
15. Brooke diary (private diary kept by Sir Basil Brooke), 8, 11 and 17 February 1944, PRONI D3004/D/31–45; also Spender diaries, *op.cit.*, 17 and 25 February 1944.
16. See minutes of meetings of Unionist Parliamentary Party, 19 September, 10 October 1944, and 2 May 1945, in PRONI: D1327/22, Ulster Unionist Council Papers, PRONI: D1327; also Cabinet Conclusions, PRONI: CAB 4/597, 15 September 1944, and PRONI: CAB 4/622, 19 April 1944.
17. See interim report of the Planning Advisory Board Committee, 1944, Cmd 224, *passim*; also Cabinet Conclusions, PRONI: CAB 4/592, 602 for 10 August and 19 October 1944; Lawrence, *op.cit.*, p. 153.
18. Brooke diary, *op.cit.*, 9, 10 October 1943; also records of Ulster Unionist Council, 1943–1944, PRONI: D1327, *passim*, and Cabinet Conclusions, 6 May 1943, PRONI: CAB 4/541.
19. See minutes of Ulster Unionist Council meetings, 2 March 1944 and *passim*, in PRONI D1327/8; also 7 March 1945, and *passim*, records of annual Unionist party conferences, PRONI: D1327/9; Brooke diary, *op.cit.* 16 January, 14 and 26 February 1945.
20. *Ibid.*, 29 July 1943 and 23 March 1945; also minutes of meetings of Ulster Unionist Council, 2 March 1944, PRONI: D1327/8.
21. See Lawrence, *op.cit.*, pp. 71–3; also John Ditch, *Social Policy in Northern Ireland between 1939 and 1950* (Aldershot: Avebury, 1988), pp. 86–8.
22. See Spender diaries, *op.cit.*, 2 December 1943; also 17 August 1943 and 28 April 1944.

23. PRONI: CAB 4/558, 14 October 1943; also Brooke diary, *op.cit.*, 21 March, 2 May 1944.
24. Cabinet Conclusions, PRONI: CAB 4/555, 556, 576, on 16, 27 September 1943 and 23 March 1944.
25. Cabinet Conclusions, 19 April 1945, PRONI: CAB 4/622.
26. See Public Record Office, London (hereinafter PRO): HO45/24213, 'Conscription 1945–46,' note by H. Morrison, 29 October 1946, and minute by C. Markbreiter, 9 May 1945.
27. Spender diaries, *op.cit.*, 16 March, 11 September 1944; see also minutes of Ulster Unionist Party Standing Committee, 11 April and 10 November 1944, 9 February 1945, in PRONI: D1327/7.
28. See J. H. Whyte 'How much discrimination was there under the Unionist regime, 1921–68?' in T. Gallagher and J. O'Connell (eds), *Contemporary Irish Studies* (Manchester: Manchester University Press, 1983); Cabinet discussion of education in PRONI: CAB 4/594, 601 on 25 July and 12 October 1945 and of family allowances, PRONI: CAB 4/628, 650 on 28 June and 15 October 1945.
29. Brooke diary, *op.cit.*, 5 September 1944, 11 July 1944.
30. See PRONI: CAB 4/606,615, Cabinet discussions on 16 November 1944 and 15 February 1945; also Brooke Diary, *op.cit.*, 2 May, and 14 July 1944.
31. Brooke diary, *op.cit.*, 7, 8 May 1945.
32. See Ulster Unionist Council Papers, PRONI: D1327/6, 7, 22, for mid-1945, also Brooke diary, *op.cit.*, 28 April 1945.
33. Barton, *The Blitz, op.cit.*, p. 286.
34. *Ibid.*, pp. 286–7.
35. Brooke diary, *op. cit.*, 9 October and 13 November 1945.
36. A. Kelly (Home Office) to R. Gransden (Cabinet Secretary, Stormont), 2 April 1946, in PRONI: CAB 9J/53 'Relations with Labour Government, 1945–50'; also Bob Purdie, 'The Friends of Ireland: British Labour and Irish Nationalism,' p. 86, in Gallagher and O'Connell (eds), *op.cit.*
37. See PRO: HO45/21996, 'The Franchise Act, 1946,' *passim.*
38. Lawrence, *op.cit.*, pp. 75–9.
39. Memorandum, by Lord Addison, dated 18 October 1946, in PRO: PREM 8/1222, 'Partition, 1946–50'; also memorandum by H. Morrison (Lord President of the Council), dated 16 October 1946, in PRO: CAB 129/13. (CAB 129 contains post-1945 Cabinet memoranda.)
40. J. E. Stevenson to E. C. Machtig (Permanent Under-Secretary, Dominions Office), 22 May 1946, in PRO: DO 35/1228/WX101/146; also see 'Summary of Relations between Great Britain and Eire' in PRO: FO 371/50364, *passim.*
41. Lawrence, *op.cit.*, Chapters 7 and 9.
42. Brooke memorandum, dated 3 March 1948, in PRONI: CAB 4/746. See B. Barton 'Relations between Westminster and Stormont during the Attlee premiership', *Irish Political Studies*, Vol. 7 (1992), pp. 6–8.
43. See Cabinet Conclusions, 13 November 1947, in PRONI: CAB 4/735; also Brooke diary, *op.cit*, 23 September 1947 and notes of Unionist Party meeting on 14 November 1947, in PRONI: CAB 9J/53.

44. Brooke diary, *op.cit.*, 7 September, 18 November 1948, 4, 26 January and 11 February 1949.
45. Memorandum by Lord Rugby (was Sir J. L. Maffey), United Kingdom Representative to Ireland, dated 4 February 1949, in PRO: PREM 8/1222.
46. Quoted in report of working party of officials, 1 January 1949, in PRO: CAB 21/1842; see also PRO: PREM 8/1464, *passim*.
47. Report by working party, 1 January 1949, in PRO: CAB 21/1842, *op.cit.*
48. 7th Earl of Longford, Minister of Civil Aviation, on 12 January 1949, in PRO: PREM 8/1464, *op.cit.*
49. Memorandum by Attlee, 10 January 1949, in PRO: CAB 129/32.
50. See notes of talks between Sean MacBride (Irish Foreign Minister) and Philip Noel-Baker, 5 May 1949, in PRO: DO35/3973, 'The Ireland Bill'; also 'aides memoires' by Irish Government, dated 7, 10 May 1949, in PRO: CAB 129/35.
51. Brooke diary, *op.cit.*, 31 December 1949, 12 May 1949; see also Brooke to Attlee, 3 June 1949, in PRO: PREM8/1464, *op.cit.*
52. Noel-Baker to E. Bevin (Secretary of State for Foreign Affairs), 9 March 1949, in PRO: DO35/3972, 'The Ireland Bill, 1949.'
53. Cabinet Conclusions, 12 May 1949, in PRO: PREM 8/1464, *op.cit.*
54. Brooke diary, *op.cit.*, 31 December 1949; also Parliamentary Unionist Party, minutes of meeting, 3 January 1952, PRONI: D1327/22.
55. See Cabinet memoranda, dated 9 January 1946 and 5 February 1946, in PRONI: CAB 9J/53; also Brooke diary, *op.cit.*, 23 September 1947.
56. Brooke diary, *op.cit.*, 12 April, 2 and 3 May 1951.
57. *Ibid*, 11 April 1948.
58. Memorandum by Morrison, dated 16 October 1946, PRO: CAB 129/13; also Brooke diary, *op.cit.*, 19 September 1946.

5 Labour in Britain and the Northern Ireland Labour Party, 1900–70

Terry Cradden

Just one among many of the conundrums associated with the Northern Ireland question is the existence of an enduring democratic socialist tradition and a high level of workplace organisation, yet the failure of the labour and trade union movement to sustain an enduring and electorally successful party of labour. Sectarian division provides some part of the answer, but there are two other aspects which demand attention. First, why did the Northern Ireland Labour Party, which began to enjoy some ascendancy in the 1960s, not find itself in the vanguard of the Northern Ireland civil rights movement? Second, why did the British Labour Party provide so little succour to its Northern Ireland comrades in toil down through the years?

IRELAND: NOT A 'REAL' ISSUE

During the twenty years preceding the partition of Ireland the attitude of the British labour movement to Ireland was superficially consistent, but in reality full of contradictions – principally because its authors were, by turns, either disinterested or exasperated.[1] In the early years of the century Labour's approach appeared to rest on two main premises: firstly, that democracy demanded the maximum devolution of political decision-making (or 'legislative independence'); and secondly, that the 'Imperial Standard' (under the influence of which the benefits of democracy were transmitted to less advanced people abroad) must be maintained. Though not the formally declared policy of the Labour Representation Committee (LRC) – the immediate predecessor of the British Labour Party (BLP)[2] – most of its members were plainly in favour of Home Rule for Ireland within the Empire.

A notable exception was William Walker, a respected member of the LRC Executive as well as being the leading light of the Belfast

LRC and its major affiliate, the Independent Labour Party (ILP). He was an ardent proponent both of the Union itself and of the fundamental unity of the workers of the whole United Kingdom of Great Britain and Ireland. The obligation to defend Walker's right to hold a divergent view, and frustration at the way the Home Rule question continued to push 'real' issues off the political stage led to a cooling of Labour's ardour for a time. But by 1912, when the Government of Ireland Bill was presented to Parliament, the Labour Party declared itself fully committed to the Liberal Government's Home Rule design.

In Ireland itself, not surprisingly, the labour movement was divided on Home Rule. In Belfast, the most active centre, there were three factions within the ILP structure: the largest, the Walkerite 'unionists', controlled the ILP's North Branch; the members of Central were broadly behind the national Labour line on Home Rule; and East was made up mainly of republican disciples of James Connolly, the Irish Marxist and socialist leader – who was to be executed by the British for his participation in the Dublin Easter Rising.[3] However, Central and East had already indicated their intention to depart from the ILP as soon as a mooted independent Irish socialist party had been formed. In the South of Ireland, by contrast, the Home Rulers within the movement had been marginalised and control lay, for all practical purposes, in the hands of those for whom nothing short of complete independence would now be enough. When the Irish Trade Union Congress (ITUC) – the only substantial all Ireland forum for socialist discourse – took the inevitably separatist decision to form itself into a combined Irish trade union centre and labour party, Belfast Trades Council was led out of Congress by the Walker supporters by whom the Council was then dominated.

The background in Belfast was of massive support by Protestant workers for the Ulster Unionist mobilisation against Home Rule. One consequence of this, following the passage of the offending Bill, was the violent expulsion of thousands of Catholic workers, together with a group of Protestants of known socialist sympathies, from the Belfast shipyards. Yet even the Walkerites were appalled when partition was suggested as a way forward in 1914, for it promised them the worst of all worlds: of being separated from their trade union and working class brothers and sisters in Great Britain, *and* from their comrades in the rest of Ireland. The Trades Council was thus able to declare its united opposition to any partition proposal, and immediately re-affiliated to the ITUC.

The British Labour Party was also opposed to partition. But in a debate in the Commons in 1914, Ramsay MacDonald entered an equivocal note. Having claimed that the Party was 'quite immovable' in its opposition to the political division of Ireland, he nonetheless went on to declare that:

> We will take the position of a detached party, listening to what is said, and noticing what is said, helping, as we have always done during the last two years in every possible way, Home Rule to be inscribed on the statute book of this realm.

A later Labour speaker in the same debate revealed the basis for this apparent willingness to contemplate the unthinkable:

> ... so long as Home Rule is being discussed year after year, questions of social reform, affecting the interests of the workers, are constantly being neglected.[4]

THE IMPORTANCE OF GETTING OUT

Back in Belfast, both the Trades Council and the ITUC were now seriously out of touch with the loyalist grass roots. With the implementation of Home Rule deferred for the duration of the Great War; with the growing apace of Northern membership of British general unions (rather than of Jim Larkin's Irish Transport and General Workers' Union (ITGWU), which was overwhelmingly successful in the rest of the country); with British patriotic fervour at a peak; and with thousands of Irishmen off fighting for the Empire, Protestant workers saw the Easter Rising in 1916 as a traitorous outrage. The efforts of the leaders of what was by then the Irish Trade Union Congress and Labour Party to distance themselves from the participation of Connolly and his Irish Citizen Army in the Rising did nothing to ease a nascent Northern unilateralism.

In 1917, therefore, despite Belfast Trades Council's earlier anti-partition proclivities, it joined with a number of individual unions and the by then mainly pro-Union remnant of the ILP in the formation of a separate Belfast Labour Party. Remarkably, British Labour had by that stage determined that Ireland was outside its territory of operation, and that the obligation to organise politically there belonged to the (again renamed) Irish Labour Party & Trade Union Congress (ILP&TUC). It was on this ground that the BLP felt obliged to reject a request from the new Belfast group for affiliation.[5] The rebuff from that quarter did not mean that Belfast Labour's eyes turned South. Indeed, the Southern connection became weaker still as time passed: Northern participation in the Congress anti-conscription campaign in 1918 was negligible,[6] and the decision of the ILP&TUC not to fight the 1918 election was also ignored.[7] The Belfast Party fielded four candidates in the city; all were defeated, but they did well enough to keep heart.

At the Labour Party Conference in London earlier in the same year a resolution supported by the leadership recognised, 'unhesitatingly', the 'claim of the people of Ireland to Home Rule.' But there was an important proviso: that such 'self-determination' should apply only to 'exclusively Irish affairs.' The concern it transpired – and it requires a leap of imagination to comprehend the anxiety – was that a separate Irish state might institute a potential threat to Great Britain from an Irish navy and/or army. In other words, as J. R. Clynes put it in a post-election parliamentary debate, the British Labour Party was 'not arguing for independence' for Ireland.[8] Labour was thus opposed to Ireland leaving, or being removed from, the United Kingdom; it was, at the same time, ideologically committed to as much legislative independence under Home Rule as the Irish people themselves demanded; and it was also against partition. After much agonising (and ignoring a common position on Home Rule agreed with the ILP&TUC in September 1920) the obvious contradictions were eventually 'resolved' by Labour giving its support to the Anglo-Irish Treaty negotiated by Lloyd George with *Sinn Féin* in December 1921 – the which, needless to say, barely met any of the BLP's conflicting requirements.[9] What the Treaty did do, of course, was to remove the Irish question from the Westminster agenda. No party desired this more than Labour.

A DARK DAWN

The 1919 '44-Hour' engineering strike and Belfast Labour Party gains in the first post-war Corporation elections suggested a change of public mood – in the industrialised part of the North of Ireland at any rate. But other events stole the movement's sting. With Labour wilfully marked by the Unionist Party as an 'enemy within', two years of bitter inter-communal strife were opened by another expulsion of over 7,000 Catholics and 'rotten Prods' (or Protestant socialists) from the shipyards in 1920. The trade union movement came poorly out of this: there was almost unbridled sectarianism on the shop floor; an insistence by the ILP&TUC that the problem was for individual unions to solve; equivocation in practice by most union executive committees in Britain; and an exhausting but fruitless search for a settlement by the Belfast Labour leadership.[10] Partly as a consequence, they were in a state of deep disillusion when the first elections for the new Northern Ireland Parliament were called in 1921. It was left to four independents to carry the Labour banner – in the event with little success.

As the much enfeebled movement faced into the future in the new Northern Ireland state, then, it had few political friends. While it can hardly have cared too much about the enmity of the Unionists, the Northern Nationalists and *Sinn Féin*, it must have been fairly wounded by the isolation imposed upon it by its ostensible comrades in socialist struggle. The ILP&TUC, for its part, while nominally the coordinating body for the whole of the Irish labour movement, was almost totally preoccupied with Southern concerns; it paid negligible attention to the North, still less to the real day-to-day difficulties of its Northern Labour brethren. Fences were mended with Dublin as the 1920s progressed, however, to the point where the ILP&TUC formally acknowledged Northern Ireland as the LP(NI)'s sole political preserve. It is perhaps worthy of comment that the British Labour Party had given the power to grant licences for this part of the United Kingdom to a party which lay outside that jurisdiction.

As for British Labour, the donor party, it was only too happy to leave the Northern Ireland movement to its own devices. Although partition had created a very different state of affairs from that envisaged in the Home Rule Ireland of long-standing Labour policy, the Party's reaction to the new situation was little more than a sigh of deliverance. So complete became its casting off from Ireland that several quite reasonable requests from Belfast for the remission of political levies on members of British unions in Northern Ireland which had ended up in BLP coffers were effectively ignored. More injurious still, British Labour later decided that it was not even prepared to grant the Northern Ireland Party the associate status enjoyed by organisations like the Isle of Man Labour Party, or the Trinidad Working Men's Association.[11] The passion to be out of Ireland obliterated fraternity.

The darkness appeared to lift for Labour as a calming of community divisions and declining wages brought it renewed local election successes. These were crowned in the 1925 Northern Ireland General Election by the victory of three trade union figures standing in the newly formed Labour Party (Northern Ireland) (LP(NI)) interest: Sam Kyle of the British Transport & General Workers' Union (known in Ireland – for

legal reasons – as the Amalgamated TGWU); Billy McMullan of the Irish
TGWU; and Jack Beattie of the Blacksmiths'.[12] Because of the Nationalist
policy of abstentionism, these three were to provide the only substantial opposition to the Unionist Government in the ensuing session. They
acted with vigour on a broad front, and harassed the Government constantly. Indeed it was these Labour gains, rather than any fear of the
Nationalists, which convinced the Unionists that proportional representation must be abolished. This required an amendment to the Government of Ireland Act, and it clearly caused some apprehensions at
Westminster. But after a delay of a few months, it was eventually
agreed to, without apparent protest from the BLP. The change achieved
its purpose in any case, and only Beattie survived in the first-past-the-
post election of 1929.

NORTHERN IRELAND LABOUR AND THE UNION WITH BRITAIN

The LP(NI) tended to focus almost all its attention on bread-and-butter
issues; it was staunchly anti-sectarian; and, appropriately enough, perhaps, was not formally committed one way or another on the Union
with Great Britain. This stance was not a consequence of irresolution,
still less of calculated ambiguity. It was simply that 'labourmen' – as
they described themselves – saw their primary role as the defence of
working-class interests. Beside that, constitutional questions were manifestly of secondary importance. This is not to say that LP(NI) members lacked opinions on the Irish national question. Its membership
was predominantly Protestant, and the majority of those members were
undoubtedly in favour of remaining within the United Kingdom. But
the Party contained an important and highly influential group – themselves overwhelmingly Protestant – who remained opposed to partition, and looked forward to an independent socialist united Ireland. As
it happens, all three of the LP(NI)'s MPs in the 1920s were of this
stamp. Kyle was an old-fashioned LRC Home-Ruler; McMullan, an
unreconstructed Connollyite, came – implausible though it may seem
– from the loyalist heartland of Belfast's Shankill Road; Beattie too
came from an LRC/ILP background – but was eventually to become
so close to the Northern Nationalists as to be almost indistinguishable
from them.

     What needs to be emphasised is that they all of them also, like their
LP(NI) colleagues of a more unionist view,[13] had a strong affection

for the British Labour movement. The old ILP tradition was probably important in this respect – and its Belfast Branch remained active until the ILP disaffiliated from the BLP in 1932.[14] British Labour was also the model of the kind of party which the LP(NI) wanted to create in Northern Ireland. That this fellow feeling was scarcely reciprocated did not seem to diminish the LP(NI)'s admiration for the BLP and its achievements.

In the early 1930s the LP(NI) became the Northern Ireland Labour Party (NILP), and the change of name was perhaps symbolic of a drift towards a more pro-Union position. Already weak political links with Dublin practically disappeared when the ITUC and the Irish Labour Party (IrLP) decided to go their separate ways in 1931. Of more immediate significance were the growing tensions within the NILP between its two leading figures. McMullen and Kyle had departed to senior trade union posts in Dublin,[15] and Beattie's only serious competitor for influence was Harry Midgley, an official of the Shopworkers Union.[16] Midgley won a seat in the Northern Ireland House of Commons (by now housed in the new Parliament Buildings at Stormont) in 1933, and as leader of the Party began to try to push it in a unionist direction.

Although a former Home Ruler, Midgley had been edging towards a pro-Union position for some time. Beattie's expulsion from the NILP in 1934 – for failing to move the writ for a by-election in a traditionally nationalist seat – helped Midgley's strategy to some extent, and he was soon taking every opportunity of providing the Party with an essentially pro-British image. Midgley also fostered links with British Labour's Headquarters in London, and was on friendly terms with several senior figures in the Labour Party hierarchy, including Herbert Morrison. While there is little evidence of formal contacts between the BLP and the NILP in the 1930s, Midgley certainly had hopes of gaining benefit for his Party by firming up the British connection.

But although Beattie had gone, there remained an influential anti-partitionist faction within the NILP, and Midgley's path was far from smooth. He finally resigned after Beattie's readmission to membership in 1942, complaining, in fact quite erroneously, that the anti-partitionists were in control of the Party.[17] Midgley immediately proceeded to set up the avowedly pro-Union Commonwealth Labour Party, and not long after, to the consternation of his former colleagues, joined the wartime Stormont Cabinet as its only non-Unionist Party member.[18] In the meantime, Beattie had won the West Belfast seat at Westminster in a by-election; he accepted the Labour whip in the Commons, and

began to build bridges to a very different group within the BLP than
that which Midgley had cultivated.

WARMING UP THE BRITISH CONNECTION

Unemployment fell dramatically in Northern Ireland during the war;
union membership more than doubled, and this was accompanied not
only by numerous episodes of militant industrial action, but also by a
surge of political mobilisation on the left. The first real attempt by the
NILP to arrive at a definitive position on partition got lost in the middle
of this, and the post-war elections were fought on a ticket which went
no further than asserting that no change could be made in Northern
Ireland's constitutional status without the consent of its people. In manifesto terms this meant that partition was a 'non-essential' issue – certainly for so long as the majority of voters wanted to remain within
the United Kingdom. Although the NILP gained only two Stormont
seats, its vote was massively up on previous performances. Intriguingly,
in the Westminster contest a few weeks later the NILP was able to
proclaim the endorsement of Clement Attlee, Labour Prime Minister-
to-be, who assured any successful NILP candidates of a warm wel-
come in the Labour Parliamentary Party. While no seats were won,
the Party polled promisingly well once more,[19] and looked forward
with justifiable confidence to the next electoral outing.

Another sign of closer contacts with the BLP came at the NILP's
1945 Annual Conference, when it was addressed by the British Party's
Assistant National Organiser. Also interesting was the decision of the
BLP National Executive Committee eight months later to put up £400
and a candidate from its own list of parliamentary hopefuls, Desmond
Donnelly, to fight a Westminster by-election on behalf of the NILP in
County Down (he did well, and gained almost 40 per cent of the vote).
More interesting still was the formation in 1945 of the 'Friends of
Ireland' group, which consisted of thirty or so Labour backbench MPs
at Westminster.[20] While its principal object was redress of the grievances of Northern Ireland's Catholic minority, it was committed also
to the ending of partition. Despite that, there came to be an interesting
affinity between the developing thinking of a substantial number of
leading NILP figures and the approach adopted by at least some of
the Friends.

Though from this distance a misconceived view, they believed that
Britain (and especially a Labour-governed Britain) was, in the words

of Geoffrey Bing MP, 'the most likely source of progressive political change' in Northern Ireland. They saw promise in the postwar performance of the NILP which, as well as doing well with the voters was also committing itself to democratic reform: 'one-man-one-vote' in local government elections (to bring Northern Ireland in line with the rest of the United Kingdom); repeal of the notorious Special Powers Act (which had, to take just one example, permitted internment without trial of suspected republicans during the war); the disbandment of the B Specials (the wholly Protestant paramilitary reserve force of the Royal Ulster Constabulary), and an inquiry into the gerrymandering of electoral boundaries. And what both the more thoughtful of the Friends and the more pragmatic of the NILP's anti-unionists both looked forward to was 'democratic Labour governments in Ireland north and south' – something which would simply render partition meaningless.[21]

Unfortunately, the Friends became entangled in the concerted all-Ireland anti-partition campaign of the late 1940s,[22] and opposition to their activities built up to the point where the NILP effectively banned members of the Friends from its public platforms – because of the electoral dangers of being identified with what was, even then, being described as 'pan-nationalism.' The real irony was that the Party to which the debarred Friends belonged had only recently decided to provide, without cost, one of its own full-time organisers to assist the NILP to develop its constituency organisation and to fight elections. Arthur Johnson, formerly the Labour Agent for Newcastle-upon-Tyne Central, took up his new post in May 1948.

Despite the activities of the Friends of Ireland, however, the Union of Northern Ireland with Great Britain also had long-standing friends in the British Labour Party, at a very senior level. Midgley's old friend Morrison paid constant tribute to Northern Ireland for its wartime fortitude; Tom Johnston, Secretary of State for Scotland, lauded the loyalty of Northern Ireland, as against Ireland's neutrality; Chuter Ede, the Home Secretary, blankly refused to inquire into how Stormont discharged its responsibilities; Labour Ministers accepted without demur the convention that matters which had been devolved to the Northern Ireland Parliament could not be discussed at Westminster; and, of truly far-reaching significance, it was the Labour Cabinet which provided the so-called 'step-by-step' financial guarantees which enabled the Unionist Government to implement the same welfare changes which had been introduced in Britain, without incurring fiscal difficulties or disturbing the Unionist Party's claim to be the only sure protector of the link by which these benefits were underwritten. Thus did British

Labour – however unwittingly – provide the NILP's Unionist enemies with a key weapon in their battle to hold back the advance of Labour in Northern Ireland.[23]

1948: A MAJOR SETBACK

The statement by *Taoiseach* John A. Costello in 1948 that he intended to take Ireland out of the Commonwealth and declare it a republic took even his own supporters by surprise. It was to be the rock upon which the NILP's hopes of an early breakthrough perished. The immediate response of the Labour Government at Westminster to the announcement was to underline that there could be no change in Northern Ireland's position within the United Kingdom 'without Northern Ireland's full agreement'. In light of this, the NILP Executive gave careful consideration to its own position and how best to make it known. It chose the debate on a motion put down at Stormont by a Nationalist MP (seconded by Beattie) which criticised the attitude of the Unionists to Irish reunification. Bob Getgood, NILP MP for Belfast (Oldpark) – who was of a mildly anti-partitionist disposition himself – emphasised three main points in his speech: firstly, that both Unionists and Nationalists had always cynically exploited the sectarian fears and passions of the divided electorate; secondly, that the Party fully endorsed the principle of consent as outlined by Attlee – which was existing NILP policy; and thirdly, in view of the gerrymandering designed to ensure continued Unionist domination, a parliamentary election was not enough. Only a straightforward plebiscite on the Union would make the will of the people truly clear. In keeping with the logic of this position, Getgood and his colleague Hugh Downey abstained in the vote.

But even among the Party's more radical thinkers there were some who felt that this approach was inadequate to the task in hand. Given the depth of the sectarian divide, the NILP could only build its strength by being clearly seen to rise above it. A former Chairman of the Party, William Leeburn, was in this camp and he tabled a discussion document which argued, in short, that the way for the NILP to avoid being labelled either unionist/Protestant or nationalist/Catholic was for it to become a regional wing of the British Labour Party. But Leeburn had underestimated the strength of the anti-partitionism of some of his fellows. Before an already arranged meeting with Morgan Phillips, General Secretary of the BLP, could take place to discuss Leeburn's proposal, details were leaked to the press. All hell broke loose. By the time

Phillips arrived in Belfast, therefore, the British Party had already decided that it did not wish to 'interfere' in the internal affairs of the NILP.

The Northern Ireland General Election of 1949 was called by Prime Minister Brooke to defend the Union against all-comers. For the NILP the results were devastating: the left attracted only just over a quarter of its 1945 vote, and the Party lost both its Stormont seats. Cutting a long and sometimes sordid story short, the upshot of the declaration of the Republic, the formal response to it of the NILP, and Leeburn's proposal to integrate the Party into the BLP was the resignation of a large number of the NILP's anti-partitionists. The Labour Government's 'copper-fastening' of partition, in clause 1(1)B of what became the 1949 Ireland Act, lay at the core of their objections – objections shared by many Labour dissidents in the House of Commons.[24] For that clause effectively transferred from the people of Northern Ireland to the *parliament* of Northern Ireland any decision on the constitutional future. So incensed were the defectors that they persuaded the Irish Labour Party to breach its time-honoured 'bailiwick' understanding with the NILP and to found a wing of its own organisation in the North. The more or less unionist remnant of the NILP replied by declaring itself in favour of the permanence of the Union with Britain.

Neither side of the Labour quarrel profited in the long run from coming off the fence on partition. Although the Northern wing of the IrLP had some early election successes, especially in local government, relations with Dublin became difficult and it was also soon riven by factionalism. The most obvious manifestation of this was that candidates describing themselves as Irish Labour, Republican Labour and Independent Irish Labour, respectively, faced each other in two constituencies in the 1953 Northern Ireland General Election. Although Beattie sat for the IrLP at Westminster, and continued to vote with the Parliamentary Labour Party on most issues, he was past his best as a vote getter and lost his seat in 1955.

In the hope of building up its support among the Protestant working class the NILP turned away from radicalism as well as anti-partitionism, and began deliberately to downplay issues such as gerrymandering and discrimination.[25] Notwithstanding that, it too entered upon a downhill slide, despite the benefit of what was generally agreed to be the unsparing work of Johnson. In 1952 British Labour's NEC decided that the cost of keeping him in Northern Ireland 'was not justified by the results', and it substituted an annual grant to the NILP – set at £300 to begin with. (The BLP's subvention lasted until 1972, by which time it had been raised to £1100 – in real terms probably a lower sum than 1952.)[26]

THE 1960s: SUCCESS BECKONS

The NILP's fortunes began to revive when the electoral system, for once, handed it a small measure of justice. In 1958, on a vote only 6,500 or so up on the Party's 1953 total of 30,000, it managed to gain four Stormont seats. Incidentally, the 'Notes for Candidates' in that election advised them to show support on the doorsteps for the B Specials and the Special Powers Act.[27] Whether this was an influence on the voters on that occasion is impossible to gauge. By the early 1960s the wind had changed, however, and a process of what might be called 'secularisation' was obviously in train. In the 1962 Stormont election the NILP gained no extra seats, but more than doubled its vote to 77,000. Of deeper significance was that nearly half the voters in the Belfast city constituencies favoured the NILP.

There were probably three main reasons for this. Firstly, the Party had clearly succeeded in gaining considerable ground in Protestant areas, especially among skilled workers in the engineering industry. Secondly, the Nationalists were never a force in Belfast (and had faded entirely by the mid-1950s), while anti-partition Labour, despite maintaining a couple of 'personality' strongholds, was otherwise a spent force. Both these factors are sure to have inclined many more Catholic voters to turn to the NILP. Thirdly, the development of local television had enabled the NILP to project as never before its image as a defender of working-class economic interests, as being opposed to discrimination on grounds of religion, and as a party 'in the middle' on the partition question – despite its constitutional commitment to the permanence of the Union.

Indeed, as the decade progressed and memories of old battles faded, the NILP began to regain much of its old anti-sectarian character. Even some of the anti-partition dissidents of the late 1940s returned to the fold. And new recruits included a host of young people of a classically 1960s militant disposition – from both sides of the sectarian divide – who saw the NILP as their only possible base of operation. The hardy annuals of one-man-one-vote, the Special Powers Act, housing and job discrimination as well as gerrymandering were all addressed. So too were fresh issues like the siting of a new university in the (Protestant) town of Coleraine rather than Londonderry (the predominantly Roman Catholic second city), the abolition of the death penalty, the extension of the free legal aid system to Northern Ireland, and the ending of the exclusion of the voluntary Catholic-managed Mater Hospital in Belfast from the National Health Service.

Yet despite the obvious gathering from the early 1960s of the pressures which were to lead to the civil rights agitation at the end of the decade, there remained a hesitancy on the part of some leading NILP members about tackling issues of democratic reform more forcefully. The main reason for this was a wish to avoid 'alienating hard-won Protestant support', even though most of their colleagues felt that the time had come when the NILP 'must champion Catholic minority rights if the possibility of a stable and non-sectarian community was not to be thrown away forever.'[28] But it was more than the cautious minority which came to see a newly-formed group in Great Britain – shades of the Friends of Ireland – as a mixed blessing.

The Campaign for Democracy in Ulster (CDU) was set up in 1965. It differed from the Friends in one crucial way, in that while many of its members were personally in favour of Irish unity, the CDU was 'concerned only with obtaining full British democratic standards for the people of Northern Ireland, to which they are entitled as British subjects.'[29] Essentially a rank-and-file organisation, it nonetheless gained the sponsorship of over one hundred Labour MPs and Peers, including Michael Foot, Roy Hattersley, Kevin McNamara, Ian Mikardo, Stan Orme, David Owen, Reg Prentice and Brian Walden – and the recently-elected MP for Manchester (Blackley), Paul Rose, who provided the CDU with its public face. There can be no doubt about the early impact of the CDU on British Labour thinking on Northern Ireland, nor about the contribution which it made to the growing clamour within Northern Ireland itself, focused on the un-British nature of democracy there.

To begin with the NILP established fairly cordial relations with the CDU. since their ambitions coincided almost precisely. In the year that the CDU was founded the NILP had publicly complained that the new and supposedly reforming Unionist Prime Minister, Terence O'Neill, had failed to deliver:

> No attempt has been made . . . to knit the community together; there has been no electoral reform, no review of electoral boundaries . . . no ombudsman. Not merely has Captain O'Neill dashed the hopes he himself raised, he has added a new bitterness and disappointment to the grievances of the minority.[30]

(This, it ought to be said, was more than a mere policy critique. O'Neill recognised a competitor for the votes of Northern Ireland's 'moderates' when he saw one, and in successive elections specifically targeted the Stormont seats held by the NILP's MPs.) A year later, having overcome the reservations of the hesitant few, the NILP allied with the Northern Ireland Committee of the Irish Congress of Trade Unions to produce a carefully crafted *Joint Memorandum on Citizen's Rights in Northern Ireland*. Published in 1967, after Unionist Ministers had rejected it out of hand, it 'was as full a programme of reform as any [later to be] brought out by an explicitly civil rights group'.[31]

It was inevitable, however, that tensions would arise between the NILP and the CDU. The Party's concerns, as they grew, were not of course about the CDU's agenda, but about the possible effects – certainly as more conservative NILP members saw them – on long-standing NILP voters of the CDU's seeming interference and its apparent siding with Irish nationalism. Even the most enthusiastic reformers were anxious to preserve their base in working-class Protestant Belfast. But both organisations were about to be overtaken by events on the streets.[20]

A DEMOCRATIC SOCIALIST FAILURE

The NILP faded out of existence in the early 1970s; and Stormont stands prorogued. Belatedly committed to Irish unity 'by consent', the British Labour Party now bestows its fraternal favour on the fundamentally nationalist Social Democratic and Labour Party – the SDLP, led by John Hume. Even so, a sometimes acrimonious debate continues within the Party about whether it should extend its own organisation into Northern Ireland, and put up candidates there as it does in every English, Scottish and Welsh constituency. Whatever the merits of that proposal, we ought first to return to the questions posed at the beginning of this chapter – which are essentially about the failure of democratic socialism to gain any more than a tiny foothold in Northern Ireland in the first fifty years of its separate existence.

Firstly, why did the NILP, a party with its own MPs at Stormont, a firmly non-sectarian image and a record of activism on issues of democratic reform, not take on the leadership of what was to become the civil rights movement? The most immediately obvious reason was the procrastination caused by the NILP's constant looking over of its shoulder to see if its traditional voters were still following after. By the time the head of steam had been released out onto the streets, therefore, it was too late to take charge. Bob Purdie provides an even more persuasive explanation for the NILP's failure to seize the initiative:

> Very largely because, as a party which was orientated to parliamentary methods, it was not a suitable instrument for creating a mass

extra-parliamentary movement; indeed most of its leaders were incapable of imagining such a course of action.[32]

He goes on to argue that the NILP could have become a *parliamentary* alternative to the civil rights movement had the possibility of an NILP-led government at Stormont, which the 1962 election seemed to hint at, been fulfilled.

The second question concerns the British Labour Party. Why did it take so little interest in Northern Ireland affairs, and give so little support to the NILP and its predecessors? The hesitancy of the NILP itself in the 1960s must provide part of the explanation. But there was, in any case, an ever present reluctance on the part of British Labour to become involved in the Irish question. It was distasteful, distracting and well off the usual Labour agenda, and too many political fingers had been burned trying to deal with it in the past. Another important reason for the arms length posture was that the Labour leadership never really believed that the Unionists were as bad as they were painted. It was the antithesis of the big lie; a truth so big that it was almost impossible to believe – and this despite the fact that testimony to the veracity of the claims about Northern Ireland's democratic deficiencies was almost always available on the Labour benches in both Houses of Parliament.

The main reason for the lack of solidarity with the NILP, however, was that there was never anything in it, either electorally or organisationally, for the British Labour Party. Indeed, it was only when it briefly seemed there might be that Johnson was sent to assist. That the BLP's annual grant to the NILP lasted for so long was purely a matter of inertia. Labour simply did not care. That perhaps suggests that any revival of democratic socialist politics in Northern Ireland – and the potential is certainly there – will have to draw upon local inspiration rather than outside intervention.

NOTES

1. The story of the labour movement in the North of Ireland during the first two decades of the century has been well documented. As well as numerous articles, see, for example, Geoffrey Bell, *Troublesome Business* (London: Pluto, 1982); John Gray, *City in Revolt* (Belfast: Blackstaff, 1985); Austen Morgan, *Labour and Partition* (London: Verso, 1991);

Henry Patterson, *Class Conflict and Sectarianism* (Belfast: Blackstaff, 1980). Although there are some gaps in his account, Bell is a particularly valuable source on the approach of British Labour to the Irish question throughout the period under consideration here.

2. This acronym is neither familiar nor felicitous, and is used here only where necessary; but is necessary because several Labour Parties are referred to in this chapter.

3. There are numerous writings on Connolly; for an acerbic, revisionist view see Austen Morgan, *James Connolly: A Political Biography* (Manchester: Manchester University Press, 1988).

4. Both quoted in Bell, *op.cit.* p. 31.

5. Campaign for Labour Representation in Northern Ireland, *The Labour Party and Northern Ireland – An Official History* (Belfast: CLR, 1986), pp. 10–11.

6. Ireland had not been covered by earlier conscription legislation, and the successful campaign against its belated introduction was supported by a wide range of organisations.

7. The ILP&TUC decision to forego the hustings was taken on the grounds that the election ought to be a once and for all plebiscite on the national question.

8. Bell, *op.cit.*, pp. 39–42.

9. There had even been a Labour 'Commission of Inquiry' (*Report of the Labour Commission on Ireland* (London: Labour Party, 1921)); it condemned the actions of the army in Ireland, as well as fully endorsing the informal policy agreement between the Labour Party and the ILP&TUC.

10. See Morgan, *Labour and Politics, op.cit.*

11. CLR, *op.cit.* pp. 11–12.

12. Kyle was an attender – and speaker – at British Labour Party conferences during this period (see Bell, *op.cit.*), presumably as a TGWU delegate. It is also possible, however, that he represented the Belfast Branch of the ILP – see below. On Kyle and Beattie, see Graham Walker, 'The Northern Ireland Labour Party in the 1920s', *Saothar 10 – Journal of the Irish Labour History Society*, 1984; and 'Jack Beattie', *Obair*, ILHS, Spring 1985.

13. That is, in the political sense.

14. The Branch then dissolved, and re-formed itself as the Socialist Party (Northern Ireland). It remained affiliated to the Northern Ireland Labour Party until the late 1930s, acting as a left-wing ginger group.

15. Kyle went to the job of Irish Regional Secretary of ATGWU, and McMullan as a National Trade Group Secretary in ITGWU (he was eventually to rise to the General Presidency of the Union). Both became active in the IrLP, and Kyle was a Labour member of the Irish upper house, the Senate, in the 1940s.

16. For Midgley's story, see Graham Walker, *The Politics of Frustration: Harry Midgley and the Failure of Labour in Northern Ireland* (Manchester: Manchester University Press, 1985).

17. For a fuller account than that which follows of the fortunes of the NILP in the war years and after, see Terry Cradden, *Trade Unionism, Social-*

ism and Partition: The Labour Movement in Northern Ireland 1939–1953 (Belfast: December Publications, 1993).

18. Midgley was the only member of his party ever to sit at Stormont. His membership of the Cabinet was as far as the Unionists were prepared to go in response to pressure from London to form a wartime cross-party coalition. He eventually went all the way and joined the Unionist Party in the late 1940s.

19. Beattie retained his West Belfast seat but was again in the wilderness, having refused to endorse the papers of an NILP candidate for a vacant, and previously Nationalist seat in the Northern Ireland Senate. He was offered the opportunity of returning to the NILP prior to the 1945 elections, and appeared anxious to take this up. But the NILP Executive refused to make a final decision until after the elections were over, and Beattie simply drifted away on his own.

20. See Bob Purdie, 'The Friends of Ireland', in T. Gallagher and J. O'Connell (eds), *Contemporary Irish Studies* (Manchester: Manchester University Press, 1983).

21. Cited in Cradden, *op.cit.* p. 150.

22. See Bob Purdie, *Politics in the Streets: The Origins of the Civil Rights Movement in Northern Ireland* (Belfast: Blackstaff, 1990).

23. See Cradden, *op.cit.* p. 152. Bell, *op.cit.*, provides copious further evidence on the sympathetic attitudes of senior Labour figures to unionism.

24. See Bell, *op.cit.*, Chapter 6.

25. See J. A. V. Graham, 'The Consensus-Forming Strategy of the NILP 1949–1968', MSSc thesis, Queen's University of Belfast, 1972.

26. CLR, *op.cit.* pp. 13–14.

27. Graham, *op.cit.* p. 53.

28. C. E. B. Brett, *Long Shadows Cast Before* (Edinburgh: Bartholomew, 1978), p. 133.

29. For more on the CDU, see Purdie, *op.cit.* (note 22), Chapter 3, *passim*.

30. Quoted in Bell, *op.cit.* p. 101.

31. Purdie, *op.cit.* (note 22), p. 71.

32. *Ibid.*, pp. 71–2.

6 Labour, Northern Ireland and the Decision to Send in the Troops
Peter Rose

INTRODUCTION

The unexpected announcement in 1948 that Ireland was leaving the Commonwealth and becoming a republic caused a crisis in Anglo-Irish relations which was to have profound implications for Labour's policy on Northern Ireland for the next twenty years. Labour Ministers were appalled by Dublin's decision, but after briefly considering retaliatory action realised that this would be futile. Commonwealth premiers brokered a deal which in effect ensured that the new republic would not be treated as a foreign country. The Cabinet's main preoccupation now was to reassure Northern Ireland that Ireland's secession did not threaten the border. Between September 1948 and March 1949 London's response to Dublin was discussed at great length at a series of Cabinet meetings. Harold Wilson, the young President of the Board of Trade, attended most of them. Other Ministers attending who were to be in Wilson's Cabinet fifteen years later included Sir Frank Soskice, then Solicitor General. When Soskice became Wilson's Home Secretary with responsibility for Northern Ireland in 1964 he was so pro-unionist that he would have qualified to be an honorary member of the Orange Order. For example, on a visit to Northern Ireland in April 1965 he said of Ulster Unionism: 'From England we watch it, we admire it and we rejoice in it'.[1] At a seminar held by the Institute of Contemporary British History (ICBH), Lord Callaghan[2] described Soskice as an odd bird. 'Frank', he said, 'had only two ambitions: the abolition of supertax and the restoration of the Tsar of Russia'.[3] Others who attended the Irish crisis meetings included Patrick Gordon Walker, Under-Secretary at the Commonwealth Office, who was to be Wilson's first Foreign Secretary.

LABOUR AND IRISH SECESSION

The Government decided that legislation was necessary to regulate the situation which would arise once Ireland left the Commonwealth. Any doubts that a 'socialist' Government might prove less steadfast in its support of Protestant unionism than the Tories had already been allayed. That commitment to Northern Ireland's special status was underlined by a remarkable memorandum prepared by a special working party for Prime Minister Attlee. It said:

> Now that Eire will shortly cease to owe any allegiance to the Crown, it has become a matter of first class strategic importance to this country that the North should continue to form part of HM's Dominions . . . it will never be to Great Britain's advantage that Northern Ireland should form part of a territory outside HM's jurisdiction. Indeed it seems unlikely that Great Britain would be able to agree to this even if the people of Northern Ireland desired it.[4]

When the Ireland Bill was published, it affirmed that 'in no event will Northern Ireland or any part thereof cease to be part . . . of the United Kingdom without the consent of the Parliament of Northern Ireland'. Moving the second reading, Attlee told MPs that the Government recognised the right of the Parliament of Northern Ireland to decide on behalf of the people of Northern Ireland to stay in or leave the United Kingdom and the Commonwealth.[5] This signified the final abandonment of Labour's long held policy of opposition to partition.

It also sparked off one of the biggest backbench rebellions of the Attlee Government. Many of the rebels claimed that because the electoral system in Northern Ireland was rigged against the Catholics it was outrageous to give Stormont a permanent veto over partition. On 16 May 1949, during the committee stage of the Bill, they refused to back the clause providing the veto. According to *The Times* on 18 May, one-third of the Government backbenchers either voted against or abstained in defiance of a three-line whip. Attlee and Bevin[6] were furious. Four of the rebels who were parliamentary private secretaries were sacked.[7] They included Robert Mellish, who was to be Government Chief Whip in Wilson's administration. Large though the revolt was, the rebels were not united in their reasons for opposing the guarantee to Stormont. Bew and Patterson have pointed out that the main division was between those who took a traditional nationalist line and a larger group who were simply concerned that British standards of democracy and justice did not exist in Northern Ireland.[8] There were similarities between this larger civil rights group and the Campaign for Democracy in Ulster (CDU) founded fifteen years later when Labour returned to power. Some of the MPs who had taken part in the revolt against Attlee were to be found in the CDU.

LABOUR AND NORTHERN IRELAND

Between the Ireland Act and the return of a Labour Government in 1964 it appeared that Ireland, North and South, was given a low priority by the Labour Party. However, it is now known that two senior Labour MPs, who were to hold top Cabinet posts in Wilson's Government, did discuss the possibility of a fundamental change of policy. In his diaries Patrick Gordon Walker[9] writes that he ought to come out against partition in Ireland, which was morally wrong and put Britain in the wrong. He put his argument to George Brown,[10] who appears to have agreed but said that trade union leaders would have to be consulted. Gordon Walker then spoke to the Irish Foreign Minister, Liam Cosgrave, stressing that a condition of ending partition would be that the Republic joined NATO.[11]

Prior to the 1964 General Election Labour drew up a statement of aims for Northern Ireland: *Signposts to the New Ulster*. In it the Party merely promised that electoral laws in Northern Ireland would be brought into line with the rest of the United Kingdom but gave no indication of when, nor was there any commitment to early action over specific Catholic grievances.[12] However, Wilson himself made three specific pledges before election day that there would be reform in Northern Ireland. This was not surprising. Leading Ulster Unionists, including Brian Faulkner,[13] considered that the Labour leader, unlike his predecessors, was sympathetic to the nationalists.[14] Also a large proportion of his constituents in Huyton were of Irish Catholic origin and he often talked of the time when he told the Republic's *Taoiseach*, Jack Lynch, that he, Wilson, had more Irish in his constituency than Lynch had in his. Three months before polling Wilson wrote to Patricia McCluskey, one of the founders of the Campaign for Social Justice in Northern Ireland (CSJNI). He promised to introduce new and impartial procedures for the allocation of houses and to set up tribunals to consider discrimination in public appointments.[15] In a second letter he wrote:

... I agree with you as to the importance of the issues with which
your campaign is concerned and I can assure you that a Labour
government would do everything in its power to see that infringe-
ments of justice are efficiently dealt with.[16]

Wilson made a similar promise to Eddie McAteer, leader of the National-
ist opposition at Stormont.[17] These commitments were published in
Northern Ireland and civil rights workers there believed that the new
Labour Government would press Stormont to introduce reform speedily.

In Northern Ireland, the Unionist administration was already considering the consequences of a Labour victory. A senior political journalist in Northern Ireland at the time recalls that the new Northern Ireland
premier, Terence O'Neill, was exceedingly nervous about the implications of a Labour victory for the region. O'Neill went out of his way
to make contact with, and try and cultivate, Wilson in this period.
O'Neill saw the likelihood of Wilson coming in and felt that this would
signal a change in the British Government's attitude to Northern Ireland, and it would not necessarily be a 'back-burner' issue any more.
According to the journalist (who knew O'Neill well), the two men had
a couple of lunches or a dinner together. This was when Wilson was
still Opposition leader but everyone knew that there would have to be
a general election in a matter of months. Wilson, to O'Neill's surprise,
seemed sympathetic towards him, which was not to say that he was
not laying down markers and giving indications that there had to be
change.[18]

Backbench MPs had a rare opportunity to demand reform in Northern Ireland during a Commons debate that took place in July 1964,
only three months before Labour came to power. Labour and Liberal
MPs demanded justice for the Catholics. However, the Conservative
Home Secretary, Henry Brooke, adhered to the traditional Government
response to charges of discrimination in Northern Ireland by repeating
the convention that the United Kingdom Government never intervened
in matters that were the sole responsibility of Stormont.[19] Nevertheless, evidence that all was not well surfaced even before Wilson got to
Downing Street. The worst communal violence seen in Belfast for thirty
years erupted during the General Election campaign, though the press
and television made little of it in Great Britain. *The Times*, however,
reported on 2 October that bystanders described the riots as reminis-
cent of the 'troubles' of fifty years earlier. The riots continued for
three nights after which *The Times* commented: 'The display of violence will disappoint those optimists who thought religious and nationalist

antagonism were dying away in Ulster ... The General Election has opened up old wounds ...'.[20]

Wilson became Prime Minister on 16 October 1964 after Labour had won the General Election by a majority of three. Early on he gave encouragement to the view that his Government's approach to Ireland, North and South, would differ from previous Conservative and Labour administrations. He promised the return to Ireland of the remains of Roger Casement, who was hanged for treason in 1916. Wilson wrote later that there was no doubt that this gesture, followed by much closer trade relations, did a great deal to improve friendship between the two countries.[21] He was also to return to Dublin the Irish flag which had been raised at the General Post Office during the Easter rebellion, gaining the gratitude of the Irish Prime Minister, Sean Lemass.[22]

As early as March 1965, Wilson proposed a possible meeting in London between the Prime Ministers of Northern Ireland and Ireland. The suggestion was made at the St Patrick's Day banquet at the London Irish club, when he referred to the recent historic meeting between Lemass and O'Neill. Wilson said:

> All of us recognise that even before your next St Patrick Day's banquet if we maintain this momentum things can be better, if we turn our backs on the past and our faces to the future I believe, speaking of the two islands, there is nothing we can not do together.[23]

These remarks, however, infuriated O'Neill, who said that it would only have been courteous if Wilson had given him an indication of what he intended to say. He would have asked Wilson what useful purpose a tripartite meeting would serve and he said that he emphasised with all the force at his command that 'our constitutional heritage ... is our most precious possession and will be maintained by all the means at our disposal'.[24]

Wilson's first administration lasted only seventeen months. He had been forced to trim his programme by the narrowness of his overall majority and the perilous economic situation. There is no evidence that during this time he seriously considered Catholic grievances in Northern Ireland, despite the assurances given to leading civil rights workers there before polling day. Sir Oliver Wright,[25] who was Wilson's private secretary at Downing Street, has stressed that it was important to bear in mind that these promises were given when Wilson was in opposition. 'When you are actually sitting at the Cabinet table in Number 10 the world looks very different, and the world *is* very different.' Wright did not consider that the gestures Wilson made to Dublin were the signal of the start of a great reform movement. He said: 'I cannot remember in my time with Wilson in Number 10 . . . that Ireland ever really rated very high in Wilson's preoccupations'.[26]

However, Labour backbench MPs were determined that the question of reform should be debated at Westminster. For more than forty years there had been a Parliamentary convention that domestic affairs in Northern Ireland could not be raised at Westminster because they were the responsibility of Stormont which, inevitably, had a permanent Unionist majority. On two occasions during Wilson's first administration they were able to bend the 'rules' because the subject of the debate was unemployment, for which the United Kingdom Parliament and not Stormont had ultimate responsibility. It was, though, a frustrating experience and afterwards Paul Rose,[27] Chairman of the CDU, complained that their protests about discrimination against Catholics had been ignored by Ministers. He wrote later: 'Not a word came from the two front benches about issues which within five years were to leave the streets smouldering and leave the stench of death on the pavements of Belfast'.[28]

Wilson wrote later that he had been convinced that Northern Ireland's best hope lay with O'Neill. Shortly after he became Prime Minister of Northern Ireland he paid Wilson a courtesy visit. But on 9 May 1965, after the latter had been in power for six months, O'Neill came to see Wilson again and this time, Wilson recalled:

> we had to get down to realities . . . I was anxious that the Unionist government under O'Neill should be encouraged to press on with their programme of ending discrimination in housing allocations and jobs and generally improving the lot of the minority in Northern Ireland. Since coming into office O'Neill had, by Northern Ireland standards, carried through a remarkable programme of easement.[29]

However, Wilson gives no evidence for this 'remarkable programme of easement' for the simple reason that there was none. Three years later CDU MPs, at their fourth annual meeting at Westminster, were in a state of despair over the lack of progress.[30]

CDU had been set up early in 1965 and soon attracted the support of a hundred backbench MPs from all sections of the Labour Party and several branches were established in the provinces. Because of the tragic events that began in August 1969 the role of CDU has tended to be ignored. However, at the ICBH seminar referred to above Callaghan and Merlyn Rees[31] had no doubt as to its influence.

THE CAMPAIGN FOR DEMOCRACY IN ULSTER

During the years before the Londonderry riot of October 1968 CDU
made ingenious attempts to circumvent the Speaker's convention on
Northern Ireland. During the debate on the committee stage of the Bill
to establish an Ombudsman for Great Britain, Paul Rose was able to
raise Catholic grievances by arguing that the Ombudsman's powers
should extend to Northern Ireland.[32] Kevin McNamara, a leading member
of CDU (and Labour's Northern Ireland spokesman, 1987–94), dis-
covered that Stormont Senators' pensions were authorised at Westminster. He therefore tabled Commons amendments to the 1966 Finance
Bill, delaying payment of pensions until various Catholic grievances,
which he listed, had been remedied. There was no chance of the amendments being called but the point was made and the convention chipped
away a little more.[33] The CDU's most important initiative was an on-
the-spot investigation of civil rights in Northern Ireland by three leading members, including Stan Orme,[34] who later became a member of
Callaghan's Cabinet. They heard allegations of discrimination in housing allocations and in public appointments. On their return they presented their report to the Home Secretary, Roy Jenkins, emphasising
how near the surface violence lay in current political life and they
demanded a Royal Commission to examine a worsening situation.[35]

The CDU received a major boost at Westminster with the arrival of
the Republican Labour MP, Gerry Fitt, who had won West Belfast in
the 1966 General Election. He skilfully deployed his maiden speech to
get round the convention. To the fury of Unionist MPs, Fitt was allowed to give a first-hand report of injustice in Northern Ireland, rarely
heard in the Commons.[36] The speech horrified the *Belfast Telegraph*,
which feared that, in Harold Wilson, Fitt had a sympathetic ear.[37]
However, by the summer of 1968 the CDU was despairing of ever
influencing the Government. At the crisis meeting at the Commons on
12 June members debated why none of their aims had been fulfilled.
The CDU secretary, Paddy Byrne, complained that letters written to
Labour Home Secretaries were treated with contempt.[38]

Despite this pessimism, only three months later the campaign finally achieved the breakthrough which they had been hoping for on
the floor of the House of Commons. It happened as a result of the
Londonderry riots, during which Fitt was beaten by B Specials. Paul
Rose later pronounced the parliamentary convention dead. 'It was killed
when the Member for Belfast West was seen by millions of television

viewers, his head streaming with blood, after a vicious batoning while surrounded by a group of members of the RUC'.[39]

RESISTANCE TO INTERVENTION

For the four years before Londonderry, Wilson had left it to the 'liberal' O'Neill to bring in the necessary changes. Just how genuine a reformer O'Neill really was is an open question. Paul Bew has written that, though O'Neill's pro-Catholic reformism was non-existent, Wilson was convinced by loyalist attacks on the premier that he must be making progress.[40] O'Neill himself regretted at the end of his life that he had led a smear campaign against the Northern Ireland Labour Party (NILP), helping to destroy Ulster's only non-sectarian party.[41] That the Catholics might have accepted partition in the late 1960s had they been given equal rights is suggested by a survey carried out in 1968 by Richard Rose that showed that only one third of the Catholics consulted disapproved of the existing constitution.[42] However, a foretaste of the violence to come occurred in the summer of 1966 with murders by the recently formed Ulster Volunteer Force and demonstrations when the Queen visited Northern Ireland. The *Irish Times* claimed in an editorial that the violence once again raised the possibility of intervention by the British Government and asked:

> Can Mr Wilson now sit back and say that the Northern Ireland government has the situation in hand when influential papers like the *Sunday Times* and *Daily Telegraph* inform its [sic] readers that there is discrimination in Northern Ireland?[43]

That Wilson was clearly worried by the deteriorating situation is confirmed by a description he gives in his memoirs of what he deemed a most important private lunch with O'Neill and Jenkins in August 1966. It was, wrote Wilson, essential that progress be maintained for, as the world learned three years later, 'time was not on our side'. Without constitutional reform it was becoming more difficult to justify to MPs the money they were being asked to vote for Northern Ireland. Wilson and Jenkins agreed not to press O'Neill to go further in the next few months. But, wrote, Wilson, more time – the most precious commodity in the explosive Northern Ireland situation – was inevitably lost.[44]

Until the Londonderry violence in October 1968 the Cabinet rarely discussed Northern Ireland. As late as September 1968 the Home Office had no civil servant devoting full time attention to the region. Lord Longford[45] admitted that he wondered what he had been doing or saying about Northern Ireland during his three years in the Cabinet:

> Every now and then one of us would raise the question of whether any steps were being taken to end the grosser forms of gerrymandering and anti-Catholic discrimination ... I was by no means alone in being aware that much was wrong.[46]

Charles Brett (now Sir Charles), one of the leaders of the NILP, personally made a number of efforts to persuade the Government to act before it was too late. During the ICBH seminar he alleged that Home Office officials were downright obstructive and were secretly furnishing Stormont with reports of the NILP's private discussions with Labour Ministers in London. However, Callaghan told the seminar that he saw nothing wrong with civil servants keeping each other informed. Whether they were in London or Belfast they were all working for the United Kingdom.

Wilson's first Home Secretary, Frank Soskice, was unashamedly sympathetic to the Unionists and ignored the CDU.[47] However, he was soon replaced by Jenkins, who was to build a reputation as a great reforming Home Secretary. With Jenkins' liberal credentials in mind and the conviction that, as Asquith's biographer, he would know something about Ireland, the CDU looked forward to great progress. They were to be bitterly disappointed. His familiarity with the turbulent history of Ireland led him to the opposite conclusion. He told the Commons:

> successive governments here have refused to take steps which would inevitably cut away not only at the authority of the Northern Ireland government but also the constitution of the province ... There is room for argument about the pace [of reform] which in practice is desirable. But we must at least be satisfied with the direction. Provided that we can be so satisfied there is a great deal to be said for not trying to settle the affairs of Northern Ireland too directly from London.

As a historian he knew England did not have a 'peculiar talent' for solving the problems of Ireland. 'Few issues in the past have shown a greater capacity to divert and dissipate the reforming energy of left-wing British governments than deep embroilment in Irish affairs'.[48] However, Jenkins now wonders whether there may have been a case after all for intervening. Whenever he had suggested visiting the region, O'Neill put him off. 'I ought to have said I am coming next month . . . but it would not have prevented 1969'.[49]

Within a year of Jenkins' plea to the Commons not to get involved in Northern Ireland, the NILP was warning Wilson that young male Catholics now felt that violence was justified. Brett recalled that after troops had to go in to prevent what would now be called ethnic cleansing, Labour politicians in London repeatedly asked him: 'Why did you not warn us of what was coming?'[50]

LEAVING IT TO O'NEILL

In the years before the troops went in an alternative strategy to 'leaving it to O'Neill' was occasionally considered. This was the threat to withhold part of the huge subsidy Northern Ireland received annually until Stormont enacted the necessary reforms. The figure that taxpayers had to fork out each year to keep the region going was about £140 million, perhaps a billion pounds in today's money. Yet the Cabinet was surprisingly ignorant about the subsidy. Crossman records that on 12 September 1968, three weeks before the Londonderry riot, the Prime Minister asked the Cabinet: 'Why should we pay vast sums to a firm in Belfast? . . . what social results do we achieve by pouring into Belfast money we deny to Millom on the North East coast?' Nobody in the Cabinet, wrote Crossman, understood the financial arrangements for Northern Ireland. Neither Jack Diamond, Treasury Chief Secretary, nor the Chancellor, Jenkins, knew the formula according to which Northern Ireland received this huge handout. In all these years, said Crossman, it had never been revealed to politicians.[51]

Stormont was well aware that the subsidy might be used as a weapon by Labour Ministers frustrated by the lack of progress in Northern Ireland. In December 1968 the Minister for Home Affairs, William Craig, whose handling of the Londonderry march was to be severely criticised by the Cameron Commission,[52] was sacked by O'Neill. O'Neill warned Craig that he was putting at risk 'the enormous subvention which makes it possible for us to enjoy a British rather than an Irish standard of living'.[53]

The little interest Whitehall took in Northern Ireland, at least until Londonderry, was reflected by the arrangements made for keeping an eye on the region at the Home Office. After he took over as Home Secretary at the end of 1967 Callaghan found that his first box of papers contained documents on everything but Northern Ireland. He was not surprised by this omission because the subject rarely if ever came before Cabinet. It was covered by the general department, which included British Summer Time, London taxi-cabs and state-owned pubs in Carlisle.[54]

The violence in Londonderry in October 1968 was a watershed in the sense that never again would it be possible for politicians in Great Britain to ignore what was happening in Northern Ireland. Until then it had not merely been a question of the parliamentary convention preventing discussion of Northern Ireland affairs in the Commons. The Labour Party were absorbed by events in Rhodesia and Vietnam and by the growing concern over immigration. As a result fraternal delegates from the NILP to the Labour Party's annual conference were treated like visitors from a friendly foreign power, despite the fact that Labour's National Executive provided a small annual subsidy to the party. Those constituency parties which tried to raise civil rights in Northern Ireland at the annual conference never got beyond the Standing Orders Committee which was responsible for the selection (and compositing) of resolutions. Ironically an unsuccessful attempt to raise discrimination in Northern Ireland was made at the 1968 conference only days before the explosion at Londonderry. Afterwards, all that changed. Callaghan himself refused to accept William Craig's argument that the IRA was behind the demonstrations. He considered that the left-wing student unrest in America and Europe which had spread to Northern Ireland was largely to blame for the commotion that autumn rather than domestic frustration and the slow pace of O'Neill's reforms.[55] However, the Cameron Commission which investigated Londonderry saw it rather differently from the Unionists or the British Home Secretary. Cameron concluded that the cause of the disturbances there, and at those immediately following, was a rising sense of continuing injustice and grievance among Catholics. The civil rights movement was not narrowly sectarian nor subversive politically. It was a movement which drew support from a wide measure of moderate opinion on many sides.[56]

After Londonderry, Wilson, for the first time since coming to power four years before, decided that the policy of leaving it to O'Neill was faltering. O'Neill and other Unionist leaders were summoned to Downing Street where they were ordered to start introducing reform immediately. Wilson threatened the use of financial sanctions and even the possibility of reducing the powers of Stormont – the first hint of direct rule.[57] But the reforms that were grudgingly brought in were criticised by the historian, F. S. L. Lyons, as being insufficient to reduce the tensions in the province.[58] Wilson's resolve seemed to weaken and he and his Cabinet could not make up their minds whether or not to intervene. Crossman recorded:

> We had been relying on O'Neill to do our job of dragging Northern Ireland out of its 18th-century Catholic–Protestant conflict . . . Callaghan told me some weeks ago in the greatest secrecy that, as Home Secretary, he was having to work out plans in case the Northern Ireland government collapsed.[59]

Wilson set up a Northern Ireland Cabinet Committee though nothing is yet known of its activities. Crossman records a full Cabinet meeting in May 1969 when Ministers frankly acknowledged that they knew nothing about the situation in Northern Ireland. Healey said: 'Northern Ireland has completely different conditions from Britain and we shall be as blind men leading the blind if we have to go in there knowing nothing about the place.' Callaghan said he was working with a very small staff. He had only two men in Northern Ireland. Crossman comments: '. . .this is the way we prepare for the possibility that we might have to take over . . .'.[60]

CONCLUSION

During 1969 the political and security situation grew increasingly grave. O'Neill was deposed and replaced by his kinsman, James Chichester-Clark, in whom Government and Whitehall had little confidence.[61] In April, British troops were used to guard installations in Northern Ireland, such as power stations and reservoirs, after bomb attacks, thought to have been carried out by the IRA but now known to have been the work of loyalist *agents provocateur*. The *Irish Times* lobby correspondent reported that direct rule from Westminster was being mentioned in corners in the Commons but it was 'no more than a horrible cloud on the horizon'.[62] A week before the violence erupted the *Financial Times* reported that, if troops had to go in, Westminster would take political control for the region from Stormont. Wilson himself was thought to be the source of this threat.[63] The violence was sparked off by the Apprentice Boys march, which Wilson had intended banning until 'unwiser counsels prevailed'.[64] Many years later Callaghan was asked whether he now believed that the Labour Government had missed an opportunity to take the policy initiatives that could have prevented the break down in law and order in August 1969. He replied that, theoretically and logically, the Government could have taken action much earlier to press Stormont to bring in reforms. In practice, he said, it was not, given the surrounding circumstances, politically possible.[65]

NOTES

1. *Belfast Telegraph*, 29 April 1965.
2. James Callaghan, Chancellor of the Exchequer, 1964–67, Home Secretary, 1967–70.
3. ICBH seminar, London, 14 January 1992.
4. Public Records Office, London (hereinafter PRO): CAB 21/1842.
5. *House of Commons Debates*, 5th ser., vol. 464, cols 1856–62, 11 May 1949.
6. Ernest Bevin, Foreign Secretary, 1945–51.
7. *The Times* 19 May 1949.
8. Paul Bew and Henry Patterson, *The British State and the Ulster Crisis* (London: Verso, 1985), pp. 9–10.
9. Foreign Secretary 1964–65, Education Secretary 1967–68.
10. Secretary for Economic Affairs 1964–66, Foreign Secretary 1966–68.
11. Robert Pearce (ed.), *Patrick Gordon Walker: Political Diaries, 1932– 71* (London: Historians' Press, 1991), pp. 212–14.
12. NEC minutes, Home Policy sub-committee, Labour Party, 2 December 1963, National Museum of Labour History, Manchester.
13. Then Minister of Commerce at Stormont and from 1971–2 Prime Minister of Northern Ireland.
14. Brian Faulkner, *Memoirs of a Statesman* (London: Weidenfeld & Nicolson, 1978), p. 130.
15. *The Plain Truth*, 2nd edn (Dungannon: CSJNI, 1969).
16. *Irish News*, 3 October 1964.
17. Recollection of Kevin McNamara MP in interview, 25 June 1992.
18. Private information.
19. *House of Commons Debates*, vol. 698, cols 1113–51, 14 July 1964.
20. *The Times*, 3 October 1964, p. 12.
21. Harold Wilson, *The Labour Government: 1964–70* (London: Weidenfeld & Nicolson and Michael Joseph, 1971), p. 75.
22. *Irish Times*, 1 April 1966.
23. *The Times*, 18 March 1965.
24. *The Times*, 19 March 1965.
25. First United Kingdom Government representative in Northern Ireland, August 1969 to March 1970.
26. Interview with Wright, 8 September 1992, London.
27. Labour MP for Manchester, Blackley, 1964–79.
28. Paul Rose MP, 'The Northern Ireland Problem (2): Breaking the Con-

vention', *Contemporary Review*, 219, 1971, pp. 284–8.
29. Wilson, *op.cit.*, p. 99.
30. CDU Newsletter, October 1968, the private papers of Kevin McNamara MP, un-catalogued, University of Hull.
31. Northern Ireland Secretary 1974–76; Home Secretary 1976–79.
32. Private papers of Paul Rose.
33. Interview with McNamara.
34. Labour MP for Salford West, Minister of State, Northern Ireland Office, 1974–76.
35. Rose, *op.cit.*
36. *House of Commons Debates*, vol. 727, cols 437–46, 25 April 1966.
37. *Belfast Telegraph*, 26 May 1966.
38. *CDU Newsletter*, October 1968.
39. *House of Commons Debates*, vol. 782, col. 263, 22 April 1969.
40. P. Bew, 'Civil Rights,' *Revue Française de Civilisation Britannique*, Vol. 11, 1991, p. 51.
41. ICBH seminar, evidence of Roy Bradford, former member of O'Neill's Cabinet.
42. R. Rose, *Governing without Consensus* (London: Faber & Faber, 1971), pp. 179–202.
43. *Irish Times*, 6 July 1966.
44. Wilson, *op.cit.*, pp. 270–71.
45. Lord Longford, Education Secretary, resigned over the school leaving age in January 1968.
46. Lord Longford, *A Grain of Wheat* (London: 1974), p. 95.
47. Interview with Paul Rose, 14 August 1992.
48. *House of Commons Debates*, vol. 751, cols 1681–88, 25 October 1967.
49. Interview, London, 13 October 1992.
50. C. Brett, *Long Shadows Cast Before Midnight* (Edinburgh: Bartholomew, 1978), p. 135.
51. R. H. S. Crossman, *Diaries of a Cabinet Minister* (London: Cape, 1977), Vol. III, p. 187.
52. *Disturbances in Northern Ireland*, Cmnd. 532 (Belfast, 1969).
53. C. C. O'Brien, *States of Ireland* (London: Hutchinson, 1972) p. 164.
54. M. Rees, 'Jim Callaghan and the Irish Problems', *Contemporary Review*, 223, 1973, pp. 33–7.
55. ICBH seminar, *op.cit.*
56. Disturbances in Northern Ireland: Report of the Committee Appointed by the Governor of Northern Ireland (Belfast: HMSO, 1969) Cmd 532.
57. L. J. Callaghan, *A House Divided* (London: Collins, 1973), p. 10.
58. F. S. L. Lyons, *Ireland since the Famine* (London: 1982), p. 764.
59. Crossman, *op.cit.*, p. 381.
60. *Ibid.*, p. 463.
61. Private information.
62. *Irish Times*, 25 April 1969.
63. *Sunday Times* Insight Team, *Ulster* (London: Penguin, 1972), p. 110.
64. Wilson, *op.cit.*, p. 692.
65. ICBH seminar, *op.cit.*

7 The Price of Containment: Deaths and Debate on Northern Ireland in the House of Commons, 1968–94

Brendan O'Duffy

April 22, 1969: Commons Debate on Northern Ireland – Mr Quintin Hogg MP (St Marylebone):

> There are two Germanies, two Koreas, two Indias, two Vietnams, two Palestines, even, God help us, two Cypruses, and, at the moment, two Nigerias . . . I have enumerated these other cases of, oppression if you like, partition if you like; but can anyone point to one in which there has been so little effusion of blood as there has been in Ireland since that Treaty?[1]

Mr Paul Rose MP (Manchester – Blackley):

> . . . it was not until heads were broken in Londonderry that the attention of the British press, public and parliament was focused on Northern Ireland. It was not until violence again erupted in Derry and other parts of Northern Ireland this weekend that the Unionist Chief Whip announced the possibility of universal suffrage in local government elections, a principal plank in the civil rights campaign.[2]

INTRODUCTION

By measuring success in Northern Ireland in terms of bloodshed the British Government practically invited an escalation of violence. Violence precipitated every major reform or constitutional initiative from October 1968, following the first civil rights marches, to December 1993 and the signing of the British-Irish Joint Declaration (the Downing Street Declaration). The central role of violence in the Northern Irish political process stems from the persistence of containment as the guiding principle of conflict regulation adopted by successive British and Irish Governments since 1920.[3] It appeared in 1994 that repeated failures to marginalise proponents of violence had led, finally, to a more enlightened approach to conflict regulation which addresses the causes rather than symptoms of violence. However, the current 'peace process' is still embryonic and therefore it is too soon to tell if the lessons of previous conflict-regulation failures have been learned. The following discussion attempts to provide a marker against which the current peace process can be compared.

FROM TURMOIL TO CIVIL WAR: OCTOBER 1968 TO MARCH 1972

By the end of 1971 significant concessions had been made to the primary demands of the civil rights movement. However, the failure of the British Government to initiate a coordinated and resolute conflict-regulation strategy meant that all of the reforms were extracted with violence. The degree to which violence was successful in imposing the Northern Irish 'problem' on reluctant British Governments is revealed by one simple statistic. As Figure 7.1 shows, between 1964 and 1973, the R-squared correlation between the number of deaths resulting from political violence and the amount of debate on political and constitutional matters in Northern Ireland was 0.91 (out of 1.0). This means that – *ceteris paribus* – 91 per cent of the variance in the amount of debate was accounted for by the number of deaths which occurred. This figure specifically excludes debate on matters related to security, violence or terrorism.

The instability generated by the civil rights movement, combined with the emergence of the Provisional Irish Republican Army (PIRA) created opportunities for the British Government to embark on a wholesale reform of the constitutional structure which had been responsible for the creation of Catholic/nationalist grievances. However, the riots and turmoil which occurred with increased frequency throughout the latter half of 1969 did not shake the British Government's determination to act as an outside advisor to the Unionist Government at Stormont. Despite the obvious signs that extremists were gaining the ascendent position, Callaghan and Wilson remained committed to the policy of non-intervention in the internal affairs of Northern Ireland. Publicly,

Figure 7.1   Deaths from political violence and debate on political and constitutional issues, 1964 to 1979

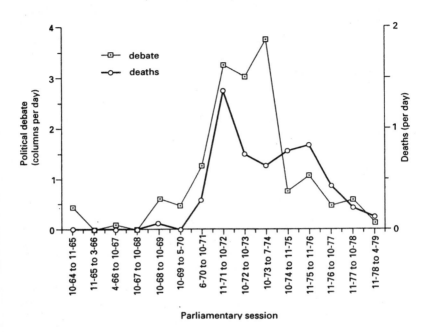

Callaghan defended non-intervention with a majoritarian version of liberal democratic theory:

> The Government's approach has sprung from the simple conception that these problems are most likely to be solved successfully and permanently if the people of Ireland solve them. They have the institutions. They have a Parliament and a Government. The Government are supported by some, rejected by others.[4]

Privately, Callaghan was more pointed in his emphasis on preventing a loyalist backlash. As both Callaghan and Healey emphasised to the Cabinet:

> [O]ur whole interest was to work through the Protestant government. The Protestants are the majority and we can't afford to alienate them as well as the Catholics and find ourselves ruling Northern Ireland as a colony.[5]

The first tentative steps towards engagement and the ambiguous goals of the intervention reflected the British Government's continued reluctance more fully to involve itself in Northern Ireland. Following the riots of August 1969 the British Army was sent in under Clause 75 of the Government of Ireland Act[6] to intervene 'in aide of the civil power'. In October, the Government moved to placate nationalist grievances against the excesses committed by the Protestant-dominated Ulster Special Constabulary or 'B Specials'.[7] Its replacement, the Ulster Defence Regiment (UDR), was a regiment of the British Army and therefore controlled, ultimately, from Westminster. However, the actual control over the security forces was ambiguous because, while the RUC was nominally under the direction of the General Officer Commanding (GOC), in fact it retained separate, and from the Army's point of view, totally inadequate, intelligence-gathering networks.[8]

The absence of forethought on security policy reflected the unanimous opinion within the Wilson Cabinet that the intervention of troops was a temporary expedient simply to restore order. On the ground the situation appeared different. After a quick baptism in the intricacies of street fighting in Northern Ireland, the GOC, Lieutenant-General Sir Ian Freeland was asked by the Stormont Cabinet how long it would take for his men to repossess the Bogside. He replied, 'three hours to take over and about three years to get out again'.[9] He underestimated by about twenty-three years (and counting).

The new Conservative Government under Edward Heath did not offer any new approach to the escalating conflict but instead decided that 'soldiering on' was the appropriate response to what they saw as essentially a law and order problem. But escalating PIRA violence and the continued existence of 'No Go' areas in Londonderry and Belfast created pressure within the unionist bloc for more draconian security initiatives. In February 1971 thirteen people were killed, including the first British soldier (Gunner Curtis) and two RUC constables, as riots erupted in Ballymurphy and Ardoyne. Five BBC technicians were killed by a PIRA bomb in Tyrone meant for the Army. In March the PIRA lured three 17-year-old Scottish soldiers from a pub in Ligoniel, a suburb of Belfast, shot them in the backs of their heads and left their bodies on a country road. These murders broke another symbolic barrier as the hardline unionists demanded the re-introduction of internment. However, Chichester-Clark believed, on Army advice, that a quick fix of repression would be counterproductive in the already polarised climate. While he declared that Northern Ireland was 'at war' with the PIRA,[10] he knew that it would be an extended campaign rather than a decisive battle. To meet the immediate demand he went to London to ask for 3,000 more troops and when he received only 1,300 he resigned. His replacement, Brian Faulkner, was considered a pragmatist by the standards of unionism. He attempted to maintain the middle ground by stocking his Cabinet with a token mix of hardliners and liberals[11] while offering the SDLP indirect participation in government through a committee system to oversee legislation in the lower house of Stormont.[12] The SDLP expressed interest but the logic of escalation intervened in July when the Army shot two Catholic youths, Seamus Cusack and Desmond Beattie in Londonderry. The Army's claim that the two were either gunmen or bombers was denied by witnesses. The SDLP demanded an inquiry into the shooting and when the British Government declined they walked out of Stormont for an indefinite period as an act of protest.

The SDLP walk-out was an important peacemaking failure. Until that moment there was still considerable competition between the SDLP and the PIRA for control of the significant minority which wavered between tacit support for rioters and active support for constitutional initiatives. By the spring of 1971 the Provisional's offensive was destabilising but it did not enjoy unbridled support across the nationalist community. The early own goals, mistakes and callous murders would not have been tolerated for long if the SDLP was able to demonstrate progress in achieving constitutional reform. The radical nationalist argument that Faulkner's committee system was 'too little too late',[13] while accurate, misses the wider point that Faulkner could not have offered a more substantial constitutional reform package, even if he wanted to, because of the outflanking pressure within the unionist bloc. Only Westminster could have insisted on a form of power-sharing, but this required a degree of resolve which the Heath Government did not have. Once again, the level of violence had not achieved a sufficient level to discredit the policy of reacting to crises.

The Heath Government's lack of resolve in addressing the root causes of the conflict contributed directly to its escalation. The reliance on Faulkner's Unionist Party to restore order with the aid of the Army was a fundamental peace-keeping error because the nationalist community was symbiotically united in opposition to the Stormont regime. Heath and his Home Secretary Reginald Maudling were more hesitant than ever to undermine the new Faulkner Government because they knew that if Faulkner fell, hardliners like William Craig were waiting in the wings. The insistence of the British Government on distancing itself from the source of the conflict encouraged the Stormont Government to use draconian powers. Emphasising the threats faced from all sides Faulkner asked in mid-July for permission to introduce internment in exchange for a ban on the Apprentice Boys Parade in Londonderry. Heath resisted but agreed to a trial run on 23 July when 2,000 troops were mobilised in an intelligence gathering operation in republican areas. Finally, even after the Army expressed its reservations about both the timing and extent of the planned operation, on 5 August, Heath agreed to allow internment.

The impact of the internment operation on the level of violence is revealed by Figure 7.2. Apart from the street violence associated with riots, a sharp increase in the number of explosions demonstrated that the Provisional command structure was still intact. On 5 September the Provisionals were bold enough to issue demands for a truce.[14] While it is true that the Provisionals had begun their offensive prior to internment it is indisputable that internment allowed them to turn an offensive into a campaign because it united the nationalist community in opposition both to Stormont and Westminster.[15] The Army's role as a neutral peace-keeper was completely undermined by their taking an offensive role: the Army killed nineteen people in August alone and forty-nine altogether between August 1971 and February 1972. By October 26,000 families were on a rent and rates strike; the nationalist ghettos of Londonderry and Belfast were sealed off by barricades; an organisation called the Northern Resistance Movement (NRM) was formed by People's Democracy (PD) in cooperation with the Provisionals while the Northern Ireland Civil Rights Association (NICRA) was effectively under the control of the Official IRA (OIRA).[16] Nationalist politicians of various hues became united as 'anti-unionists'; hundreds resigned from local government positions and public appointments.

Internment sparked a cycle of escalation which the police and Army were unable to control: The escalation of republican violence naturally led to a loyalist response: the Ulster Defence Association (UDA) was formed in September and the Ulster Volunteer Force killed fifteen Catholics in McGurk's Bar in December. Then, in January 1972, the Army's Parachute Regiment killed thirteen unarmed Catholics in London-derry in what became known as Bloody Sunday. More atrocities followed and on 24 March Stormont was prorogued when Faulkner resigned in protest against the removal of all law and order powers. The passive approach to peace-making had finally resulted in a sufficient level of violence for the Heath Government to take a more active interest in Northern Ireland. The nationalists had finally brought down Stormont but the fact that it took violence to destroy it legitimated the use of

Figure 7.2   Monthly deaths from political violence before and after internment*

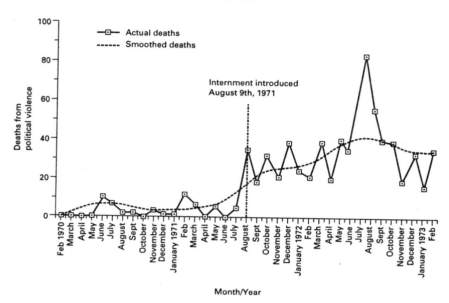

Source: Calculated from RUC data.
   * The data were smoothed using the technique known as 'Hanning' as de-
    scribed in F. Hartwig (with B.E. Dearing), *Exploratory Data Analysis*
    (Beverly Hills, CA: Sage, 1979), pp. 36–9.
  ** 34 of 35 deaths in August 1971 occurred on or after August 9th.

violence as a means of de-constructing an illegitimate government. This
lesson was not lost on loyalists, especially after Whitelaw agreed a
ceasefire with the PIRA and flew its leaders to London for talks.

DIRECT RULE

By proroguing Stormont the Heath Government had taken advantage
of the instability caused by violence and was presented with an opportunity to implement a form of devolved government which would gain
the acceptance of the majority within both the nationalist and unionist communities. The culmination of the Heath Government's conflict-
regulation strategy was the Sunningdale Agreement signed by the leaders
of the SDLP, Alliance and UUP in December 1973. The agreement

represented an attempt to elevate the moderate sub-blocs of the nationalist and unionist communities to positions of ascendence over the radical sub-blocs.

Given the strength of the radical sub-blocs within both communities, an active rather than passive conflict regulation strategy was required. Instead, an agreement was reached, its contradictions thinly veiled in ambiguity. Nationalists were given a share of executive power and the Irish Dimension was established in the form of a Council of Ireland which was comprised of executive and parliamentary tiers with representatives drawn equally from both parts of Ireland. While the structure of the power-sharing dimension was unambiguous, the actual powers devolved were lacking in one major area: security. At one point during the Sunningdale negotiations it appeared that the British Government were going to offer devolved security powers to the Executive. Francis Pym, who had just replaced Whitelaw as Northern Ireland Secretary, circulated a policy paper which suggested that a future Northern Ireland Executive would be given control over the security apparatus. Upon hearing the offer Heath publicly renounced Pym's offer and stated that 'no British Government would agree to restore security powers'.[17]

The Council of Ireland was the centrepiece of the deal and its ambiguous construction reveals the weakness of the foundation upon which the agreement rested. The SDLP had to sell the Council of Ireland as a significant step towards Irish unity in order to appease both republicans as well as the 'green' nationalists within the SDLP. For Faulkner on the other hand, the Council of Ireland had to be sold as a minimalist concession based on inter-governmental recognition of Northern Ireland as a part of the United Kingdom. However, Faulkner's position was seriously undermined in January when the Irish Supreme Court ruled in *Boland* v. *An Taoiseach* that articles two and three of the Irish Constitution, which the Court interpreted as *de jure* claims to sovereignty over the entire island of Ireland, took precedence over clause five of the Sunningdale Agreement, which the Court interpreted as mere *de facto* recognition of the current position of Northern Ireland as part of the United Kingdom.

Based on this tenuous agreement the power-sharing Executive stumbled into existence on 1 January 1974 with Faulkner as Chief Executive and Gerry Fitt of the SDLP as his deputy. The Executive had been standing less than a month when Heath called an election to confront the growing power of British miners. By calling the election Heath clearly demonstrated that the Northern Ireland problem was of secondary concern to domestic politics. The end result was that Heath lost his gamble to the miners and the power-sharing experiment was emasculated by the results of the election which in Northern Ireland took the form of a referendum on the power-sharing Executive. Unionists opposed to the agreement formed the United Ulster Unionist Council (UUUC) and won 11 of the 12 Westminster seats.

Wilson's second Labour Government was almost immediately faced with the prospect of upholding an unpopular agreement in the face of a massive strike organised by the Loyalist Association of Workers in May 1974. Given the formation of bloc alignments, a game-theoretic response by a neutral and resolute arbiter would have called for intervention in order to uphold the Executive and give the moderate sub-blocs (the SDLP and Faulkner Unionists) an advantage in their competition with the radicals. However, the strength of the loyalist sub-bloc compared to the weakness of the Executive required just the type of forceful intervention which the British Government had been trying to avoid since 1921. On the ground the Army GOC, Sir Frank King, was determined to avoid a two-front war and wrote a memorandum to Northern Ireland Secretary Merlyn Rees outlining reasons why the Army should not intervene in the strike. While the GOC emphasised that the Army had the technicians, but not the manpower to maintain electricity supplies, the main reason for the Army's hesitancy to intervene was that it did not have faith in the ability of the Executive to survive without a dependence on sustained intervention.[18] The new Northern Ireland Secretary, Merlyn Rees, refused to negotiate with the Ulster Workers' Council (UWC) as a matter of principled opposition to the use of extra-constitutional methods, a position which epitomises the British Government's refusal to recognise the reality of violent politics. He also rejected the passive approach (future SDLP leader John Hume's preference) of letting the strike continue until the sewers overflowed in order to test the popularity of the UWC.[19] Instead, Wilson played into the hands of the UWC by accusing the people of Northern Ireland of 'sponging on Westminster and British Democracy'.[20] Rees then ordered several half-measures which proved to be too little, too late: a few UDA men were arrested and on the tenth day the Army was ordered in to man the petrol pumps. The UWC merely threatened to escalate the power-stoppages if the Army intervened and on the fourteenth day of the strike Faulkner announced the resignation of the power-sharing Executive.

Most academic attention to the failure of Sunningdale focuses on the lack of resolve on the part of the British Government in facing up to the loyalist strike.[21] Critics point to Rees' indecision in the first week; the reluctance of the Army to get involved in a two-front war with loyalists and republicans; and the unwillingness of the Wilson Government to set a precedent for strike-breaking which would then have to be applied in Britain. All of these factors were important but none more important than the fact that the power-sharing agreement was inherently flawed and in the estimation of both the Government and the Army, not worth the price required to save it. The agreement was flawed because it was an elaborate containment exercise rather than a thorough reform which confronted and addressed the primary source of the conflict: the competing national aspirations of the two communities. The Irish Dimension was flawed because its ambiguous construction allowed it to be interpreted in diametrically opposite ways by the SDLP and Faulkner's Unionists. The power-sharing dimension was flawed because it did not include security powers, the one issue which had the potential to raise the moderate sub-blocs into positions of ascendency over the radical proponents of violence. Without security powers the Sunningdale agreement represented power-sharing without power. It was reliant on the British Army and Protestant-dominated security forces to act as peace-keepers even though they had been alienated from a large section of the nationalist community through violence and intrusive measures such as internment. Sunningdale was an attempt at a quick fix of a bothersome problem. Other issues such as the economy, membership of the EEC and the miners took precedence over attempts to address the core issues which fuelled this extended and increasingly expensive conflict.

POST-SUNNINGDALE: FROM PASSIVE INTERVENTION TO ACTIVE CONTAINMENT

The failure of the power-sharing experiment led to a return to a narrow containment exercise. In the debates which followed the fall of the Executive there was considerable cross-party agreement that the Irish should be left to sort out their peculiar problem. In July 1974 Rees announced plans for the establishment of a Constitutional Convention which would be mandated to offer proposals for devolved government which would be acceptable to 'the people of the United Kingdom as a whole'. Despite the resounding victory of the anti-Sunningdale forces of the UUUC Rees indicated that any viable solution must be based on the Sunningdale principles of power-sharing and an Irish

Dimension (though not necessarily an institutionalised one) and must also be based on agreement among the protagonists in Northern Ireland. As he told the Commons:

> The Convention will be a Convention of Northern Irish people, elected by Northern Irish people, and considering the future of the Northern Irish people. We do not think it right that the Government should take a part in the Convention, or should seek to influence either its deliberations or conclusions.[22]

Rees and others interpreted the mobilisation of the Ulster Workers' Council as an indication of the emergence of non-sectarian, progressive politics. While unconstitutional politics was not, as Pym had declared, 'the British way of doing things'[23] it was the reality of irrational Irish politics. As Julian Critchley saw it, the Convention was:

> an attempt to persuade those who have recently exercised power to show responsibility, an attempt to persuade the UWC in particular – where the power resides – that it is its turn to exercise a degree of responsibility. *If this is so, then it looks as if at last the problem is being returned to Ireland.* The genius of the first Lloyd George settlement after the First World War was that if the Irish were sufficiently irrational to practise murder in the pursuit of their political ideals, they should have the responsibility for it . . . [T]he path towards an eventual settlement has been eased by the lesson which the Ulster workers have administered to the Republicans north and south of the border. A Constitutional Convention ought to incline both sides toward moderation. It should make the Loyalists more likely to concede something on the sharing of power as the price for the UK economic subsidy, and might even incline Catholics in the convention to moderate their demands for a united Ireland if only because of the fear of the consequences for them were Northern Ireland ever to achieve independence.[24]

The expectation that the UWC would suddenly emerge as a moderate political force was a serious mis-reading of the bloc alignments within unionism. Such wishful thinking reflected the desperate hope that the British Government would be able to wash its hands of the problem. Predictably, no new mood of compromise emerged from the Convention as the UUUC repeated their electoral success of the previous February by taking forty-seven of the seventy-eight seats (54.2 per cent). No compromise was offered in the Convention deliberations on either power-sharing or an Irish Dimension and the Convention was eventually wound up in March 1976.

'NORMALISATION' THROUGH 'ULSTERISATION' AND 'CRIMINALISATION'

The second successive failure of a constitutional approach led to a renewed emphasis on the security dimension and away from constitutional initiatives. Before the Convention significant policy changes had been undertaken on the security front. The policy of criminalisation was introduced following the publication of the Gardiner Report in January 1975 which recommended that political status for convicted terrorists should be removed; that detention without trial should continue until the level of violence dropped; and that non-jury Diplock courts (first introduced in August 1973 under the provisions of the Emergency Provisions Act) should continue to be used to try people charged with scheduled offences. The findings in the Gardiner Report were undoubtedly influenced by the ferocity of the PIRA's British bombing campaign in the second half of 1974. The bombings in Guildford, Woolwich, the M62 and Birmingham left twenty-eight dead and hundreds injured, many maimed for life. These bombings led to the speedy passage of the Prevention of Terrorism Act (PTA) which gave British authorities two main powers: to exclude from any part of the United Kingdom anyone suspected of involvement with terrorism in Northern Ireland; and to detain suspected terrorists for up to forty-eight hours and a further five days with approval of the Home Secretary.[25] The direct effect of the British bombing campaign was expressed by Home Secretary Roy Jenkins:

> I hope and believe that the House will proceed expeditiously – more so than it would in normal circumstances – with these measures ... [W]e must bear in mind that there will be disappointment in the country if the Bill is not on the statute book by late Thursday night or early Friday morning.[26]

In order to compensate for the continued use of draconian security measures Rees also made overtures to the PIRA, which resulted in a series of ceasefires from the end of 1974 through to November 1975. The Provisionals were enticed into a series of discussions by hints that the Wilson Government was seriously considering withdrawal from Northern Ireland following the failures of Sunningdale and the Constitutional Convention. Incident centres were established to monitor the ceasefire and a series of meetings took place between PIRA leaders and officials from the Northern Ireland Office (NIO). Whether the Government's hints at withdrawal were serious or merely a ruse to entice the PIRA into a cessation of violence is a matter of continuing debate.[27] In the end, the increase in loyalist violence (primarily against Catholic civilians) and the PIRA's tit-for-tat response precluded moves towards withdrawal, if ever it was a serious option.

Roy Mason succeeded Rees as Northern Ireland Secretary in September 1976 and immediately announced that no new constitutional initiative would be offered until the security situation was 'normalised' because such initiatives merely raised expectations which in turn resulted in more violence when such expectations were not met. The Mason 'offensive' (as his Opposition shadow Neave favourably described it) against the PIRA consisted of a greater use of the Special Air Service (SAS) in rural trouble-spots like South Armagh, increased undercover operations by the RUC and regular Army, and the Ulsterisation of the security forces by increasing the number of locally recruited personnel into the RUC and UDR and a reduction in both the number and role of the Army in favour of 'police primacy'. The proportion of 'Ulsterised' forces subsequently increased relative to the Army force levels so that the proportion of locally recruited forces increased from 45 per cent in 1970 to 51 per cent in 1977 and reached 67 per cent by 1989.[28] Of course, the Ulsterisation of the security forces also increased the Ulsterisation of victims of PIRA violence, an effect intended further to insulate British politicians from the results of the war.[29]

The degree to which violence had become de-politicised after 1974 is revealed in Figure 7.1. From 1974 to the middle of 1976 as the number of deaths climbs the level of debate first drops and then rises only moderately before dropping again through 1978. In the House of Commons Northern Ireland had become primarily a law and order problem rather than a political or constitutional crisis. In June 1977 Mason confidently told the Commons:

> Politically-motivated violence enjoying a measure of community support has been much reduced. Therefore, those responsible have no realistic political cause and no political or democratic backing. The gap is widening between these criminals and the community in whose interests they claim to act. They really are being isolated.[30]

While the reduction in PIRA violence made the problem appear to be more manageable, the failure to confront the sources of intransigence merely bought some time before the umpteenth rising of the Phoenix and its counterpart, the Red Hand.

The normalisation policy began to unravel by the end of 1978 for at least three reasons. First, the shift away from detention towards a re-

liance on criminal prosecutions led to the increased use of forceful
interrogation by members of the security forces. Charges of mistreat-
ment of suspects were investigated by Amnesty International (1978)
and the Government's own Bennett Inquiry (1978) both of which led
to adverse international publicity against British security policy, including a decision by the United States State Department to ban the
sale of weapons to the RUC. Secondly, the removal of political status
for paramilitary prisoners led to the H-Block campaign in the Maze
Prison which evolved from a blanket protest to a dirty protest to a
hunger strike by 1980. Each stage of this protest increased international
exposure of the Northern Ireland problem and led directly to a re-
politicisation of the republican movement under the leadership of the
'Northern Command' of Gerry Adams, Danny Morrison and Martin
McGuinness.[31] Thirdly, the very success of the Mason offensive led to
a reorganisation of the PIRA into a near impenetrable cell-structure
which also facilitated the development of a wider range of terrorist
tactics. By the end of 1978 it was apparent that the PIRA was ready to
initiate a new bombing campaign in both Northern Ireland and Britain.
Over fifty bombs, many of them incendiaries, exploded in Northern
Ireland in the last two months of the year and in the same period in
Great Britain bombs exploded in Liverpool, Manchester, Bristol (seven
injured), Coventry, Southampton and London (one injured).

SYMBOLIC WATERSHEDS

The killing of Airey Neave by the Irish National Liberation Army
(INLA)[32] on March 30 1979 with a car-bomb planted in the Commons
car-park was another serious blow to the normalisation strategy. Attacks in Great Britain always carried disproportionate weight but the
killing of a senior Conservative minister-in-waiting in the heart of
Westminster was especially influential. Neave was targeted by the INLA
because, as Opposition spokesman on Northern Ireland from 1975 to
1979, he advocated more forceful security measures and was also the
author of the Conservatives' integrationist electoral manifesto which
called for the establishment of regional councils in Northern Ireland.
His death had several other important repercussions: it was an indication that a potentially more extremist republican group was waiting in
the wings even if the Provisionals could be successfully contained. He
was also a close friend and advisor to Margaret Thatcher and his death
strengthened her resolve to defeat terrorism. Finally, the outcry over

Neave's death provided an opportunity for the future leader of the UUP, James Molyneaux, to make political capital in the Commons:

> ... [O]n numerous occasions ... we who come from Northern Ireland have told other honourable Members that the Ulster experience is not unique. We said that they would see the same drama enacted on the mainland before their very eyes. It gives me no pleasure to say that the drama is now unfolding.[33]

It may not have given him pleasure, but Molyneaux's subsequent pleas for greater security and more devolved powers certainly carried more weight after atrocities occurred in Britain.

The threat of an escalation of violence was brought closer to home to the British public and Government on 27 August 1979 when the PIRA committed two separate attacks against the Crown and her forces. On that morning, off the coast of Sligo, the yacht of Earl Louis Mountbatten was blown up by a thirty-pound bomb set by the PIRA. The explosion killed Mountbatten, his 14-year-old grandson, the Dowager Lady Brabourne and a boatman. In the afternoon of the same day eighteen soldiers were killed near the border at Warrenpoint, County Down when the PIRA set up an ambush involving two separate bombs and machine-gunners planted along the road on the Republic's side of the border. The killings at Warrenpoint and the killing of Mountbatten, the Queen's cousin, decorated war hero and last Viceroy in India, produced an international outpouring of hostility and acrimony towards the republican movement. Nevertheless, before the dust had even settled politicians of all persuasions began to ride the wave of instability generated by this double atrocity. A poignant example of symbiotic opportunism was offered by the Irish Premier Jack Lynch in the aftermath of 27 August. When asked whether he believed that these events would delay a British initiative in Northern Ireland he replied to the contrary by saying, 'It might well accelerate it'.[34] In his last meeting with Thatcher in 1979 Lynch attempted to use the crisis to broaden the discussion beyond the issue of security towards the issue of a wider political settlement.

The renewed level of instability led the new Conservative Government to adopt a familiar response: an initiative in the form of a Constitutional Conference chaired by the new Northern Ireland Secretary Humphrey Atkins. That this was yet another exercise in containment is supported by Atkins' statement in the Commons announcing that the Conference would not consider the return of law and order powers to a devolved government:

Responsibility for law and order in the Province, *[which] remains the Government's overriding priority in Northern Ireland*, would not be transferred . . . I must tell the House that political advance – or even the prospect of it – will not solve the security question, because those who are responsible for the violence in Northern Ireland will, if anything, feel that this move is a threat to them . . . We must be just as resolute in seeking to control violence and bring terrorism down from its present level.[35]

Not even this limited mandate could lead to any form of consensus among the constitutional parties in Northern Ireland. The Official Unionist Party (OUP) refused to participate on the grounds that the proposals for devolved government were a repudiation of the Conservative's election manifesto which had promised an integrationist approach. The Democratic Unionist Party participated but refused to share power at executive level and the SDLP participated but refused to go along with proposals which did not include executive power-sharing and an institutionalised Irish Dimension.

FROM ULSTERISATION TO ANGLO-IRISH CONTAINMENT

The failure of the Constitutional Conference and the continued threat posed by the resurgence of both PIRA and loyalist terrorism led to an important change of strategy by the Conservative Government from a unilateral containment exercise to the development of an Anglo-Irish inter-governmental process. The adoption of the Anglo-Irish approach represents another example of turning the threat of instability into an opportunity to advance the political process over the heads of intransigent Northern Irish political leaders, just as the Heath Government had done by prorogueing Stormont in 1972. Haughey and Thatcher met three times between May 1980 and November 1981 culminating in the establishment of the British-Irish Inter-Governmental Conference, the institutional structure used to negotiate the Anglo-Irish Agreement of 1985.[36]

Instability produced by the failure of the 'containment through Ulsterisation' strategy was crucial to the negotiating position of both the British and Irish Governments. The negotiating strength of the constitutional nationalist position was based on the argument that violence was a *product* rather than a *cause* of the constitutional impasse in Northern Ireland (as expressed in articles 4.3 and 4.4 of the New

Ireland Forum Report). Therefore the instability caused by PIRA violence and loyalist retaliation was proof that Northern Ireland was, in
Haughey's words, a 'failed political entity'.[37] In his first meeting with
Thatcher in May 1980 Haughey attempted to move the discussion beyond the issue of cooperative security measures to the wider issue of
a political settlement based on the principle of unity by consent. Haughey
knew that Northern Ireland was a low-priority item for Thatcher and
also believed that her visit to the border security posts following the
Mountbatten and Warrenpoint deaths reinforced her belief in the necessity
of securing formal security cooperation with the Republic.[38] It was
Haughey's intention, like Lynch before him, to use the leverage of the
security situation to gain concessions on an Irish Dimension. However,
the pressure for such a concession by Thatcher was lessened as the
death toll diminished in the first few months of 1980. The drop in the
level of violence was caused by a combination of more effective surveil-
lance and intelligence strategies implemented by the new GOC, Richard
Lawson, and the new RUC Chief Constable, John Hermon, as well as
a shortage of arms and money within the republican movement.[39]

The reduced level of instability allowed Thatcher to reassure unionists prior to the May meeting with Haughey that 'The future of the
constitutional affairs of Northern Ireland is a matter for the people of
Northern Ireland, this government and this parliament and no one else'.[40]
Yet the absolutist position on sovereignty had apparently changed by
the time of the December 1980 summit when Thatcher and Haughey
issued a joint-communique which stated that future meetings would
address the 'special consideration of the totality of relationships within
these islands' and would discuss the formation of 'new institutional
structures' which would express the uniqueness of the relationship
between the United Kingdom and Ireland.[41] The apparent shift in emphasis between the two meetings cannot be accounted for without a
consideration of the changed security situation.

The most immediate security threat was caused by the combination
of political and paramilitary fallout from the hunger-strikes of 1980–1.[42]
Thatcher's decision not to concede an inch on the prisoner's demands
represents a hang-over from the 'law and order' containment approach.
The unintended consequence of her 'crime is a crime is a crime' mantra
was to produce a massive outpouring of support for the prisoners which
eventually coaxed *Sinn Féin* into entering constitutional politics. Since
Bobby Sands was elected MP for Fermanagh-South Tyrone in 1981
Sinn Féin has consistently received between 10 and 15 per cent of the
popular vote overall, which represents between 30 and 40 per cent of

the nationalist vote. However, the real impact of *Sinn Féin*'s 'New Departure' was based on its ability to combine electoral success with its military campaign through the tactical combination of the 'armalite and ballot box'. While the level of PIRA violence in Northern Ireland dropped from 1980 to the first half of 1983 for electoral purposes, this void was filled by a renewed bombing campaign in Britain. From October 1981 to December 1983 bombs at Chelsea barracks, Hyde Park, Regent's Park and Harrods killed nineteen people and injured 189.

The threat to stability posed by *Sinn Féin*'s emergence is reflected in the level of debate concerning the next constitutional initiative: rolling devolution (see Figure 7.3). Despite widespread opposition to both the timing and content of the initiative, there was a certain degree of consensus that direct rule was unable to bring stability to Northern Ireland. As Prior told the House:

> [D]irect rule is most people's second-best option. It could not prevent the upsurge in violence brought on by the hunger-strike or the events of last autumn. Despite the most intense and dedicated efforts by the security forces, violence continues and tensions between the communities are quickly roused.[43]

Figure 7.3   Deaths from political violence and debate on political and constitutional issues, 1979 to 1992

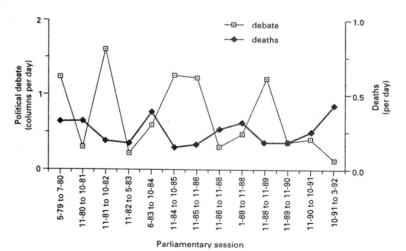

Given these conditions it should have been no surprise that rolling devolution failed to lead to any agreed form of power-sharing. Both the SDLP and *Sinn Féin* contested the election for the new Assembly in October 1982, but both declared that they would abstain from participation in the Assembly. Without the participation of the intended opposition the Assembly merely acted as a forum for Unionist politicians to denounce the activities of the British-Irish Inter-Governmental Council where the external political process was gaining momentum.

The inter-governmental approach took precedence over the internal approach for three primary reasons. First, the successive failures of the Constitutional Conference and the rolling devolution Assembly suggested that neither continuing violence nor the related economic crisis were sufficient to induce significant compromise among local leaders. Secondly, the threat of *Sinn Féin*'s challenge to the SDLP was turned into an opportunity by John Hume to create a united constitutional nationalist position on political progress. The report of the New Ireland Forum was published in May 1984 and while its proposed options (a unitary state, a federal state and joint authority) were all rejected by Thatcher, the report was approved by both houses of Congress in the US and praised (though not endorsed) by Ronald Reagan. The Forum Report contributed directly to the inter-governmental process because it presented a semblance of unity among the constitutional nationalist parties which could be used to deliver a compromise agreement. Finally, the escalating threat of violence was demonstrated by the attempt on Thatcher's life in the bombing of the Grand Hotel in Brighton during the Conservative Party Conference in October 1984. Before the bombing a seven-ton shipment of arms from America was seized aboard the *Marita Ann* off the coast of Kerry. The shipment was an indication that the PIRA was preparing for the 'long war'.[44] These factors all contributed to the momentum for an agreement between London and Dublin which would contribute at a minimum, to cooperation on security, and more hopefully to a new momentum for a form of devolved government based on power-sharing and an institutional Irish Dimension.

FROM ANGLO-IRISH CONTAINMENT TO PROGRESSIVE CONFLICT REGULATION

In the aftermath of the Agreement there were hopeful signs that its intended aims of marginalising *Sinn Féin* and inducing unionist movement were working. *Sinn Féin*'s vote dropped slightly in subsequent elections and there were signs, most notably the meeting between Hume and Adams in 1988, that *Sinn Féin* was interested in joining the constitutional process. The feared unionist backlash did not materialise despite early shows of force and Unionist leaders eventually came around to participate in constructive proposals in the form of the talks process started by Northern Ireland Secretary Peter Brooke in 1989. As Figure 7.3 shows: the peaks of violence have declined continuously throughout the 1980s and early 1990s, and their timing reveals an indirect, and possibly reactive effect, rather than a direct effect upon constitutional debate.

However, the Anglo-Irish containment approach was gradually strained by an escalation of PIRA violence from 1987, the loyalist response from 1989, and the failure of any internal progress among the constitutional parties. *Sinn Féin* did not wither away in the aftermath of the Agreement but instead solidified its basis of support. It consolidated its support despite (or because of?) the hugely negative publicity resulting from the atrocities in Enniskillen in November 1987, the bombing in Deal which killed 10 bandsmen in September 1989, the killing of Conservative MP Ian Gow in July 1990, the use of human proxy-bombs in the border areas in 1990–91, the Teebane Cross massacre in January 1992 and the attacks in Warrington in March 1993 and the Shankill Road in September 1993. To a certain degree the damage to the republican movement caused by these atrocities has been offset by widely publicised abuses by the security forces: the Gibraltar incident; the Stalker, Sampson and Stevens Inquiries into shoot-to-kill operations and collusion between UDR and Protestant paramilitaries; abusive interrogation at Magherafelt; and more shoot-to-kill ambushes at Loughgall have all contributed to the impression that a two-sided war is being fought rather than a one-sided terrorist campaign.

The most important factor in the continued threat posed by the republican movement was the tactical shift towards commercial bombing in Northern Ireland and Britain since 1991. This shift was partly a response to the limited efficacy of its campaign of assassination of security force members and their suppliers as loyalist paramilitaries were able to counter and even exceed the annual republican death tolls from 1992 through to the ceasefires of 1994. The result was a shift to 'spectaculars' in Britain, starting with the Downing Street mortar attack in February 1991, the Baltic Exchange bombing in April 1992 and Bishopsgate in April 1993. The latter two caused an estimated billion pounds' damage between them and threatened the City of London's

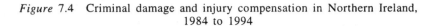

Figure 7.4   Criminal damage and injury compensation in Northern Ireland, 1984 to 1994

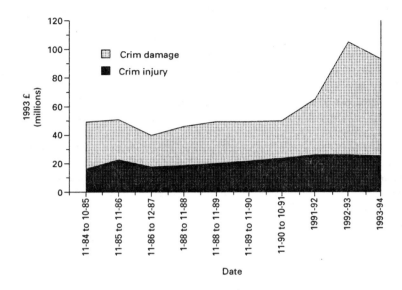

Date

stature as a secure capital of world finance. The City bombs were followed in early 1994 by mortar attacks on Heathrow Airport as the PIRA attempted to present a similar threat to one of the major air transport hubs. The commercial bombing of Northern Ireland towns also led to a significant increase in the amount of bomb-damage compensation as revealed in Figure 7.4, with a doubling of the amount of expenditures on claims from £42 million in 1990–1 to £102 million in 1992–3. The effect of the bomb damage in Northern Ireland and Great Britain on Government thinking was revealed in an off-the-cuff remark by Sir Patrick Mayhew to the German paper *Die Zeit* in April 1993:

> A number of nationalist people have been encouraged by the terrorists to believe that the British Government would never release Northern Ireland, we would very happily release Northern Ireland, to be perfectly frank with you, because we have no selfish interest, strategic interest.
>
> It's not quite right to say, I withdraw that, I don't want to say we would very happily do it. I don't want to say that. We would be no obstacle in the way. It costs us three billion a year net. Three billion for one-and-a-half million people – we have no strategic interest, we have no economic interest, in staying there.[45]

Despite claims by John Major that the PIRA would not be able to bomb its way to the negotiating table it is clear that the upsurge in instability from 1989 created threats which were then converted by the British and Irish Governments into opportunities for political progress which by-passed the stalled strand-one process in Northern Ireland. In November 1990 Northern Ireland Secretary Peter Brooke had made an important speech which pre-dates Mayhew's declaration of British neutrality. Brooke also emphasised that PIRA violence was among the last remaining reasons for British involvement in Northern Ireland and by the spring of 1992 the Government was involved in secret discussions with Republican leaders.[46] Still, the Republican leadership pressed for a clear commitment by the Government to exercise active neutrality by becoming 'persuaders' of unionists towards the cause of a united Ireland. Towards this end the campaign of violence continued with the spectaculars and spectacular mistakes mentioned above. The Downing Street Declaration of December 1993 cannot be explained without reference to the stimulation of the inter-governmental process by recent atrocities and spectaculars. Following the Shankill and Greysteel killings the Irish Foreign Minister, Dick Spring, in a speech to the British-Irish Association Conference on 10 September 1993 emphasised the urgency of political progress:

> The horrific upsurge of killings recently, which plunged yet more families into grief, and widened the circles of communal fear still more, cries out for a different and more urgent response than a complacent sense of the conflict being manageable.[47]

In November 1993 the climate of urgency generated by renewed violence led Major to declare in the Commons:

> The Government will now intensify its efforts to find a basis for the constitutional parties in Northern Ireland to carry forward the talks process . . . We are determined to do all we can to bring peace to Northern Ireland. The further killings over the weekend make that search for peace all the more urgent.[48]

The Downing Street Declaration signed by the British and Irish Governments in December 1993 represents a step beyond Anglo-Irish containment towards a more progressive framework for a regulation of the conflict. The two Governments declared their commitment to achieving the consent of the two communities for any change in the constitutional status of Northern Ireland. While the commitment to consent was not new, the recognition of the equal legitimacy of the two traditions was also a recognition of the legitimacy of the goals, if not the means, of both loyalist and republican movements. In combination with the British declaration of neutrality in 1990, the Downing Street Declaration convinced the Republican leadership that violence had gotten the movement as far as it could and that their remaining goals could only be achieved through constitutional means. The PIRA declared a ceasefire on 31 August 1994 and loyalist paramilitaries reciprocated on 13 October.

CONCLUSION

The desire to remove the Irish question from British politics led to a various forms of containment, the most successful and enduring of which was provided by the Unionist regime at Stormont from 1921 to 1972. The fact that Stormont was brought down with a combination of moral and physical force legitimated the use of force to seal the margins of compromise within both the nationalist and unionist communities. The clear determination of significant portions of each community to promote/defend their interests with violence called for a more thorough conflict regulation initiative than that embodied by the Sunningdale Agreement. However, the supposedly un-British physical force means used to force the Northern Ireland conflict onto the British political agenda also contributed to a re-enforcement of the determination to contain rather than resolve the conflict. The option of withdrawal, which had been used in former colonies such as Palestine, Cyprus and Aden, was considered by the Labour Government in 1975 but rejected because of the historic links, proximity, and certainty that a bloodbath would follow.

The repeated failures of the containment approach to produce an internal settlement led to a shift towards Anglo-Irish containment based on a combination of increased security measures and an external agreement with the Republic of Ireland. The gradual unravelling of this form of containment at the hands of sustained paramilitary violence again placed Northern Ireland onto the agenda of British politics and contributed to the momentum which led to the Downing Street Declaration. However, the repeated reliance on the threat of instability to produce opportunities for constitutional initiatives merely reinforces the efficacy of violence as a tool in the political process. Since the ceasefire both Nationalist and Unionist politicians have used the implicit threat of violence to back their opposing positions on the future constitutional and institutional structures. For example, when a draft of the two Governments' framework document was leaked in February 1995, David Trimble (Unionist MP for Upper Bann) warned: 'We are very worried that the greed of Dublin and the weakness of Stormont Castle are going to prejudice the peace process. Believe me, coming forward with proposals of this nature will derail the peace process.'[49] This was countered by Seamus Mallon (SDLP MP for Newry and Armagh) who said the leak of the document was a 'fairly cynical political game' being played by Conservatives who sympathised with hardline unionism. 'It is also a very deadly game because what is at stake is the peace that has been painstakingly created.'[50]

What is required to break the cycle of violence permanently is a proactive rather than reactive approach to the fundamental source of conflict: the opposing national aspirations of the two communities. To date the process undertaken since the Downing Street Declaration does appear to address these core issues. However, given the current Government's dependence on Unionist votes to maintain its slim majority in the Commons, there remains the distinct possibility that peace will be sacrificed at the altar of incumbent politics.

NOTES

1. *House of Commons Debates*, 5th ser. vol. 782, col. 313, 22 April 1969. Quintin Hogg later became Lord Hailsham of St Marylebone. He served as Shadow Home Secretary from 1966 to 1970 and Lord Chancellor from 1970 to 1974, and from 1979 to 1987.
2. *House of Commons Debates*, 5th ser., vol. 782, cols 263–4, 22 April 1969. Paul Rose was chairman of the Campaign for Democracy in Ulster (CDU) from 1965 to 1973.
3. D. G. Boyce, *The Irish Question and British Politics, 1868–1986* (London: Macmillan Education, 1988), p. 65.
4. *House of Commons Debates* 5th ser., vol. 782, col. 320, 22 April 1969, emphasis added.
5. R. Crossman, *The Diaries of a Cabinet Minister: Vol. III Secretary of State for Social Services, 1968–70* (London: Cape, 1977), p. 622, quoted in D.G. Boyce *op.cit.*, p. 108.
6. Clause 75 of the Government of Ireland Act (1920) states:

    Notwithstanding the establishment of the parliament of Northern Ireland or of anything contained in this Act, the supreme authority of the parliament of the United Kingdom shall remain unaffected and undiminished over all persons, matters and things in Northern Ireland and every part thereof.

7. P. Buckland, *A History of Northern Ireland* (Dublin: Gill & Macmillan, 1981), pp. 138–40.
8. D. Hamill, *Pig in the Middle: The Army in Northern Ireland 1969–1984* (London: Methuen, 1985), pp. 51–67.
9. Quoted in *ibid.* p.24. Hamill does not provide a source for this quote but it appears to be from an interview with an un-named Cabinet member. According to Army leaders, the primary criticism of the Government's approach was that it was hoping to suppress violence within the legal framework of a liberal democracy. .
10. K. Kelly, *The Longest War* (London: Zed, 1988), p. 150.
11. The hardliner brought in was Harry West and the liberal was David Bleakley of the Northern Ireland Labour Party, whose nomination was brought under a rarely used clause in the Government of Ireland Act (1920) which allowed the selection of a non-sitting member for a period of six months.
12. Under the proposal, the committees would be composed of members in relation to party strength and two of four committee chairs would be chaired by Opposition members. The committees proposed were: Social Services, Environmental Services, Industrial Services and the already existing Accounts Committee. The Green Paper of October 1971 also proposed enlarging the Stormont Commons by between twenty and thirty to increase minority representation; and the possible introduction of the Single Transferable Vote to replace 'first past the post'. Faulkner explicitly ruled out any form of power-sharing with nationalists at the Executive level. See M. J. Cunningham, *British Government Policy in Northern Ireland 1969–89: Its Nature and Execution* (Manchester: Manchester University Press, 1991), pp. 44–5.
13. M. Farrell, *Northern Ireland: The Orange State* (London: Pluto, 1976), pp. 279–81.
14. The Provisionals' five-point demand included: 'an end to the British forces' campaign of violence; the abolition of Stormont; a guarantee of non-interference in the election of a nine-county Parliament (*Dáil Uladh*); the immediate release of detainees; compensation for those who had suffered from British violence', quoted in R. Deutsch and V. Magowan, *Northern Ireland, 1968–74: A Chronology of Events*, Vol. 3 (Belfast: Blackstaff, 1975), pp. 124–5. The fact that the demands did not include a united Ireland suggests that the Provisional leadership had already developed the theory that a federal structure would both ease the unionist transition to acceptance of a united Ireland and allow the Provisionals to reform the entire Irish state according to its version of 'Gaelic Socialism'. See K. Kelly, *op.cit.*, pp. 120–34, and P. Bishop and E. Mallie, *The Provisional IRA* (London: Corgi, 1988), pp. 211–17.
15. For an Army version of internment which emphasises the escalation of the PIRA campaign prior to internment see M. Dewar, *The British Army in Northern Ireland* (London: Arms and Armour, 1981), pp. 49–56.
16. M. Farrell, *op.cit.*, pp. 285.
17. B. White, *John Hume: Statesman of the Troubles* (Belfast: Blackstaff, 1984), p. 151.
18. For the Army's view of the UWC strike see D. Hamill, *op.cit.*, pp. 145–54; and M. Dewar, *op.cit.*, pp. 100–3.

19. B. White, *op.cit.*, p. 170.
20. From a televised speech quoted in the *Irish Times* on 27 May 1974.
21. See R. Fisk, *The Point of No Return: The Strike which Broke the British in Ulster* (London: André Deutsch, 1975); also D. Anderson, *14 May Days: The Inside Story of the Loyalist Strike of 1974* (Dublin: Gill & Macmillan, 1994). Both Fisk and Anderson reproduce the words of an Army source, also quoted in *Fortnight* (No.333, November 1994), who wrote: 'The Army has shown that it is not prepared to act under certain circumstances, it has shown a considerable distrust of Socialist politicians.'
22. *House of Commons Debates* 5th ser., vol. 876, col. 1167, 9 July 1974.
23. *House of Commons Debates* 5th ser., vol. 866, col. 670, 13 December 1973.
24. *House of Commons Debates* 5th ser., vol. 876, cols 1197–8, 9 July 1974, emphasis added.
25. The Prevention of Terrorism Act also allowed the authorities to proscribe terrorist organisations and made illegal any show of support for proscribed organisations through the solicitation of funds or the withholding of information.
26. *House of Commons Debates* 5th ser., vol. 882, col. 36, 25 November 1974.
27. Rees claimed in a letter to *The Times* in 1983 that the Government had 'seriously considered' withdrawal but that the increase in loyalist violence and Dublin's resistance to the idea of British withdrawal had precluded it. See P. Bew and G. Gillespie, *A Chronology of the Troubles* (Dublin: Gill & Macmillan, 1993), p. 99. Lord Donoughue, head of Wilson's Policy Unit, said at an ICBH conference on 13 July 1995 that a short-lived Cabinet Committee was set up to consider this option.
28. Calculated from Irish Information Partnership's *Irish Information Agenda: Update 1987–89* (London: IIP, 1990).
29. For an analysis of the Ulsterisation of victims see B. O'Duffy, 'Violence in Northern Ireland 1969–1994: Sectarian or Ethnonational?', *Ethnic and Racial Studies* (forthcoming, 1995).
30. *House of Commons Debates,* 5th ser., vol. 934, col. 635, 30 June 1977.
31. The shift to control of the PIRA by the northern command is explained in L. Clarke, *Broadening the Battlefield: The H-Blocks and the Rise of Sinn Féin* (Dublin: Gill & Macmillan, 1987).
32. The INLA, established in 1975, was the military wing of the Irish Republican Socialist Party. The INLA was comprised primarily of members of the Official IRA who disagreed with that organisation's renunciation of violence in 1972.
33. *House of Commons Debates,* 5th ser., vol. 969, col. 956, 2 July 1979.
34. Quoted in D. Barzilay, *The British Army in Ulster*, Vol. 4 (Belfast: Century, 1981), p. 96.
35. *House of Commons Debates,* 5th ser., vol. 972, cols 626, 634–5, 25 October 1979.
36. See G. FitzGerald, *All in a Life: An Autobiography,* (Dublin: Gill & Macmillan, 1991), pp. 504–30, and M. Thatcher, *The Downing Street Years* (London: HarperCollins, 1994), pp. 393–406. A comparison of the accounts of Thatcher and FitzGerald of the negotiations of the Anglo-Irish Agreement reveals that, while they naturally emphasised their own

contributions, they both utilised the implicit threat of violence to buttress their opposing positions.

37. See K. Kelly, *op.cit.*, pp. 307–8.
38. Quoted in *Irish Times*, 13 October 1986.
39. For a detailed account of the period see J. B. Bell, *The Irish Troubles: A Generation of Violence 1967–1992* (Dublin: Gill & Macmillan, 1994), pp. 586–7.
40. *House of Commons Debates*, 5th ser., vol. 985, col. 250, 20 May 1980, quoted in P. Bew and G. Gillespie, *op.cit.*, p. 139.
41. See M. Thatcher, *op.cit.*, p. 390, where she claims that she paid insufficient detail to the *communiqué* released after the December 1980 summit and would have objected specifically to the term 'special consideration of the totality of relationships within these islands', which implied that the constitutional status of Northern Ireland was open to change.
42. The most detailed account of the hunger strikes is D. Beresford, *Ten Men Dead: The Story of the 1981 Hunger Strike* (London: Grafton, 1986). For a discussion of the political context see P. O'Malley, *Biting at the Grave: The Irish Hunger Strikes and the Politics of Despair* (Belfast: Blackstaff, 1990).
43. *House of Commons Debates*, 6th ser., vol. 23, col. 469, 10 May 1982.
44. For details of the Libyan shipments see B. O'Brien, *The Long War: The IRA and Sinn Féin* (Dublin: O'Brien, 1993) pp. 133–53.
45. This is the Northern Ireland Office's own version of the interview as quoted in the *Irish Times*, 27 April 1993.
46. For the republican leadership reaction to Brooke's November 1990 speech, see B. O'Brien, *op.cit.*, pp. 209–23.
47. Quoted from a transcript of the speech in the author's possession.
48. *Evening Standard*, 1 January 1993.
49. *Independent*, 3 February 1995.
50. *Independent*, 2 February 1995.

8 Conservative Politics and the Abolition of Stormont

Philip Norton

The issue of Ireland was one of high politics in the nineteenth century and for the first three decades of this century. For the Conservative Party, the commitment to the Union was a fundamental one. In the second decade of this century, so strong were feelings on the issue that Party leaders were prepared to toy with unconstitutional action in order to maintain that union.

Yet in terms of domestic politics – and certainly in terms of issues that were to occupy Conservative politicians – the Irish question largely slipped from the agenda following the establishment of Stormont and the devolution of executive powers to a Northern Ireland Cabinet and Civil Service. The issue was, in effect, hived off from the national agenda of the Conservative Party and, indeed, of successive governments. The politics of Northern Ireland were complex, fragmented, and conducted in a culture that was not the culture of mainland British, and certainly not English, politics. English politicians were content to leave the governing of Northern Ireland to the Prime Minister and Cabinet at Stormont.

English politicians consequently had little contact with the affairs of Northern Ireland. There was no Cabinet Minister with exclusive responsibility for the region. Some English politicians made an issue of Northern Ireland, but they were the exception. At Westminster, Ireland was not so much an issue of high or low politics, but essentially a non-issue. A 'desire for non-involvement on the part of Westminster in "internal" Northern Ireland affairs' was, as Brigid Hadfield recorded, one of the dominant features of the system that existed from 1921 to the 1960s.[1] From 1922 onwards there was a parliamentary convention that no MP could raise in the House of Commons an issue that was the direct responsibility of a Minister at Stormont.[2] Ulster Unionist Members appeared to adopt a parochial attitude and interest by other MPs, especially Labour or Liberal Members, in Northern Ireland was not encouraged.[3] Between partition and the latter half of the 1960s, the House of Commons spent an average of two hours per year on the subject of Northern Ireland.[4] As O'Leary and McGarry have observed, the Stormont regime may not have constituted a state, but it did constitute a semi-state.[5] Some issues were reserved to the United Kingdom Government, ranging from defence to the Post Office. Other issues were left to Stormont, while the Westminster Government got on with administering the rest of the United Kingdom.

Northern Ireland politicians, for their part, had little significant input into deliberations in Whitehall and Westminster. Their concerns were essentially provincial, with little interest in the affairs of state in London. At Stormont, a Speaker's ruling determined that issues reserved to the United Kingdom Government were not discussed. The leading politicians in the province had their own power base at Stormont. They had no power base in London. Given that Northern Ireland had its own parliament, it had fewer seats at Westminster than its population would normally have justified. For most of the period under study, it had twelve seats. Those seats were normally won by Ulster Unionist MPs with large majorities. The Ulster Unionists formed a subsidiary part of the Parliamentary Conservative Party, but they were a distinct and largely ignored element. 'As a group, they tended to enter politics later in life, which meant their careers at Westminster were relatively short, averaging about ten years'.[6] They spent little time at Westminster and, when there, were rarely of a calibre to attract attention from the Whips and Ministers. The more talented party leaders went to Stormont, not Westminster. Westminster MPs were viewed as 'political eunuchs'.[7] Some senior Ulster Unionists made it to ministerial office in the 1920s and 1930s. The Marquess of Londonderry served as Lord Privy Seal. In the Commons, one Ulster Unionist served for nine months as a Parliamentary Under-Secretary.[8] From 1940 to 1972, no Northern Ireland MP served as a departmental minister. One – Robin Chichester-Clark – served as a Parliamentary Private Secretary (PPS), or unpaid ministerial assistant, in 1958 and as a Government Whip from 1958 to 1964. A few others made it as far as Parliamentary Private Secretaries[9] but no further. Even so, they shone individually more than collectively. As a group, their political visibility was low to nonexistent.

The result was an era of 'dual politics',[10] Northern Ireland politics being the preserve of the executive of Northern Ireland, English politics being the preserve of the Government in London. The era of dual politics came to an end in the latter half of the 1960s, but the existence of this duality is important for helping explain the central feature of events within the Parliamentary Conservative Party when Stormont came under attack: that is, the failure of the Ulster Unionists to have any notable impact. They were to prove essentially marginal actors.

THE FALL OF STORMONT[11]

The rise of the civil rights movement in Northern Ireland and the clashes in the province between civil rights marchers and the police brought the issue of Northern Ireland on to the political agenda in Westminster. Later rioting could not be contained by the police and in 1969 troops were deployed in Northern Ireland in support of the civil power. Troops had been used during the Irish Republican Army (IRA) campaign of 1956 to 1962, but they now had a new peacekeeping role while the politicians attempted to find a political solution.[12]

The Conservative Government of Edward Heath was returned in June 1970. During the first session of the new Parliament, there were meetings between the eight Ulster Unionist MPs at Westminster[13] and Home Secretary Reginald Maudling. The meetings were concerned more with detail than strategy, covering the basic nuts and bolts of the security operation. Believing that the Government was not being tough enough, the Ulster Unionists tried to pressure Ministers to strengthen security measures and to ensure that the Northern Ireland Government had a greater voice in determining the deployment of forces in the region. Two of them – ironically, the two most liberal (Robin Chichester-Clark and Stratton Mills) – abstained in a vote on a three-line whip and all apparently threatened to withdraw their support from the Government if troops were not put under the control of the Stormont Government.[14] The Defence Secretary, Lord Carrington, refused. The Ulster Unionists did not withdraw their support.

However, a deteriorating security situation put more pressure on the Government. The Government failed to take action sufficient to prevent the Northern Ireland Prime Minister, James Chichester-Clark (brother of Robin), from resigning in March 1971. Ulster Unionist MPs responded by abstaining in two Commons' votes on the Industrial Relations Bill. Edward Heath reiterated in the Commons the Government's determination to support the army in rooting out terrorism, but the statement was not sufficient to still growing backbench worries about the situation in Northern Ireland. A meeting of the backbench Home Affairs Committee, convened at the request of the Ulster Unionists, attracted more than 160 backbenchers. Critical comments were made by Ulster Unionists and some Conservative backbenchers, but the Home

Secretary offered nothing new to the meeting.[15] The Ulster Unionists met to decide what to do: they decided to continue their support of the Government.

As violence in Northern Ireland worsened in subsequent months, the Ulster Unionists demanded more decisive action and four of them again threatened to withdraw their support from the Government in the division lobbies. However, the other four did not, with James Kilfedder criticising the threatened withdrawal of support; it would, he said, be bewildering to Conservatives who were supporters of the Union.[16] The House entered the summer recess with the Ulster Unionists critical of the Government but nonetheless divided as to how to express their disquiet.

In the summer, the Government responded to violence in Northern Ireland by agreeing to the introduction of internment. The House was recalled to debate the decision. The debate took place on an adjournment motion, with Labour critics of the decision forcing a division. The Government carried the division by 203 votes to 74. The official Opposition line was to abstain from voting. The Ulster Unionists supported the Government, though not enthusiastically. (One of them felt the policy was 'crazy'.) Their support remained conditional and in the following session it disappeared.

The internment policy proved a failure and the security situation in Northern Ireland worsened in the early months of 1972. The Heath Government decided to attempt a political, rather than a military, initiative in order to reduce the violence. This decision was welcomed by the Opposition but greeted less enthusiastically by some Conservative backbenchers. At a meeting of the backbench Home Affairs Committee on 6 March, several of the fifteen or more MPs who spoke expressed the view that 'rather than wave peace symbols, the government should go fiercely on the attack'.[17] With the exception of Peter Tapsell, those who spoke were on the right of the Party.

On 22 March, senior Government Ministers met with the Northern Ireland Prime Minister, Brian Faulkner, to discuss the Cabinet's proposed initiative. Three principal proposals were put to Faulkner: periodic plebiscites on the issue of the border, a start made on the phasing out of internment, and the transfer of responsibility for law and order from Stormont to the Westminster Government. Transfer of responsibility for law and order proved unacceptable to Faulkner and his Cabinet. The following day, Faulkner told the British Government that, if the proposal was implemented, the Northern Ireland Government would resign. On 24 March, Heath informed the House of Commons that the

British Government was left with 'no alternative to assuming full and direct responsibility for the administration of Northern Ireland until a political solution to the problems of the Province can be worked out in consultation with all those concerned'.[18] A Bill to give effect to this would be introduced and a new post of Secretary of State for Northern Ireland would be created, to be occupied by the then Lord President of the Council, William Whitelaw.

The announcement was welcomed by the Labour and Liberal Parties but received a divided response on the Conservative benches. Ulster Unionists who spoke condemned the move, as did John Biggs-Davison, an established backbench critic of Government policy. On 27 March, the day before the second reading of the Bill, the Northern Ireland (Temporary Provisions) Bill, critics took the opportunity to air their views at a meeting of the backbench Home Affairs Committee. Of fifteen Members to speak at the crowded meeting, at least eight are believed to have voiced criticisms. The presence of William Whitelaw helped temper the mood of the meeting but, as *The Times* noted the following morning: 'it is touch and go whether the criticism stirring among backbenchers finds expression when the second reading of the bill is put to the Commons tonight'.[19]

In the event, doubts about the Government's actions failed to incite a significant level of public opposition from Conservative backbenchers. The Whips estimated initially that between twenty and twenty-five backbenchers would join the Ulster Unionists in voting against the Bill. During the debate, two known critics of Government policy – John Biggs-Davison and Enoch Powell – rose to speak against the Bill; another critic, Hugh Fraser – who had reportedly voiced doubts at the meeting of the Home Affairs Committee – rose to support it. The Bill was given a second reading by 483 votes to 18. The twenty Members, including tellers, to oppose the Bill comprised nine Conservatives, eight Ulster Unionists, two Irish Unity Members and the Democratic Unionist MP Ian Paisley.[20] A further twelve Conservatives abstained. The following day, the remaining stages of the Bill were taken, with an all-night sitting being used in order to complete them. The Ulster Unionists forced a number of divisions, but in none of them were they joined by more than six Conservatives.[21] The Bill was given a third reading by 191 votes to 13, with four Conservatives joining the MPs from Northern Ireland in the 'No' lobby.[22]

Public opposition from Conservative MPs was thus on a small scale, and smaller than originally anticipated. The Ulster Unionists were vehement in their public condemnation of the Bill, but privately were far from united. They had previously discussed the issue of Stormont and some had accepted that it might have to go. However, they had been reminded by Faulkner that support of Stormont was a condition of membership of the Ulster Unionist Party, and they therefore felt that they had no option but to oppose the Bill.[23]

The Bill actually served to unite the Ulster Unionists, who were already showing signs of splitting in two. Three (Chichester-Clark, Mills and Pounder) formed a moderate group, supporting the Faulkner reform programme in Northern Ireland, the others (Kilfedder, Molyneaux, Maginnis, McMaster and Orr) forming a more hardline grouping. Even the hardliners were not united. McMaster was later to split from them and support the Sunningdale agreement. Kilfedder favoured the full integration of Northern Ireland into the United Kingdom.

The united opposition of the Ulster Unionists was broken the following week when Robin Chichester-Clark joined the Government as Minister of State for Employment. Chichester-Clark was leader of the Ulster Unionists at Westminster. Orr and Mills were nominated to replace him. Both received four votes each (McMaster, of the hardline group, apparently voted for Mills). Orr was eventually chosen. Both Orr and Mills were nominated for the post of Vice-Chairman of the newly-formed backbench Northern Ireland Committee. Conservative MPs elected Mills. These event served to reveal the split within the ranks of the Ulster Unionists – exacerbated when the three moderates ceased to attend group meetings – and the preference of Conservative MPs for the more moderate brand of Ulster Unionism.

A lack of unity was also apparent when the Ulster Unionists met to decide their tactics in response to the Government's actions. They decided to withdraw their general support from the Government and to keep the Whips guessing as to how they would vote. This approach was opposed by Kilfedder, who wanted them to be fully integrated within the Conservative Party. Chichester-Clark then accepted Government office. There were thus only six Ulster Unionists left to pursue this policy and they did so only sporadically. Orr was variously absent because of illness. The most Mills did in support of the policy was not tell the Whips how he would vote on the guillotine motion on the European Communities Bill. The effect of their action on the Bill was, as the Government Chief Whip was later to observe, 'terribly marginal'.

Though Ulster Unionists thus had little impact in the House, the Government could not afford to take its support in the House for granted. The Government's conciliatory approach and rumours of contact between the Secretary of State and the PIRA fuelled unease on the backbenches. Government policy came in for repeated criticism at meetings of the backbench Northern Ireland Committee in July. At a meeting on 12 July, attended by forty to fifty MPs, thirteen criticised Government policy; only three supported it.[24] Explosions and more deaths in Northern Ireland increased the pressure on the Government. In an emergency debate in the House, the Secretary of State announced that he would never again sit down with representatives of the Provisional IRA.[25] The following week, the Army occupied so-called 'no-go' areas in Northern Ireland. The successful completion of the dawn operation, known as Operation Motorman, was announced to the House and received support from all sides. It had the effect of stilling criticism from Conservative backbenchers. Previous critics – such as Peter Tapsell, who had called for Whitelaw's resignation at the backbench Committee meeting on 12 July – now swung round to support the Government. So too did one of the Ulster Unionists, Stratton Mills. The introduction of direct rule, in his view, was now 'water under the bridge'. In December, Mills resigned from the Ulster Unionist Party, though retaining the Conservative whip.

Following Operation Motorman, the Government then took the political initiative. Whitelaw convened a conference at Darlington attended by Ulster Unionists, the Northern Ireland Labour Party, and the Alliance Party. The following March (1973) a White Paper on constitutional change in Northern Ireland was published, proposing a power-sharing executive. The White Paper was attacked by the now diminished band of Ulster Unionists, but they could muster little support among Conservative MPs. When the House debated the White Paper, an amendment moved by Orr – regretting that the White Paper did not provide for adequate representation of the people of Northern Ireland at Westminster – was defeated by 332 votes to 13. Ten Conservatives voted for the amendment, one doing so in error.[26] That was the maximum support the Ulster Unionists could muster. The motion to approve the White Paper was carried by 329 votes to 5.[27] Only two Conservatives – Enoch Powell and Nicholas Winterton – joined three Ulster Unionists in voting against. A number of Members, including Maginnis, were content to abstain.

The marginalisation of the Ulster Unionists was demonstrated in later divisions. The Ulster Unionists forced votes during passage of the Northern Ireland Assembly Bill and the Northern Ireland Constitution Bill.[28] Their main opposition was directed at the latter Bill (they failed to divide against the former on second and third reading) but they never managed at any stage to attract more than six Conservatives into the lobby with them. Their only consistent supporter on the Conservative benches was Enoch Powell. On the second reading the Constitution Bill, only Powell and Harold Soref joined Ulster Unionists in voting against it – the Bill was carried by 230 votes to 7 – and only Powell stayed the course and voted against third reading.

The Ulster Unionists not only failed to rouse Conservative MPs to support their stance, they also faced difficulties within their own ranks. They had already lost Mills. Chichester-Clark was a Minister. Pounder did not vote against the Government during the passage of the Bills. McMaster declared that, as the Constitution Bill had now been passed, he wanted to see it work and hence would support it (a decision that was to cost him his seat). Even on the second reading of the Constitution Bill, Maginnis had described it as a half-way house that he would vote neither for nor against. In the event, he acted as a teller against it. Even so, his speech pointed to the difficulty of maintaining a united front among the increasingly tiny band of Ulster Unionists opposed to Government policy.

In November 1973, Whitelaw announced agreement on the formation of an executive in Northern Ireland and the following month announced that agreement had been reached at Sunningdale on the formation of a Council of Ireland. The four remaining hardline Ulster Unionists voiced their opposition and took their opposition to the division lobbies. (Or rather three did – Kilfedder was absent.) They were joined by only one Conservative, Enoch Powell. Pounder and McMaster, along with Chichester-Clark and Mills (who by this time had joined the Alliance Party), supported the Sunningdale Agreement. The disintegration of the Ulster Unionist Party in the House was complete.

The security situation in Northern Ireland created a serious problem for the British Government and it took a number of measures in order to address the problem. The way it did so caused disquiet on the Conservative backbenches. Ministers and the Whips had to anticipate and to assess backbench reaction. The mood on the backbenches was especially worrying for Ministers in the period from the introduction of the Northern Ireland (Temporary Provisions) Bill in March 1972 through to the completion of Operation Motorman in July of that year. Yet what is remarkable is the fact that, in parliamentary terms, a major constitutional change – the suspension of Stormont and the introduction of direct rule in Northern Ireland – was achieved with relative ease. Far from the Ulster Unionists rallying a substantial number of Conservative MPs – members of the Conservative and Unionist Party – in opposition to the Government's policy, the actions of the Government served essentially and ultimately to split the Ulster Unionists, rendering them a marginal force in the House of Commons.

EXPLANATIONS

The Ulster Unionists and their allies within the Conservative Party failed to prevent the demise of Stormont. As our narrative of events has shown, their impact during the critical period was negligible. Given the commitment of the Conservative Party to the Union, and the action of Party leaders earlier in the century, it might plausibly have been expected that the Conservative Party would be more receptive to the views of the Ulster Unionists within its midst. Yet when the crisis came, Conservative MPs rallied behind the Government. William Whitelaw recalled that, as the new Secretary of State for Northern Ireland, he thought he could rely on a broad consensus of support throughout Parliament: 'This meant that, carefully handled, Westminster was a potential source of strength to me at moments of extreme stress. So it proved'.[29]

What, then, explains the failure of the Ulster Unionists to mobilise Conservative MPs in opposition to the imposition of direct rule? There is no single explanation. Rather, the combination of one constant and three variable factors produced the marginalisation of the Ulster Unionists in 1972.

(1) The nature of their position in relation to the United Kingdom. The Ulster Unionists were, and remain, dependent on the British Government for maintaining the thread of Union. Unionists, by definition, are committed to that Union. As Bulpitt has noted, 'By definition the Unionists lacked the ultimate weapon of any party of territorial defence, the threat of "exit" . . . there was really nowhere else to go, other than to a united Ireland'.[30] The threat of breaking the ties of Union was not one so much in the hands of the Unionists but in the hands of the British Government. Furthermore, for those Unionists who wanted to move away from the position of dual politics towards the integration of Northern Ireland within the United Kingdom, the abolition of Stormont was not necessarily a threat. Unionists lacked the ultimate deterrent. That, however, was not all they were lacking. In terms of Westminster politics in 1972, they lacked two other features that would have given them some political leverage: allies already in place and voting leverage.

(2) The Ulster Unionists had failed to ensure that they had allies in

place to support their stance. This is where the background of neglect – that is, neglect of Westminster – becomes significant. To quote Bulpitt again:

> Most Ulster politicians stayed at home; few, if any, played politics at Westminster or Whitehall. With hindsight it can be argued that this strategy was a mistake. It meant that the Unionist cause was not articulated at Westminster. Even worse, Ulster had few friends at the Centre. The Unionist elite were to suffer from this after 1968.[31]

Fifty years of dual politics – of Northern Ireland not being an issue of political salience – had meant that the emotional attachment to Union was no longer so strong among Conservatives as it had been at the beginning of the century. There was no strong commitment to be tapped at a moment's notice. Ulster Unionists had not been a visible presence at Westminster and had made no effort to ensure that it was an issue. When it became an issue, they had neither the time nor, in some cases, the personal commitment to garner allies on the Conservative benches.

Furthermore, what general concerns there were on the Conservative benches were less about the existence of Stormont than about maintaining law and order in Northern Ireland. This is clear from our preceding narrative. Opposition to the abolition of Stormont was confined to a handful of Conservatives led by Enoch Powell and, on occasion, comprising no more than Enoch Powell. Wider disquiet was expressed over the level of violence within Northern Ireland. Much of the disquiet in 1972 was dispelled not by any action by Government concerning the constitutional framework of Northern Ireland but by the successful completion of a military operation, Operation Motorman. The deaths of British soldiers in Northern Ireland had an impact on public opinion in Great Britain. The constitutional framework for the former had less, if any, political salience. Conservative MPs generally, according to one of their number (a leading critic of Government policy), mirrored public feeling. They simply wanted the issue to go away.

(3) The abolition of Stormont came in a Parliament in which the Government enjoyed a modest overall majority, but an overall majority nonetheless. (The Conservative Party was returned to power in the 1970 General Election with an overall majority of thirty.) Ulster Unionist MPs by themselves were not sufficient in number to threaten that majority, assuming a straight whipped vote between the Government and the Opposition parties. On the issue of direct rule, the Ulster Unionists – even if they had managed to garner a substantial body of supporters among Conservative backbenchers – would not have been

able to deny the Government a majority. The stance of the Labour and Liberal Parties denied them that opportunity.

Where they might have had an impact was in divisions on other issues in which the Opposition parties were voting against the Government. This, as we have seen, was a ploy they tried. But they lacked the organisation and the internal unity necessary to exploit this strategy effectively. One of their number was brought into Government, thus neutralising his vote, another was variously ill, and the others split as to what to do. Thus a strategy that was to be employed later and to effect during a period of minority Labour Government – the Ulster Unionists exploiting the situation more effectively than the Liberals, obtaining an increase in the number of Westminster parliamentary seats in Northern Ireland – was to fail them during this crucial period.

(4) One final variable may have contributed to the failure of the Ulster Unionists to garner more support for their cause in the Parliamentary Conservative Party: the competition with other issues. The troubles in Northern Ireland constituted a major political issue in the early 1970s. The security situation was a serious problem for Government and an issue that caused unease on the Conservative benches at Westminster. It was, though, not the only issue. Negotiations for British membership of the European Community were completed in 1971 and the House invited to approve membership in principle on the terms negotiated. The issue badly split both parties. The following year the European Communities Bill was introduced and was a central item on the parliamentary agenda from February until third reading on 13 July. Fifteen Conservatives voted against the second reading of the Bill even though it had been a made a vote of confidence.[32] The same year saw the Heath Government's U-turns on industrial policy and the economy.

This is not to downplay the importance of the issue of Northern Ireland. Rather, what it points to is the fact that other issues were also occupying the minds of Conservative MPs at the same time. Northern Ireland had to compete with those issues. Perhaps unfortunately for Ulster Unionists, those who were closest to them politically within the Parliamentary Party were MPs on the right who were also opposing the Government on a number of these other issues. There was a significant correlation between opposing the Government's policy on Northern Ireland and opposing its policies on the European Community, immigration and Rhodesian sanctions.[33] This was a problem for Ulster Unionists in that their allies could be dismissed by Ministers and the Whips as the established rebels. Though some respected backbenchers who were not persistent rebels voiced concerns, they tended to voice those concerns privately in the backbench Party Committee meetings and to focus on the security situation rather than the issue of retaining Stormont.

CONCLUSION

The Ulster Unionists were thus in a weak position in resisting Government in its insistence on direct rule. The Government took steps to assuage doubts on the Conservative benches concerning the security situation and were assured that direct rule would not face opposition from the Labour and Liberal Parties in the House. Lacking a notable voting clout of their own, there was little Ulster Unionists could do. The actions of the Government briefly united them but served ultimately to divide them. With the end of Stormont came the end of the united Ulster Unionist Party within the Conservative Party. The Ulster Unionists separated from the Conservative Party in the House. The effect, in terms of using their parliamentary position to influence public policy, was to be slight.

The withdrawal of the Unionists from the Conservative Party had profound effects for the Party in the February 1974 General Election. According to John Campbell, 'the enmity of the Ulster Unionists cost Heath his majority in February 1974'.[34] This is not quite accurate. Had the Ulster Unionists still been in the Conservative fold, the Conservatives would not have had an overall majority in the election – but they would have been the largest single party. However, in terms of using their parliamentary activity to influence public policy, the Unionists could claim little success. The features of the Stormont period – a body of parochially-oriented MPs, poor attendance records and attracting little interest from other MPs – have remained to the present day.[35] At Westminster, the Ulster Unionists persuaded the minority Labour Government of James Callaghan in 1978 to increase the number of Northern Ireland seats and the Conservative Government of John Major in 1994 to establish a Select Committee on Northern Ireland. Against that must be set their failure to influence the signing and implementation of the Anglo-Irish Agreement in 1985. Despite mass rallies in Northern Ireland, the resignation from office of one middle-ranking Government Minister (Ian Gow), and resignations by Unionist MPs in order to force by-elections, the Thatcher Government held firm. Unionists could not rally support on the Conservative benches to threaten the Government's position.

Variations in party strength in the House of Commons may give the Ulster Unionist MPs some political leverage. But that variable has to be put alongside one constant. The fact that the Unionists are dependent on the British Government for maintaining a commitment to the Union. They cannot afford to make too much of an enemy of the one body they need to retain as a friend.

NOTES

1. B. Hadfield, 'The Northern Ireland Constitution', in B. Hadfield (ed.), *Northern Ireland: Politics and the Constitution* (Buckingham: Open University Press, 1992), p. 4.
2. J. Loughlin, 'Administering Policy in Northern Ireland', in Hadfield (ed.), *op. cit.*, p. 64.
3. When in the mid-1960s one Liberal MP tabled some questions about Northern Ireland, one Ulster Unionist MP– who by chance had a home in the Liberal MP's constituency – claims to have retaliated by tabling questions about issues in the Liberal Member's constituency, with the result that the questions about Northern Ireland ceased to be asked. Told to the author by the Ulster Unionist MP in question in the latter half of the 1960s.
4. F. S. L. Lyons, *Ireland since the Famine* (London: Fontana, 1973), cited in B. O'Leary and J. McGarry (eds), *The Future of Northern Ireland* (Oxford: Clarendon Press, 1990), p. 28.
5. O'Leary and McGarry, *op. cit.*, p. 11.
6. W. A. Hazleton, 'A Breed Apart? Northern Ireland's MPs at Westminster', paper presented at the annual conference of the American Political Science Association, New York, 1994, p. 3.
7. J. F. Harbinson, *The Ulster Unionist Party 1882–1973* (Belfast: Blackstaff Press, 1973), quoted in Hazleton, *op. cit.*
8. Sir Hugh O'Neill, Parliamentary Under-Secretary for India and Burma from September 1939 to May 1940. O'Neill had previously been Chairman of the Conservative backbench 1922 Committee, but it was not then as influential a body as it was later to become. James Craig, the first Prime Minister of Northern Ireland, had served as Parliamentary Secretary at the Ministry of Pensions from 1919 to 1920 and then as Financial Secretary to the Admiralty before taking up his post at Stormont.
9. Knox Cunningham served as Parliamentary Private Secretary to Prime Minister Harold Macmillan (his reward was a knighthood in Macmillan's resignation hours); Robert Grosvenor served as a PPS 1957–59, Stratton Mills 1961–64 and Rafton Pounder 1970–71.
10. See J. Bulpitt, *Territory and Power in the United Kingdom* (Manchester: Manchester University Press, 1983).
11. Unless otherwise indicated, material in this section is drawn from the

relevant sections of Chapters 2–5 in P. Norton, *Conservative Dissidents* (London: Temple Smith, 1978). Quotations and views attributed to individuals are derived from interviews conducted by the author for that work.

12. M. Wallace, *British Government in Northern Ireland* (Newton Abbot: David & Charles, 1982), p. 36.
13. The eight Ulster Unionists to sit in this Parliament were Robert (Robin) Chichester-Clark (Londonderry), James Kilfedder (Down, North), Stanley McMaster (Belfast, East), John Maginnis (Armagh), Stratton Mills (Belfast, North), James Molyneaux (Antrim, South), Capt. Laurence Orr (Down, South), Rafton Pounder (Belfast, South). Kilfedder and Molyneaux were serving in their first Parliament.
14. *Economist,* 6 Feb. 1971.
15. *The Times,* 23 March 1971.
16. *The Times,* 31 July 1971.
17. *Daily Mail,* 7 March 1972.
18. *House of Commons Debates,* 5th ser. vol. 833, col. 1860, 24 March 1972.
19. *The Times,* 28 March 1972.
20. P. Norton, *Dissension in the House of Commons 1945–74* (London: Macmillan, 1975), pp. 423–4. The nine Conservatives were John Biggs-Davison, Julian Critchley, Angus Maude, Enoch Powell, Trevor Skeet, Harold Soref, Anthony Trafford, John Wilkinson and Nicholas Winterton.
21. The only Conservatives to join the Ulster Unionists in the lobby, apart variously from the nine to join them in voting against the second reading of the Bill, were Bernard Braine, Anthony Buck, David James, Robin Maxwell-Hyslop and C. M. (Monty) Woodhouse.
22. Norton, *Dissension in the House of Commons 1945–74,* pp. 429–30.
23. Norton, *Conservative Dissidents,* p. 84n.
24. *The Times,* 13 July 1972.
25. *House of Commons Debates,* 5th ser. vol. 841, col. 1373, 24 July 1972.
26. The nine who voted deliberately for the amendment were Ronald Bell, John Biggs-Davison, John Cordle, Walter Elliot, Angus Maude, Enoch Powell, Harold Soref, John Wilkinson and Nicholas Winterton. Norton, *Dissension in the House of Commons 1945–74,* p. 537. Six of the nine had voted against the second reading of the Northern Ireland (Temporary Provisions) Bill in 1972. See above.
27. *House of Commons Debates,* 5th ser. vol. 853, cols 1661–68.
28. See Norton, *Dissension in the House of Commons 1945–74,* pp. 539–42, 555–6 and 562–78.
29. William Whitelaw, *The Whitelaw Memoirs* (London: Headline, 1990), p. 113.
30. Bulpitt, *op. cit.,* pp. 145–6.
31. *Ibid.,* p. 153.
32. Norton, *Dissension in the House of Commons 1945–74,* pp. 404–6.
33. Norton, *Conservative Dissidents,* p. 90.
34. J. Campbell, *Edward Heath: A Biography* (London: Jonathan Cape, 1993), p. 434.
35. Hazleton, *op. cit.*

9 From Whitewash to Mayhem: The State of the Secretary in Northern Ireland

David Bloomfield and Maeve Lankford

NORTHERN IRELAND IN BRITISH PRIORITIES

Kevin Boyle remarked to the Opsahl Commission in 1993 that, around the dinner tables of England, Northern Ireland is not considered a polite topic for conversation. He spoke as one of the large number of people recently referred to in an Irish Sunday paper as Northern Irish Professional People Living in England, or 'nipples'. Few of them would disagree. His tone was one of resignation. His point was that, when mainland political or social problems surface, British society at large loses interest in, and accords little importance to, Northern Ireland. Most of Professor Boyle's fellow nipples would endorse his views with little surprise, and look with sanguine resignation at those British dinner tables. But they, and their compatriots in Northern Ireland, share a suspicion that the same disinterest applies to the British Cabinet table too. And on that point, they are less forgiving.

So when the British Government declares that it has no 'selfish strategic or economic interest' in Northern Ireland, many in Northern Ireland interpret it as meaning that the British Government has little or no interest at all in Northern Ireland. Few people there argue very much when the phrase is used. Had the Government declared that it no longer had any selfish strategic or economic interest in Yorkshire, or the borough of Camden, say, reaction would surely have been one of justified outrage.

The good people of Yorkshire or of Camden could be forgiven for thinking that the amount of attention given to Northern Ireland is unfairly greater than that given to their own regional concerns. Northern Ireland represents 3 per cent of the United Kingdom population. Per head of population, or per square kilometre, it is quite arguable that Northern Ireland gets more than its fair share of British attention. But there is one obvious difference between Northern Ireland and any other United Kingdom region: that is of course the protracted violent conflict. From an English perspective, Northern Ireland is a security problem, a problem of unrest. In Charles Townshend's words, 'the struggle to govern Ireland may fairly be regarded as Britain's longest counterinsurgency campaign'.[1] In practice, this has meant tackling the paramilitaries with both military and economic means, the aim being to defeat terrorism. Implicit in this, as in political history for eighty years, is a sense that Britain prefers an armslength role as manager of the conflict, as arbiter between the locals in *their* search for compromise. O'Leary and McGarry point out that to base policy on such 'disinterested pursuit of rational compromise would ensure that Irish politics was kept from the centre of the political stage, an objective shared by successive generations of the British governing class since 1868.'[2]

The very fact that this problem refuses to go away, or to yield to solutions that look, in British eyes, eminently satisfactory, breeds scepticism in us all, participants and observers alike. For the people of Northern Ireland, this in turn breeds cynicism. One of the cruellest paradoxes of the conflict is that its solution is beyond any one person or faction, and that it thus requires co-operation between a plurality of elements whose basic positions are described in such mutually exclusive terms as to allow little room for co-operation without compromising the basic principles of those positions. There are many players in this conflict: communities, political parties, military forces, paramilitary forces, governments. On their own they have impossible jobs. The British Secretary of State for Northern Ireland is not excepted: Britain may be the most powerful player in the game, but not even Britain can solve the problem independently. The point to be made here is that political progress towards a constitutional settlement demands a high degree of co-operation.

Northern Ireland, however, lies low on the domestic British political agenda, and this in itself contributes to Britain's difficulties in gaining the degree of co-operation necessary to address the problem successfully. The process of appointment of Secretary of State for Northern Ireland exemplifies this. Specifically, Northern Ireland's low-priority ranking means that Secretaries, and their Ministers, may get appointed for reasons that have more to do with that domestic agenda than with the requirements of the job. This in turn shapes negatively the reception of successive Secretaries by people in Northern Ireland. And this negative reception in itself reduces a Secretary's capacity to carry out successfully one critical aspect of the role: progress on the constitutional front.

The following journalistic commentary, from James Naughtie in 1989, is by no means unusual:

> In all the traditional reshuffle foreplay . . . the position of Northern Ireland has been secondary, a disposition to be made when other moves are complete . . . And what that demonstrates, of course, is that the Province is no priority . . . a commitment to calm and little else. More adventurous appointments seem unlikely.[3]

We must make a clear distinction here between reality and perception. It is important to note that this does not mean that Secretaries are in any way incompetent or unmotivated or second-rate. Rather, the appointment process permits or encourages people and politicians in Northern Ireland to *perceive* them in a negative light, and such a bias of perception in itself makes the job more difficult, since it predisposes them against co-operation. Nor does it mean that the failure to find a constitutional settlement in Northern Ireland can be entirely explained by flaws in the appointment process of Secretaries, but this is still a significant contributory factor. The important point here is not whether Secretaries are in reality good at their job or bad, committed or lukewarm to the task in hand. What matters is that those with whom the Secretary must deal see things in these terms. Consequently, any incoming Secretary is facing an added obstacle – a dearth of goodwill, and a default position of suspicion until proved otherwise. As one journalist noted:

> There was a time when kids ritually spent several nights pelting newly-arrived Army regiments with stones. It was their way of testing the incoming soldiers' mettle. Something similar occurs in politics when a new Secretary of State takes office.[4]

Because Northern Ireland is indeed secondary to other considerations during the 'foreplay of reshuffles' the resulting perception of the outcome is a foregone negative conclusion. Hence we should not be surprised at statements such as that of David McKittrick:

> As for Northern Ireland, it has for the second time running been insulted by the appointment of an amiable, second-rank politician . . . the Province deserves better.[5]

In more outspoken terms, *Fortnight* magazine made the same complaint in an open letter to one Secretary:

> Let's face it: you inherited an NIO [Northern Ireland Office] stuffed full of non-entities both at junior-ministerial level – why oh why

did you not insist on some decent material at the outset? – and in terms of the intellectual calibre of the senior civil servants both in London and at Stormont.[6]

Whether such criticism is valid is not the focus here; but the appointment process encourages such negative perceptions, and such a view predisposes the people of Northern Ireland to receive new Secretaries in a manner which hinders rather than helps their progress.

THE ROLE OF THE SECRETARY

The post of Secretary of State for Northern Ireland differs from other Cabinet posts in at least three significant respects. The most obvious of these stems from the region's over-riding unique feature: the 'Troubles'. Northern Ireland is post-war Europe's most enduring violent conflict. That fact alone should mark the Northern Ireland Secretary's post out for special consideration within the Cabinet. Specifically, it is a particularly delicate and dangerous post, where people can save or lose lives dependent on political decisions made at Stormont Castle or at Westminster. This is not only an argument for taking a sympathetic and supportive view of those who bravely try to do it, but also indicates the need for sensitivity and reflection in the appointment process to ensure that this greatly demanding post gets the incumbent it needs.

Secondly, the Secretary has a non-elective relationship with the recipients of policy. In the 'democratic deficit' of direct rule, no-one in Northern Ireland feels that they ever put into power the ruling British party of the day, whether Labour or Conservative. It becomes all too easy for Northern Irish people to gain a sense of having Secretaries foisted upon them. Even in Scotland and Wales, where the respective Secretaries have a geographic commonality with the other departments of state, the electoral relationship exists at least between the electorate and the party of government. In sum, no other Cabinet Minister is charged with responsibility for the welfare of a geographically distinct clientele to such a wide degree and with so little accountability.

But further, once 'foisted', the Secretary, and the administration at the NIO, appears to rule over most aspects of life. In this sense, the Secretaries play a role that James Prior likened to a Governor-General.[7] Within Northern Ireland, no-one elects them. Within Northern Ireland, no-one even appoints them. Unlike in England, where some section of the voters, even if it is a minority, will always feel that 'our' Party is in power and therefore it is 'our' Government and 'our' Cabinet, in Northern Ireland the incumbents at Stormont Castle are always somebody else's choice. While that should in no way constrain the ability of Secretaries to act fairly and representatively towards the opinions they find in the Northern Ireland population, it colours fundamentally the view of a Secretary formed by those in his or her care before the new arrival even sets foot in Stormont. And if that impression is unfavourable, it may well inhibit the Secretary's scope for initiatives.

The fortunate Secretary will simply be treated with general suspicion from all sides on arrival. As Alf McCreary counselled the incoming Douglas Hurd:

> Remember, it's lonely up there at Stormont. If in doubt, ask Jim, Humphrey, Roy, Merlyn, Francis and Willie, who were there before you. The day that your foot steps on Ulster soil is the day you begin to discover who your real friends are.[8]

A less fortunate one may find him or herself rejected in advance by one side in particular. Speculation abounds as to which side the Secretary is closest to. While such speculation regarding the affiliations or vested interests or ideological leanings of any newly-appointed Cabinet Minister is normal, it impinges to a disproportionate degree on the work of the Northern Ireland Secretary. If the Secretary is seen as particularly sympathetic to the grievances of one side in Northern Ireland, and thus received with added suspicion by the other side, the whole initial period in office may simply be taken up with protracted attempts to offset the perception, however inaccurate it may be. A Foreign Office diplomat, for example, who has been involved in previous negotiations with the PIRA, as Hurd was, will be damned in the eyes of most unionists before they take the time to find out whether or not he has any sympathy for their views. Similarly, an ex-British Army officer, with a period spent as security adviser to the Unionist Government, as Michael Mates was, is facing an uphill battle to win the confidence of nationalists simply on the basis of his past record, despite his overt support of the Anglo-Irish Agreement and his chairing of the all-party Anglo-Irish group in the Commons.

Thirdly, the Secretary has, by comparison with Cabinet colleagues, an excess of powers directly to affect the recipients of policy. From the perspective of a Northern Ireland citizen, the Secretary is effectively the full range of Cabinet roles in one: defence, home office, health, education, social security, trade and industry, exchequer, and so on. Given the democratic deficit, this imbues Secretaries with even more of the appearance of Governors-General, answerable in the first place not to those they govern but to those by whom they were appointed. Some may relish the potency of the office, others may share Tom King's unease:

> The longer I have had the wide powers that a Secretary of State exercises, the more it has convinced me that people in the province and elected representatives in the province should take a greater share of those powers and responsibilities.[9]

But none will deny the power of the post, however diligently they may work towards the goal of transferring it to a local administration.

Both these latter factors – the lack of direct electoral responsibility, and the extraordinary powers of the office – are merely accentuated by the Westminster system. The procedure for Orders in Council differs from that for Bills in two important respects: they cannot be amended in Parliament, but only accepted or rejected in their entirety; and the time allotted for debate is traditionally extremely limited. Orders in Council and the lack of a Select Committee (until recently) do not go far to offset the sense of imperialistic rule from afar.

Given that it is a hugely complex, draining and demanding job, a bed of nails for even the most able politician, all three factors might also suggest the need for particular sensitivity when it comes to the post, not only in the execution of the task, but in the process of selection and appointment. Sadly, people in Northern Ireland are doubtful if that is the case all the time. They have seen ten Secretaries and dozens of junior Ministers appointed since 1972, ranging from the confused and unmotivated to the overtly reluctant, and from the genuinely concerned and talented to – that rarest of all – the keen volunteer. In response, they have created a wide variety of epithets over the years – Willie Whitewash, Humphrey Who?, Gentleman Jim, Tom Cat King, Babbling Brooke, Paddy Mayhem, and so on, ranging from the affectionately informal to the downright rude. They have seen a succession of appointees who represent the broad sweep of British parliamentary opinion. They have seen a broad range of skill-levels. They have failed to see any great consistency of style, skill or approach among appointees that might lead them to assume some systematic thought going in to the process. Even the biggest single factor which might explain consistency or variance in policy – which party is in power at Westminster – is decided with no involvement by the electorate of Northern Ireland. Consequently, it is a matter of some confusion as to what the criteria for appointment might be. In particular, it is informative to examine how those criteria are interpreted in Northern Ireland. Whatever the reasons for appointment, the common perception of the appointment process – as at best apparently inconsistent and at worst apparently irrelevant to the needs of the job – in itself promotes antagonistic perceptions of incoming Secretaries, which immediately constrain their capacity to do the job as well as they otherwise could and would.

Specifically, these constraints operate in the area of constitutional initiatives, as distinct from the Secretary's other responsibilities of managing Northern Ireland's internal affairs, including economic and security issues. The freedom provided by the Secretary's breadth of powers and lack of localised accountability refers only to the latter: the post carries great freedom to develop and shape broad social policy without obstruction. By and large, local acquiescence is not a vital requirement for such decision-making or implementation. But where co-operation from local politicians is a *sine qua non* is in the area of constitutional initiatives. And it is in the pursuit of such co-operation that the negative perceptions of Secretaries mitigate against success. A predisposed antagonism, or even scepticism, about any incoming Secretary's abilities or commitment in this vital field will clearly affect the amount of room for manoeuvre given to him or her by the politicians and, indeed, by the two communities at large. Secretaries begin their task already handicapped by such perceptions, which stem in large part from a general understanding in Northern Ireland that the post is given low priority at Westminster. To develop this argument, it is useful to examine some of those perceptions.

PERCEPTIONS OF THE SECRETARY OF STATE FOR NORTHERN IRELAND

A number of observations can be made about the possible criteria applied to the selection of candidates for the post of Secretary. It is possible that Secretaries and junior Ministers are sent to Northern Ireland as a testing ground, a means by which their party can test their calibre as politicians; it is possible that they are appointed for their relevant expertise in specific policy areas; it is possible that appointments are made on the basis of the inherent "message" contained in a particular choice of candidate, be it for the unionist community, the nationalist community, the Governments of the Republic of Ireland and United

States of America, or any combination of these; it is possible that Secretaries are chosen as a means of removing them from the British domestic political scene or, alternatively, as a means of rewarding them with a marginal Cabinet post for service in that scene; it is possible that Secretaries are appointed as an outcome of internal struggles which persist in the ruling political party; and, finally, it is possible that Secretaries are appointed to or removed from Northern Ireland depending on the needs and constraints imposed by the British domestic political agenda. It is also quite feasible that a combination of these factors will apply to any particular appointment.

Observing the choices made by political parties of candidates for Cabinet office it is almost impossible to tell for certain which, if any, of the criteria suggested above apply to appointments. And because we cannot know for certain, speculation and perceptions inform our reality. It is in this respect that perceptions of the criteria applied to the appointment and removal of successive Secretaries and perceptions of the post of Secretary of State itself are extremely important. They play a major part in potentially enhancing or inhibiting an individual Secretary's capacity for making progress on a constitutional settlement to the Northern Ireland conflict. It is the realm of perceptions that is of interest here. Most of the quotes used to illuminate the perceptions held by the people of Northern Ireland have been taken from the *Belfast Telegraph* newspaper and *Fortnight* magazine, unless otherwise stated. As highlighted below, the most commonly held perceptions appear to be negative, ie perceptions of the reasons for appointing or removing Secretaries are seldom seen as having any relevance to the needs of the people and politicians of Northern Ireland. Similarly, perceptions of the post of Secretary appear to be such that the Secretary can be easily circumvented when it comes to making serious political progress on negotiating a constitutional settlement to the conflict. Both these factors inhibit and constrain the capacity of a Secretary to achieve significant progress on this all important aspect of the conflict.

From the list of possible criteria outlined above, the most common perceptions of the selection criteria applied to the post of Secretary come under the broad headings of 'punishment', 'reward', 'party political concerns', and 'over-riding domestic political agenda'. Moreover, the choice of candidates for the post over the past twenty-odd years has variously been considered to have 'consign[ed] Northern Ireland politics to the backburner' and to have involved the choice of 'political lightweights' who are perceived by the people and politicians of the region as being in no position to develop new or novel means of tackling the conflict and the search for a constitutional settlement. This has particularly been the case during the period of Tory rule after 1979, during which the post of Secretary has been seen, on occasion, as a gift to bequeath to a loyal supporter considered deserving of a Cabinet position but not one of the 'important' ones, or as a means of exiling an awkward colleague, too powerful to be completely removed from Cabinet office but needing to be sidelined from mainstream domestic politics. Either way, as reward or punishment, the manipulation of appointments to the position of Secretary, particularly in recent years, has been interpreted in Northern Ireland as indicative of the relative unimportance of the region on the British domestic political agenda. The following are some examples of those selected, the apparent intentions behind the appointment, and the consequent perceptions of the appointee on arrival at Stormont.

'PUNISHMENT'

The most obvious example of the use of the post of Secretary as a means of punishing or exiling a political opponent was the appointment of Jim Prior as Secretary in 1981. As one commentator observed: 'At one stroke, in the biggest Cabinet reshuffle since 1957, she [Thatcher] has rid herself of almost all her critics, and exiled her most dangerous political opponent to Northern Ireland, humbling him [Prior] in the process.'[10] Perhaps partly because Prior had held a previous high Cabinet post and was so well known as an opponent of Thatcher he was regarded locally 'as the first Tory political heavyweight in the job since Mr Whitelaw'.[11] However, it was widely held that he had been sent to Northern Ireland as a means of getting him out of the way, not because he was identified as the person who could best deal with the intensifying problem of the hunger strikes in the Maze, the most significant item on the Northern Ireland domestic political agenda at the time. Even Prior himself commented, at a later date, 'I think it is a pity that Northern Ireland is always regarded as if it were a dustbin. I went there because Mrs Thatcher was fed up with me at home'.[12]

Tom King is also perceived as having been more or less exiled to Northern Ireland to make room for the Prime Minister to appoint someone at the Department of Employment more faithful to her dogma. As David Watson and Robin Morton reported at the time: 'Mr King is understood to have been somewhat reluctant to take on the Northern Ireland portfolio, a move which is generally regarded as being a demotion within the Cabinet, as Mrs Thatcher is keen to come to grips with the high unemployment levels'.[13] King's replacement of Douglas Hurd was both unanticipated by the local population and regarded as a sign that Northern Ireland was less important than the concerns generated on the domestic British political agenda, in this case, unemployment. As John Hume argued at the time, the switch was something which no one had forecast, particularly since Hurd had barely spent a year in the post. 'It underlines how unimportant Northern Ireland is when the interests of the Conservative Party are at stake'. He continued: 'It would appear that the office of the Secretary of State for Northern Ireland has been a purgatory for those on their way up and a limbo for those on the way down'.[14] Harold McCusker, the Ulster Unionist MP, felt similarly: 'One clear thing is that to switch people in and out of Northern Ireland at this speed clearly indicates that Northern Ireland is not top of the list of priorities on Mrs Thatcher's agenda'.[15] Seamus Lynch of the Workers Party concurred: 'Mrs Thatcher's appointment of a failed Employment Secretary to preside over the country's worst unemployment blackspot, suggests that she views Northern Ireland and its problems with contempt'. It was clear, he said, that in Mrs Thatcher's eyes Northern Ireland was 'the Siberia of her empire, a punishment for those who offend her'.[16]

'REWARD'

On the other hand, the appointment of Peter Brooke to the post of Secretary was regarded as a reward: 'Mr Brooke's promotion into the Cabinet last night, as successor to the long-serving Tom King in one of the Government's most arduous posts, was a clear recognition of Mrs Thatcher's regard for his able and loyal service during the past 21 months'.[17] Again there appeared to be no real consideration of whether or not Brooke was a 'good person for the job', it was simply that he was to be rewarded for services rendered. And, although some of the locals perceived that Brooke had a 'safe pair of hands' – a feature which according to the accepted wisdom, is a 'pre-requisite for the Stormont job'[18] others argued that 'Brooke . . . at first sight appears to be a lightweight politician for such an onerous task . . .'.[19] Moreover, the *Independent* claimed that:

> As for Northern Ireland, it has for the second time running been insulted by the appointment of an amiable, second-rank politician.

Peter Brooke can be relied upon not to introduce clever, counter-productive initiatives, but the province deserves better.[20]

The appointment of Sir Patrick Mayhew to the position of Secretary can be interpreted in the same vein as Brooke's, i.e. as a reward. It is no secret that Mayhew had pursued the job for many years. It was not until 1992, however, that Mayhew got what he wanted. His appointment was, in many respects, a case of the then Prime Minister rewarding or acknowledging a previous good turn. Noted by one observer at the time: 'Almost overlooked in the post-election reshuffle was that Mr Major's first step up the greasy pole was as parliamentary private Secretary to Sir Patrick'. And one Tory MP said: 'There is a real symmetry to the appointment. The prime minister does have enormous loyalty to people, so it does not surprise me that he gave Northern Ireland to Paddy. He would never have got it from Thatcher'.[21]

'PARTY POLITICS'

In some respects, whether the appointment to Northern Ireland is by means of punishment or reward for the appointee, the issue at stake is sometimes seen as being the internal needs of the political party in power at the time. The following is a comment from a *Belfast Telegraph* editorial at the time of the appointment of a particular Secretary of State, but it could easily have served at many points over the last twenty-two years:

> The new Secretary of State at first sight appears to be a lightweight politician for such an onerous task. Certainly it seems unlikely that any initiatives will be forthcoming during his tenure of office. His deputy ... is an even more anonymous figure. [The Prime Minister's] obvious priority is to win the next election. Nationally, the party may have a more vigorous image. In Ulster terms, there is little to fire the imagination.[22]

This suggests that a prevailing perception in Northern Ireland is that party political issues are more relevant to the appointment of a Secretary than the needs of the people of the region. It is hard to avoid the conclusion that party politics does indeed play a role on occasion, during the tenure of Secretaries in office, as well as at the time of their appointment or removal. The corollary of this conclusion is the perception that Northern Ireland can be used to British party political ends when it suits Downing Street: the Maastricht deal is clearly a matter of Conservative Party politics, just as Callaghan's concession of five new Northern Ireland seats at Westminster bought Unionist support for a Labour Government that lacked a parliamentary majority. Even for the hard-nosed and unidealistic politicians of Northern Ireland, such manoeuvres breed a realisation that one means of furthering political progress is to indulge in such cynical bargains. Moreover, evidence of such deals constrains a given Secretary's ability to negotiate progress on the constitutional issue in Northern Ireland. No real political initiative was pursued by Roy Mason, partly because of Mason's perceived contempt for local politicians,[23] but perhaps more so because the SDLP denounced Mason as being 'in the pockets of the unionists' following the deal on representation at Westminster and refused to take part in talks with him.

'OVER-RIDING DOMESTIC POLITICAL AGENDA'

The removal of Secretaries from office has also been seen, on occasion, as having been conducted without due regard for the internal needs of the region. Two examples immediately suggest themselves. One involved the first Secretary, William Whitelaw, or 'Whitewash' as he was colloquially known. Not for the last time, there was deep unrest in Britain between the Government and the miners. Despite the fact that Whitelaw was well in the throes of the pre-Sunningdale negotiations the pressure was on to get him back to England to deal with the impending industrial crisis. As Barry White of the *Belfast Telegraph* pondered retrospectively:

> ... the real crisis of 1974 was the confrontation with the miners, not Northern Ireland. And I remember missing any acknowledgement of how vital Mr Whitelaw's presence in Northern Ireland was to the whole concept of power sharing ... nor of the disastrous consequences of an early election.[24]

The demands of the British domestic political agenda superseded the needs of the Northern Ireland political agenda. One can only speculate as to whether or not Whitelaw could have built a lasting agreement at Sunningdale. That he never had the chance, however, can only be deeply regretted, particularly when one contemplates the twenty-odd years of bloodshed which followed. The enduring negative effect of removing a Secretary during such a significant point in political negotiations affecting the constitutional future of the region is evident in the fact that White's observation was made ten years after the event.

This was not a one-off 'mistake'. Perhaps equally disturbing was that the lesson of the adverse consequences of removing the main strategic British player at a key-point in negotiations about a constitutional settlement was not learned, or if learned, certainly not abided by. Again, in 1985, the then Secretary was removed from office at a crucial point. Hurd had been an important player in negotiating the Anglo-Irish Agreement. His role was potentially even more important with regard to implementing the Agreement against predicted Unionist opposition, but still he was removed. Moreover, Hurd had been in office for little over a year at the time, something which made his swift removal all the more strange and seemingly inconsistent with the needs of the people and politicians of Northern Ireland. As the *Belfast Telegraph* noted at the time:

> Mr Brittan had to be prised out of the Home Secretary's job . . . and Mr Hurd was seen as a safe replacement. The time was not ripe, with the Anglo-Irish process reaching a climax, but British politics dictated that Mr Hurd should go, and Mr King, reluctantly, should step into his shoes.[25]

Indeed, as another reporter put it in somewhat stronger terms:

> It makes as much sense, frankly, as Ted Heath's recall of Willie Whitelaw, as soon as power-sharing was agreed, but we have got the message by now that when duty calls, it's goodnight Northern Ireland.[26]

To sum up these sections, therefore, both the appointment of Secretaries and their removal are viewed with a certain cynicism by the people of Northern Ireland. The needs and concerns of British political parties, and perhaps more importantly, the British domestic political agenda, are undoubtedly seen as preceding those of Northern Ireland and all the evidence indicates that this perception is quite accurate. Little surprise therefore, that the same cynicism is carried over in regard to the post of Secretary itself.

PERCEPTION THAT THE POWER LIES WITH THE PM IN LONDON

The post is extremely powerful within the confines of Northern Ireland itself. However, when crises arise like that brought about by the Maze hunger strikes and, more significantly, when it comes to negotiating a constitutional settlement to the Northern Ireland conflict, it is widely perceived that the real power lies with the Prime Minister in London and not with the Secretary in Northern Ireland. This is an obvious constraint on the ability of the Secretary to force political progress. Such a view arises from observation of the occasions when Secretaries have developed political initiatives without the apparent support of the Prime Minister, e.g. James Prior's rolling devolution Assembly, legislation which Thatcher referred to as 'a rotten bill' – or when the initiative seems to be taken out of the Secretary's hands by the Prime Minister, e.g. Major's overruling of Brooke in early 1992 by pressuring the Northern Ireland parties to resume the Strand One Talks. As a result, Northern Ireland politicians are encouraged to by-pass the Secretary and go directly to what they see as the seat of power. This perception of power residing at Westminster, in the hands of the Prime Minister, predated the Anglo-Irish negotiations of the early 1980s and the resultant Anglo-Irish Agreement, although these factors and the more recent Downing Street Declaration obviously intensify the perception.

It was during Atkins' time in office that the power of the Prime Minister was highlighted as superseding that of the Secretary. During August 1979, Thatcher 'paid the first of a number of surprise visits to the province during his term. These gave rise to suggestions that the real power in Northern Ireland lay not with Mr Atkins at Stormont but with Mrs Thatcher at Downing Street'.[27] It is frequently suggested that Atkins was never at ease with his position in Northern Ireland. Perhaps that had something to do with the murder of Airey Neave by the PIRA and the forced choice of Atkins, who had no previous Cabinet experience nor any knowledge of Northern Ireland, as the alternative appointee to the post of Secretary following the Conservative victory in the May 1979 General Election. Whatever the case, Paul Arthur suggests that between 1979 and his removal to the Foreign Office in September 1981, Atkins never really got to grips with Northern Ireland: 'He departed as he arrived. . . . bewildered and bemused'.[28]

Although Thatcher's visits to Northern Ireland diminished during Prior's time as Secretary, the perception remained that he was not in an independent enough position to determine the future of Northern Ireland in association with the people of the region. As Barry White observed at the time of his departure:

> I don't blame him for not coming up with a solution for I think he was always constrained by what he could squeeze out of the cabinet

and Mrs Thatcher. He wanted to make a few grand gestures, and propose something far more radical than his weak-kneed Assembly but he was talked or voted out of them.[29]

Similar perceptions lay with the London press at this time: as the *Daily Mail* expressed it at the time of Hurd's appointment: 'We wish the Hurd–Boyson duo well. Our only advice to them would be to leave fresh initiatives – if any – to the Prime Minister'.[30] And another quote in a similar vein: 'Mr Prior left a sadder and wiser man and Mr Hurd could well take his advice not to embark on policies which do not have the full support of the Prime Minister and the Cabinet, let alone Northern Ireland opinion.'[31] The same perception was expressed by the leader of the SDLP: 'his ability to do anything to solve the Ulster problem would depend on the backing the new Minister [Hurd] got from the Prime Minister and the Government'.[32]

Recent developments in the political scene in Northern Ireland indicate ample evidence of a strong perception remaining that the key British player, when it comes to negotiating a constitutional settlement to the Northern Ireland conflict, is the Prime Minister. This was evident in the way in which Hume went directly to the Prime Minister following his talks with Gerry Adams, not to the Secretary, albeit that Mayhew was undoubtedly informed of developments throughout the proceedings. The deal struck between Major and the Ulster Unionists over Maastricht can be interpreted in a similar light. Having now apparently got what they bargained for – a Northern Ireland Select Committee – the UUP seem less inclined than ever to co-operate in Mayhew's attempt to restart three-stranded talks. It seems that, if they see the goods being delivered not from the NIO but from Downing Street, the Secretary's capacity for local political progress is once again constrained by such a perception. He is seen as having restricted powers for independent action.

IMPORTANCE OF WHERE THE SECRETARY OF STATE STANDS ON ISSUES INTEGRAL TO THE GOVERNING OF NORTHERN IRELAND

Given that the Secretary of State is thus seen as having increasingly restricted power to act independently in attempting to resolve the conflict, the perceived position of the Secretary on economic and security issues assumes increasing relative importance. During the early 1980s the perception of Prior as a Tory 'wet' when it came to Thatcher's monetarist orthodoxy was greatly welcomed and appreciated in Northern Ireland. As David Watson reported at the time of his appointment: 'members of various political parties sounded relieved that a new man – and a 'wet' when it comes to monetarist economics – was taking over the Northern Ireland Office.'[33]

When Hurd was appointed, concern was expressed not so much about his own position with regard to economic issues but about that of his deputy, Rhodes Boyson, who was thought to have been chosen to keep 'a close eye on public spending' in the region. With regard to Hurd himself, Molyneaux said: 'I'm disappointed in the sense that we have got someone who up to now has been aloof from the security and economic aspects of Northern Ireland'.[34]

Tom King's ability to develop political initiatives was inhibited by unionist opposition to and outrage at the Anglo-Irish Agreement. The only area where he had an opportunity to shine was in relation to internal regional issues, most of which King himself perceived as his concerns:

> It [security] is a very important part of the battle against terrorism, as are a number of other approaches – not least to give people the hope of a job and a better future, a home and a safe environment, a decent education for their children and a decent health service, which is a major consideration as well. In other words to establish here the opportunity for people to live in peace with the prospects of a different future and in circumstances in which there is fairness and equality of opportunity for all in Northern Ireland – that I see as my concerns.[35]

Brooke's position on the economy was also considered very important, not least since King had highlighted the importance of the role of the Northern Ireland economy in the conflict throughout his time in the region and also in his parting remarks. As one reporter observed:

> . . . the new ministerial team at Stormont will be more interested in economics than politics, as most of Mr King's last utterances indicated. One of Mr Brooke's first ones placed the economy on a par with the previous official priority, 'law and order'. Mr Needham, moved to the DED, almost sounds like the anti-political Roy Mason when he stresses the redeeming power of 10,000 jobs for west Belfast.[36]

Indeed, since 1989 targeting social need has become the Government's third public spending priority, behind law and order and the economy.

Mayhew's appointment has been perceived as incorporating a change in Government policy towards Northern Ireland:

> The initial perception is that there is a tougher team at the Castle –
> more decisive and less likely to let itself be pushed around by the
> local politicians. Sir Patrick has already let it be known that secur-
> ity will be a priority, and the arrival of Michael Mates reinforces
> his words.[37]

It is the perception of Mayhew as a strong voice on security which is behind much of his appeal to unionists. That he was accompanied by Robert Atkins, a former junior Trade Minister who was 'set to take on the task vacated by the long-serving Richard Needham of promoting the recovery of the Northern Ireland economy',[38] made him all the more attractive.

CONCLUSION

In conclusion, therefore, the Secretary has an extremely important role to play in the governing of the region itself. The role of the Secretary of State has been likened to that of a Governor-General and although the Secretary, like a Governor-General, is seen as being responsible to the authority which appoints it and not to the local population which he or she oversees, the Secretary of State in Northern Ireland has considerable internal autonomy and considerable executive control when it comes to regional developments. As Tom King said on reflection of his time as Secretary: 'The longer I have had the wide powers that a Secretary of State exercises, the more it has convinced me that the people in the province and elected in the province should take a greater share of those powers and responsibilities'.[39] Using these powers, to the great appreciation of the people of Northern Ireland, individual Secretaries of State have frequently preserved the region from some of the worst aspects of monetarism and public spending constraints imposed by central government.

With regard to their role in working towards bringing about a negotiated settlement to the constitutional aspect of the Northern Ireland conflict, however, Secretaries are widely perceived as being delegates of the British Government in Northern Ireland, unable to develop substantial new initiatives on the constitutional issue without central backing. This is not to undermine the creativity and effort that many Secretaries of State have brought to tackling the constitutional problem; it merely contributes to our understanding of why such initiatives have been so singularly unsuccessful. Undoubtedly the impression that Secretaries of State are relatively powerless in this regard has constrained their ability to make a positive contribution to political progress on the constitutional issue. Moreover, that impression has been fostered and intensified by ever-increasing co-operation between the Governments of the United Kingdom and Ireland. Even when the Anglo-Irish relationship is under strain it is widely perceived that the primary actors are the Prime Ministers of each country. The Secretary of State is but the envoy of the British Prime Minister, a position which at times makes it difficult to build positive relationships with the nationalist community and a position which can safely be by-passed when a major breakthrough has occurred in the thoughts and/or actions of either the nationalist or the unionist communities.

Further, negative perceptions arising from the appointment process undermine the Secretaries' ability to build the degree of co-operation necessary to make political progress. If the Secretary is thus inhibited, so, by extrapolation, is the British Government. Northern Ireland is given a low priority on the domestic political agenda, and this is a root cause of the cynicism which so inhibits political progress. Raising Northern Ireland on the agenda might not only focus British minds more closely on the problem, but could also go a long way to encourage co-operation from local parties in the trust-building process which is so vital to political progress. Thus, so long as Northern Ireland remains a low priority, a resolution remains a dim prospect.

NOTES

1. C. Townshend, 'Britain's Civil Wars', cited in B. O'Leary and J. McGarry (eds), *The Politics of Antagonism: Understanding Northern Ireland* (London and Atlantic Highlands, NJ: Athlone Press 1993), p. 8.
2. O'Leary and McGarry (eds), *op.cit.*
3. *Fortnight*, July/August 1989.
4. *Belfast Telegraph*, 14 September 1984.
5. *Fortnight*, September 1989.
6. *Fortnight*, September 1990.
7. J. Prior, *A Balance of Power* (London: Hamish Hamilton, 1985), p. 183.
8. *Belfast Telegraph*, 12 September 1984.
9. *Belfast Telegraph*, 27 July 1989.
10. *Belfast Telegraph*, 15 September 1981.

11. *Ibid.*
12. *Belfast Telegraph*, 3 September 1985.
13. *Ibid.*
14. *Ibid.*
15. *Ibid.*
16. *Ibid.*
17. *Belfast Telegraph*, 25 July 1989.
18. *Ibid.*
19. *Ibid.*
20. Quoted in *Fortnight*, September 1989.
21. Richard Ford MP, *Fortnight*, May 1992.
22. *Belfast Telegraph*, 25 July 1989.
23. P. Arthur, *Government and Politics of Northern Ireland*, 2nd edn (London: Longman, 1984), p. 119.
24. *Belfast Telegraph*, 13 September 1984.
25. *Belfast Telegraph*, 3 September 1985.
26. *Belfast Telegraph*, 5 March 1985.
27. *Belfast Telegraph*, 15 September 1981.
28. Arthur, *op.cit.*, p. 119.
29. *Belfast Telegraph*, 6 September 1984.
30. *Belfast Telegraph*, 11 September 1984.
31. *Ibid.*
32. *Ibid.*
33. *Belfast Telegraph*, 18 September 1981.
34. *Belfast Telegraph*, 11 September 1984.
35. *Fortnight*, July/August 1989.
36. *Fortnight*, September 1989.
37. *Belfast Telegraph*, 15 April 1992.
38. *Ibid.*
39. *Belfast Telegraph*, 27 July 1989.

10 The Inter-relationship of the Press and Politicians during the 1981 Hunger Strike at the Maze Prison

Michael von Tangen Page

INTRODUCTION

Northern Ireland is very rarely a subject of intense journalistic news coverage. Since the Troubles broke out in 1969 there have been relatively few occasions when it has been able to command the front pages over a significant period.[1] One such period has been the sustained coverage of the developing peace process following the ceasefires by the three largest paramilitary groups in Northern Ireland. The previous period of enduring press coverage was probably following the Anglo-Irish Agreement of November 1985, and prior to that events surrounding the hunger strike of 1981 secured steady coverage. At these times the media is in a position to put the Troubles into its proper context, explaining to the people of Britain why they have been involved in this protracted and seemingly unresolvable conflict for the last twenty five years. Yet, it is clear that the media have failed to do this.

MEDIA COVERAGE OF THE 1981 HUNGER STRIKE

In 1981 republican prisoners decided to launch a hunger strike to support their campaign for the recognition of their status as political rather than criminal prisoners. This was an escalation of a campaign fought by both republican and loyalist prisoners since Merlyn Rees, the then Secretary of State for Northern Ireland, ended the differentiation of criminal and scheduled prisoners in 1976. The abolition of special category status led to the introduction of cellular based confinement for paramilitary prisoners convicted for crimes committed after 1 March 1976. The 1981 hunger strike was the culmination of a protest that

162

republicans and to a lesser extent loyalists had fought since 1976.

The republican protest was concentrated initially within the prison system. It took the form of a refusal to conform with the new system (principally the wearing of prison convicts' uniform) in a campaign known as the 'blanket protest'. The republicans also refused to carry out prison work and after a period also refused to wash or use sanitary facilities in the so-called 'dirty protest'.[2] During this period a simultaneous assassination campaign was conducted by the Provisional Irish Republican Army (PIRA) and the smaller more extreme Irish National Liberation Army (INLA). The targets of this campaign were the prison officers who had to enforce the new regulations within the prisons. This campaign, lasting from April 1976 to January 1980, claimed the lives of eighteen prison officers along with a number of civilians.[3]

Combined with the campaign within the prison system, an attempt to mobilise popular support amongst Irish nationalists on both sides of the border was made with only limited success. The campaign signally failed to change Government policy in regard to penal policy in Northern Ireland. Indeed, despite the change of government in 1979, hostility to the restoration of special category status from the Northern Ireland Office (NIO) remained constant. The failure of the prison protest in either changing Government policy or receiving a large amount of public support led to the decision in 1980 by the Republican prisoners in the Maze Prison (also known as Long Kesh) to launch a hunger strike by seven protesters, although at least initially the Republican leadership outside the prison was opposed to this escalation of the dispute. This protest ended in some confusion, on 18 December 1980, as the prisoners believed the British were willing to change policy. This, however, did not happen. As a result, a second hunger strike was launched on 1 March 1981 when Bobby Sands refused his breakfast.

The hunger strikes were a problematic area for reporters to cover. One journalist – Mary Holland – writing about the event described the main task of a journalist as that of separating fact from propaganda.[4] (In the case of the hunger strikes both sides in the conflict attempted to use the media for their own propagandist purposes.) She also felt that the media had, by concentrating on violent events rather than explaining the context of this violence, failed to cover the Troubles properly. This has also been said in a report by the left-wing media pressure group Article 19:

The British readership, which foots the bill for the troubles and is entitled to be kept informed, is thus taken quite unawares by events, such as the election to the Westminster Parliament of Bobby Sands on a hunger strike, a logical development for those following the story from closer at hand.[5]

The broadsheet media had, in the hunger strike, an ideal news peg which would have allowed it to contextualise the Troubles, but it failed to use the opportunity. The reason for this omission was not journalistic but political.

In order to discuss this point and look at the reasons behind it, it is useful to consider a model of media behaviour developed by the American writer Daniel Hallin to examine the United States media's coverage of the Vietnam war. Hallin argued in his book – *The Uncensored War*[6] – that, contrary to the accepted wisdom that United States politicians turned against the involvement in Vietnam because of hostile media coverage, it was in fact the reverse: that is, the media turned against the Vietnam war because the politicians turned against it or at least made questioning of their country's involvement respectable. To illustrate his argument Hallin produced a model of the spheres of consensus, controversy and deviance.

He argued that mainstream media news coverage would contain the sphere of consensus, which was the uncontroversial side of news coverage, or what Hallin describes as the 'region of motherhood and apple pie' where the 'journalist's role is to serve as an advocate or celebrant of consensus values'. Then there is the sphere of legitimate controversy, which would also be covered and is defined by the United States two party system and the perimeters of the debate between the Democrat and Republican parties. In this region 'objectivity and balance reign as the supreme journalistic virtues'. Beyond this lies the sphere of deviance. This was 'the realm of those political actors and views which journalists and the political mainstream of the society reject as unworthy of being heard'. The borders of these separate spheres are, he maintains, blurred and can change.

In the early stages of the Vietnam war the mainstream media and the politicians were largely in agreement about United States' involvement, so coverage was largely uncritical and could be described as belonging to the sphere of consensus. However, when Congressmen began to question the war, the debate entered the sphere of legitimate controversy, with the anti-war position coming out of the sphere of deviance. The important aspect was that it was the political elite rather than the journalists who legitimised the debate. One could draw a parallel in Northern Ireland with the revelation of contacts between

Figure 10.1   The Hallin model

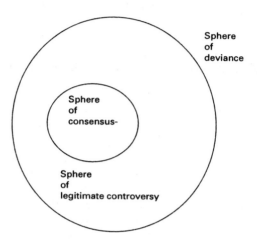

Source: Daniel C. Hallin, *The Uncensored War* (New York: Oxford University Press, 1986), pp. 116–17.

the Government and *Sinn Féin* suddenly making media interviews with Gerry Adams legitimate.

But does Hallin's theory explain the broadsheet press coverage of the hunger strike of 1981? In this chapter, it is tested by examining coverage of three Fleet Street broadsheet newspapers on four selected events during the hunger strike. The papers are: the liberal *Guardian*; the more conservative *Times*; and, finally, the business-orientated *Financial Times*. The events examined will be: the start of the fast by Bobby Sands on 1 March; Sands' election to Westminster in the Fermanagh and South Tyrone by-election of 9 April; his death on 5 May; and the end of the fast on 3 October.

THE START OF THE FAST

At this stage the prisoners' position is definitely relegated to the sphere of deviance. Sands' refusal of his breakfast was treated to event-based news coverage by *The Times* and the *Guardian*. While both papers did explain that the fast was a development of the feeling that the authorities had reneged on their promises to the protesters before Christmas,

the issue of political status was not discussed by either of the papers.[7]
The *Financial Times* relegated the story to eighteen words in its summary of the news.[8]

THE FERMANAGH AND SOUTH TYRONE APRIL BY-ELECTION

The election of Sands to Westminster with 51 per cent of the vote was an issue which could not be ignored. However, the news coverage was still extremely limited. The issues that all three newspapers addressed were the embarrassment which the Government suffered and how the House of Commons would react to Sands' election. Principally the question of whether Sands should be expelled or not was debated. Further, the leaders of *The Times* and *Guardian* both felt that the vote was partly sectarian in character, with Catholics voting for the sole nationalist and Protestants voting for the sole unionist candidate. Thus, the position of Sands in parliament was part of the sphere of legitimate controversy, but the issue over which he had fought the election campaign, and the reason why he had starved himself for over forty days, were still not discussed.

This reflected the view in the British Parliament on the few occasions that the issue was discussed in the House of Commons. Both Labour and the Liberals were supportive of the Government, as was Gerry Fitt, the sole Nationalist sitting in the House at this time. There were no attempts to criticise the criminalisation policy from the political mainstream and thus this was not an angle pursued by the media.[9] Yet by conventional news values one would have expected the background of the hunger strike and the demands of the prisoners to be addressed.

THE DEATH OF SANDS

Sands died as a result of his sixty-six day fast early on 5 May, the news of his death leading to serious rioting throughout Northern Ireland and world-wide publicity for the prison struggle. Partly as a result of the election to Westminster his death was given lead coverage. The principal concern of *The Times* was the ramifications that his death would have on public order in Northern Ireland. Further, the political reaction given first was that of the Secretary of State, Humphrey Atkins.

The reason for his fast was not given until half way through the article after it was noted that he had ignored appeals from the Irish Prime Minister, the Pope and his mother to end the fast.[10] The *Guardian* was also concerned about the violence that Sands' death would bring, also examining the last minute attempts by the Irish Government to achieve a solution to the dispute through the intervention of the European Commission on Human Rights.[11] On 6 May the *Guardian* was still preoccupied by street disturbances caused by the death but it also gave coverage of Margaret Thatcher's refusal to grant concessions to the republican prisoners when she was quizzed by 'grim-faced MP's' (*sic*) during Question Time.[12] In longer articles inside the newspaper the lack of sympathy for the prisoners' cause inside Parliament was looked at and the fact that normal life went on in Belfast despite the Troubles was noted.[13] The leader for the day supported the British position whilst bemoaning Mrs Thatcher's aggressive style when refusing to see a delegation of backbench TDs from Dublin. The leader also worried about the failure of the Government to put across the British position to 'uninformed international opinion against Britain'.[14]

The Times on 6 May did attempt to put Sands' death in a historical context, looking at other republican prison martyrs such as Terence MacSwiney in 1920 and Sean McGaughey in 1946. It did not, however, even question the British refusal to give any form of concession, although it did carry the leading articles from the previous day's *Irish Times* and *Irish Independent*, which were mildly critical of British policy. Both, however, were far stronger in condemning the PIRA and the armed struggle than they were critical of the British Government.[15] In its leader, titled 'Who killed Bobby Sands?', the history of the dispute is traced back to the report, by the judge Lord Gardiner, that recommended the end of special status. *The Times* felt that the reasons for refusing political status were still as strong as ever and it ended by answering its own question, stating that: 'There is only one killer of Bobby Sands and that is Sands himself.'[16]

The *Financial Times* led its front page on the 6th with the Prime Minister's refusal to grant political status. In another front page story the fear that Irish-American sympathizers would react to the death of Sands by sending arms was emphasised. This story also contained the caveat that the majority of Americans were sympathetic to Britain's problem in dealing with the dispute.[17] The leader page used Sands' death to debate the future of Northern Ireland. The paper made the telling point that it did not really matter what went on in the Maze/ Long Kesh if the Troubles continued. Unlike the other two newspapers it actually treated the issue of political status as a legitimate issue of debate. It questioned the British position on prison conditions. It felt that critics had a point when long sentences were handed out by a single judge with no jury. It also attacked the Protestants for showing no flexibility and said that if United Kingdom citizenship was a privilege then they should respect the responsibilities that went with being British and 'show some regard for the Government' (this was almost certainly an attack on unionist hostility to the Anglo-Irish talks that had been going on between Thatcher and Haughey).[18]

Sands' funeral on 7 May was a major story by any means, with between 50,000 and 100,000 mourners in attendance, according to *The Times*' estimates of numbers.[19] This did not prevent a unionist counter-demonstration of 4,000 people getting equal billing in the headline 'Republicans bury their hero as Protestants honour their dead'. Further, after describing the funeral, the article ended by referring to the murder of an RUC officer, PC Ellis, saying, 'His [Ellis'] will be a rather more lonely affair.' Inside the paper the concern was still about public order and the threat of an increase in violence because of the fast. In another shorter article there were reports that Michael Foot, the Leader of the Opposition, was under attack from some backbenchers for supporting the Government stand. However, it failed to mention the names of the MPs who were attacking the bipartisan policy.[20] The *Guardian* of 8 May concentrated on the spectacle of the funeral, remarking on Japanese journalists covering an event where the 'Catholic church . . . claiming him as a son, the Iranians who sent their ambassador, as a freedom fighter; and the IRA as a martyr'.[21] Meanwhile the political corespondent covered the Government's way of addressing the problem of Sands' election to Westminster by passing a new law preventing convicted prisoners standing for election to Parliament.[22] The *Financial Times* covered the funeral of Sands and the counter-demonstration by unionists in the centre of Belfast as well as a republican demonstration in Dublin and the renaming of a road in Tehran after Sands.[23]

THE END OF THE FAST

The fast continued over the summer, resulting in a conveyor belt of prisoners dying, being buried and then replaced by a new prisoner. In this period Sands' election agent, Owen Carron, won the by-election caused by the death, while two other prisoners were elected to the *Dáil* in the Republic's General Election. By 3 October 1981, after ten deaths had failed to move the authorities on the issue of political status, the prisoners' families had grown disillusioned with the hunger strike tactic. Under the influence of the part-time prison chaplain, and human rights campaigner, Father Denis Faul of Dungannon, the relatives of most of the remaining hunger strikers announced that they would give consent for the authorities to intervene and save the lives of those fasting after they had fallen into comas. This effectively emasculated the fast, and the prisoners had no choice but to announce an end to the hunger strike. This was not a great surprise and both the *Guardian* and *The Times* had articles predicting the end of the fast on 3 October. However, neither paper saw fit to balance the story as it would if it were a legitimate area of debate. It was simply given a standard reportage.[24]

On 5 October the *Guardian* carried an assessment of the previous seven months. This included a chronology of the fast as well as an in-depth article about the suffering of the prisoners' relatives.[25] The *Guardian*'s Northern Ireland correspondent also gave a personal account of the fast, assessing the political impact that it would have and its importance to the PIRA in winning sympathy and help from overseas.[26] The news pages of all three papers carried the story that now the hunger strike was over the newly appointed Secretary of State, James Prior, would launch a new series of prison reforms.[27] Editorially *The Times* welcomed the end of the fast by emphasising that it was a victory for the Government cause, which had been 'manifestly just'. The newspaper felt this was despite the double standards of the Labour Party which supported Irish unity by consent but without the loyalist veto. This was attacked for being contradictory and it was suggested that it was up to the Irish to make themselves more appealing to the unionists. However, it ended on a more conciliatory note, welcoming the flexibility which Prior seemed to promise.[28] The *Guardian* felt that the republican prisoners had been defeated but was now willing to discuss future prison conditions in the Maze/Long Kesh in the context of Prior's proposed reforms. Like *The Times* it went on to discuss the wider constitutional ramifications of the Troubles but called for an end to the loyalist veto and for more talks between London and Dublin.[29]

CONCLUSION

As can be seen in the coverage of the four events outlined above, with the notable exception of the *Financial Times'* editorial of 6 May, the three papers were in basic agreement about the issues raised by the hunger strike. Where the *Guardian* and *The Times* differed it reflected the division between the Opposition and the Government. That was over the long term future of Northern Ireland and the so called 'loyalist veto' on constitutional change. This editorial policy, at least in the *Guardian*, was different from the views of one of its Northern Ireland corespondents, David Beresford, who put across a quite different view in his book *Ten Men Dead*.[30] However, the papers seemed to respect the cross-party consensus on criminalisation that existed in Westminster. Liz Curtis has also argued that the media coverage of the fast was based not on an examination of actual developments but rather conditioned by the requirements of government policy'.[31]

This is certainly reflected in the *Guardian* and *The Times* coverage, which placed the demands of the prisoners firmly in Hallin's sphere of deviance. This, however, need not have occurred for any sinister or propagandistic reasons. A news reporter will take a large amount of his or her information from establishment sources, be they the army, police, politicians or civil servants. It is therefore not surprising that many of the value judgements of a journalist's sources might be represented in the reporter's own version of the story. This would bear out Hallin's contention that it is the political elite rather than the media that sets the boundaries of legitimate political debate within society. This could be the reason for the slight difference in the *Financial Times*' editorial position after Bobby Sands died. The *Financial Times* as a business paper would not be as reliant as the other two papers on Government sources and thus may be more relatively free to make such decisions. Further, representing business rather than political interests means that the *Financial Times* is more interested in stability than the fine print of legitimising the PIRA by giving them political status. Thus it may have had a slightly different agenda to the other two newspapers in this study.

It is by no means novel to arrive at a conclusion that media coverage of the troubles in Northern Ireland has failed to get to grips with the core issues of that conflict. What is interesting, however, is the application to that coverage of Hallin's model, which rejects any conspiracy theories with regards to media coverage in favour of an explanation where the key is a more structural relationship between journalists and politicians. If we accept this explanation it raises some fundamental questions about politicians as well as journalists. Recently we have witnessed the Scott inquiry showing how the Government has attempted to limit discussion of issues which are politically embarrassing but not dangerous to the state by using public interest immunity certificates in court. This is a formal way of trying to close an issue from public debate. However, exactly the same was achieved by a cross-party consensus on the issue of political status for paramilitary prisoners in Northern Ireland. At no one time was this issue raised in the media, primarily because there was no political split for journalists to exploit. It was an issue too deviant to address for politicians and hence it became too deviant for the public to learn about despite the fact that wide concessions were in fact given to the prisoners in Northern Ireland two days after the hunger strike was called off.

The first to appreciate this informal power of the politicians should of course be journalists and therefore they are to blame too. Caught up at the time in rhetoric about the dangers of providing a platform for 'terrorist propaganda', journalists shied away from explaining exactly what the hunger strike was about when that debate was not legitimised by politicians. Meanwhile, in Northern Ireland the hunger strike gained a momentum of its own with tens of thousands of people supporting Bobby Sands. If violence had escalated at the time and spilled into the rest of the United Kingdom, did the citizens of Britain not deserve a better explanation of what was happening so they could exercise their right to influence politicians through public opinion? In the event, that particular conflict did not spiral out of control. However, one can not help speculating on what journalists would have done if a similar thing happened in West Yorkshire with hunger strikers in Armley prison, thousands of people in the streets and one of the hunger strikers elected to Parliament. Would journalists not have questioned politicians about their motives? Of course they would. Therefore it seems fair to conclude that when media coverage of Northern Ireland is wanting it is not because of a particular conspiracy between journalists and the politicians but because Northern Ireland has geographically been firmly rooted in a Sphere of Deviance and therefore not regarded as a newsworthy topic.

NOTES

1. 'Pack Up the Troubles', *Critical Eye* (London: Exco Television for Channel 4, first broadcast on 24 October 1991).
2. Full accounts of this period can be found in Liam Clark, *Broadening the Battlefield* (Dublin: Gill & Macmillan, 1987) and in Tim Pat Coogan,

On The Blanket: The H-Block Story (Swords, Co. Dublin: Ward River Press, 1980).

3. Michael von Tangen Page, *The IRA, Sinn Féin, and the Hunger Strike of 1981*, unpublished M. Phil at the University of St Andrews, 30 July 1992, pp. 104–9.

4. Information from this paragraph is taken from Mary Holland, 'The Journalist's Perspective' in *Terrorism and the News Media*, Conference Papers (London: Centre for Contemporary Studies, 1983), pp. 12–13.

5. Article 19, *No Comment, Censorship, Secrecy and the Irish Troubles* (London: Article 19, 1989), pp. 67–8.

6. Information in this paragraph and the figure come from Daniel C Hallin, *The Uncensored War* (New York: Oxford University Press, 1986), pp. 116–17.

7. Christopher Thomas, 'IRA prisoners' leader begins hunger strike', *The Times*, 2 March 1981 and David Beresford, 'IRA leader begins Maze hunger strike', *Guardian*, 2 March 1981.

8. 'Hunger strike on', *Financial Times*, 2 March 1981.

9. Hugh Noyes, 'Foot backs government policy', *The Times*, 2 May 1981.

10. Christopher Thomas, 'Sands dies in Maze prison after 66 days', *The Times*, 5 May 1981.

11. David Beresford, 'Bobby Sands dies after 66-day fast', *Guardian*, 5 May 1981.

12. Julia Langdon, 'Thatcher adamant on refusing concessions', *Guardian*, 6 May 1981.

13. Simon Hoggart, 'One man and his shadow are unmoved', and John Cunningham, 'The voice of triumph speaks softly for Sands', *Guardian*, 6 May 1981.

14. 'One more death, as scheduled', *Guardian*, 6 May 1981.

15. John Witherow, 'Why the Irish use hunger strikes as a weapon', *The Times*, 6 May 1981.

16. 'Who killed Bobby Sands?', *The Times*, 6 May 1981.

17. 'Prime Minister firm on refusing political status for prisoners', and 'Fear of US arms flow to Northern Ireland', *Financial Times*, 6 May 1981.

18. 'In face of suicide', *Financial Times*, 6 May 1981.

19. Christopher Thomas, 'Republicans bury their hero as Protestants honour their dead', *The Times*, 8 May 1981.

20. 'Ulster police warning of terrorist attacks & Labour pressure for action', *The Times*, 8 May 1981.

21. John Cunningham, 'Milltown, and making of a martyr and a myth', *Guardian*, 8 May 1981.

22. Julia Langdon, 'Ministers try to plug "Sands loophole"', *Guardian*, 8 May 1981.

23. Stewart Dalby and Walter Ellis, 'Thousands watch Bobby Sands funeral', *Financial Times*, 8 May 1981.

24. David Beresford, 'Maze fast may be halted by families', *Guardian*, 2 October 1981 and Richard Ford, 'End of Maze hunger strike is in sight', *The Times*, 2 October 1981.

25. 'Relatives tell of the suffering behind the fast and 216 days of protest in the Maze', *Guardian*, 5 October 1981.

26. David Beresford, 'The deaths that gave new life to an IRA legend', *Guardian*, 5 October 1981.

27. David Beresford, 'Ulster gaol reforms "this week"', *Guardian*; 'Prior to unveil prison reforms', *Financial Times*; and Richard Ford, 'Prior flies to talks on Maze reforms', *The Times*, 5 October 1981.

28. 'Ten wasted lives', *The Times*, 5 October 1981.

29. 'Ten graves, another milestone', *Guardian*, 5 October 1981.

30. David Beresford, *Ten Men Dead* (London: Grafton Books, 1986).

31. Liz Curtis, *Ireland: The Propaganda War* (London: Pluto Press, 1984), p. 206.

11 BBC Current Affairs Coverage of the 1981 Hunger Strike
Howard Smith

INTRODUCTION

This chapter examines, with extensive quotation from BBC Current Affairs programmes, the statement by Liz Curtis, in her book *Ireland: The Propaganda War*, that the media 'treated the Hunger Strike as if it had been concocted out of thin air by the IRA: as if there was no real feeling behind either the prisoners' action or the support given them by the nationalist community'; and that the media's analysis was 'based not on an examination of actual developments, but rather conditioned by government policy'.[1] It suggests that – as far as BBC current affairs programmes are concerned – this criticism is both inaccurate and misleading. It also, incidentally, shows how the BBC resisted strong right-wing pressures which started from the assumption that it was the BBC's job to help the Government defeat the PIRA, and that any statement of the reasons for the widespread support for the hunger strike or any visible demonstration of such support, let alone any statements from members of *Sinn Féin*, was wrong.

Over eight hours of current affairs material about the hunger strikes was shown on BBC television between March and October 1981, including substantial reports in twenty-five editions of *Newsnight* and five editions of *Panorama* (including one complete edition on 21 September, called 'The Provo's Last Card'), an edition of *The Heart of the Matter* and one of *The Editors* devoted to BBC television coverage of Northern Ireland. The following are summaries of eleven of the most significant of these programmes, with some account of their context.

PANORAMA (27 APRIL 1981)

In her only quotation from any of this material, Curtis uses the reporter's (Philip Tibenham) statement that Bobby Sands' impending death 'has to be seen for what it is – a potentially tragic end to a skilful piece of exploitation and propaganda' as if this was characteristic of the overall editorial tone of Tibenham's report. It is not. The statement precedes a historical sequence which indicates how the hunger strike weapon was used in the 1916–21 period, and includes an interview with Bernadette MacAliskey in which she claims that the British Government has suspended democratic rights in Northern Ireland and rejected a protest democratically endorsed by the people. The report continues with an account of the British Government's successive changes of policy about political status since 1972, illustrating the difficulty in maintaining its logicality and consistency. It also includes a discussion of the relationship between the ending of the 1980 hunger strike and the start of the 1981 strike and of Sands' crucial role in both, of the reasons for Sands' by-election victory, and a statement from Martin Bell in Washington about the possible effect of the intransigence of the British Government's policy on American public opinion. On the other hand, the report is called 'The Politics of Suicide' and also includes a comment by Tibenham that some PIRA prisoners in the Maze/ Long Kesh are 'living in appalling conditions of their own making' (accompanied by the official pictures of the 'Dirty Protest' which graphically underline its unpleasant nature), both of which could be construed as evidence supporting Curtis' view.

The report also includes statements from both Gerry Fitt and Merlyn Rees that the hunger strikers should not be granted political status, vigorously supported by the Unionist Harold McCusker, though this simply reflects the considerable opposition to political status not only in the House of Commons (Michael Foot, the leader of the Labour Party, was criticised in *Newsnight* on 13 May for 'excessively uncritical support' for the Government's policy) but also in Dublin and Washington. Overall the tone of the report is far from that of uncritical support for the British Government position implied by Curtis. Indeed the BBC could hardly be seen to be doing its job of reflecting the views of the *entire* population of Northern Ireland if this was the case.

PANORAMA (20 JULY 1981)

This report, perhaps significantly called 'A Time to Compromise', contains one of several accounts of the historical background to the hunger strike – from the establishment of Special Category status in 1972, through the blanket and dirty protests of the late 1970s (previously dealt with at length in a *Panorama* report of 12 February 1979), to the hunger strikers' five demands (repeated in a number of other programmes) and the Government's response (from an extended interview with the Secretary of State, Humphrey Atkins, in the *Panorama* of 1 June). It also includes a statement by John Hume that Sands' death had been the PIRA's best recruiting sergeant since Bloody Sunday (a claim later amply justified by events), and – even more significantly – the suggestion (in an account of the negotiations between Michael Allison and the Irish Commission for Justice and Peace) that an agreed compromise had been countermanded personally, in Allison's own words, by 'the lady behind the veil' (an obvious reference to Mrs Thatcher).[2] The report includes a film report of the startlingly violent dispersal of crowds, demonstrating in favour of the hunger strikers in Dublin, by the Irish police, and an interview with the Labour Party's Northern Ireland spokesman, Don Concannon, in which he supports the Government's position. One of the strongest impressions left by this programme is the increasing intransigence of both sides – indeed one of the most significant benefits of this kind of retrospective analysis is to observe how the intransigence of both sides fuelled the other's, the more so since each side expected the other to give way.

NEWSNIGHT (21 APRIL 1981)

Whilst the Government position was fully stated several times, notably in the *Panorama* of 1 June mentioned above, the republican position was given equal prominence, notably in this edition of *Newsnight* when Humphrey Atkins and Danny Morrison appeared in the studio together, and were both subjected to rigorous and detailed questioning about their respective positions. Morrison claimed that the British Government was in an indefensible position, since 500 PIRA prisoners were already being allowed the same privileges which were now being demanded by the hunger strikers. Atkins claimed that no concessions were possible, since this would amount to the granting of political status.

NEWSNIGHT (5 MAY 1981)

In another report which gave full weight to the republican point of view, there was an interesting confrontation between Danny Morrison and John Tusa on the day Sands died, in which Morrison – reiterating his point about the inconsistency of British Government policy – managed to unsettle one of the BBC's safest pairs of hands.[3] The report includes an interview with John Hume, in which Hume claims that the addition of two concessions by the Government – which would not amount to the granting of political status – would bring the strike to an end; he also complains that the worldwide publicity which the hunger strike has achieved can only strengthen the PIRA. This is an early indication of the way in which the SDLP's position was damaged by the Government's intransigence. Hume's claim is denied by Ian Paisley, who fully supports the Government's position with the traditional unionist cry (frequently heard in these programmes) that the hunger strikers have a choice as to whether they die, but gave their victims none. The report ends with an account of growing opposition to British policy abroad, especially in the USA, and with a brief interview with a *Fianna Fáil* Senator expressing the Dublin Government's increasing exasperation with Westminster.

The Dublin Government's view – of opposition to the hunger strikers' demands but with a growing inclination to achieve some kind of agreement which might end the strike – was not substantially affected by a change from *Fianna Fáil* to a *Fine Gael*/Labour coalition half way through the year; its view is frequently reflected in these programmes, which in turn clearly reflects the new realities of the rapprochement between Dublin and Westminster which had begun at the end of the previous year. It is interesting therefore to note that in the early weeks of the hunger strike much more attention was paid in BBC Current Affairs programmes to this rapprochement and to the reaction of Dr Paisley's DUP than to the hunger strike.

HEART OF THE MATTER (21 MAY 1981)

This programme – called 'A Righteous Hunger?', from a long-running series made by the BBC's Religious Programmes Department concerned with ethical issues, contains one of the most striking of a number of reports which illustrate the range and depth of popular feeling inside the nationalist community in Northern Ireland. It includes interviews with Father Brian McCreesh, whose brother was actually on hunger strike, and with Father Denis Faul, who – though he is prepared to justify the hunger strike as having 'a grave and proportionate cause' – was very influential in bringing the hunger strike to an end. But, most significantly, there is a substantial interview with Bishop Edward Daly of Londonderry. This interview is introduced with pictures of Bloody Sunday, notably those featuring Father Daly (as he then was) which carry a strong (though implicit) editorial message about the situation. The Bishop says that he believes that Northern Ireland is 'an artificial political entity created out of political expediency' suffering oppressive legislation which distorts people's attitudes. He adds that the hunger strike is not morally justifiable, but that it can only be understood in the political context which the British Government fails to acknowledge.

NEWSNIGHT (7 MAY 1981)

This report, on the day of Sands' funeral, juxtaposes this 'display of republican pomp' (and the images of Sands' funeral are extremely striking) with the much smaller – but for the unionists equally significant – commemoration of unionist dead outside Belfast City Hall (a similarly even-handed report was carried on the BBC *Nine O'Clock News* on that day). For the purpose of this investigation however the significant thing is not the personalisation of the unionist ceremony through the widow of a Protestant shot by the PIRA, but the strength of support for the hunger strikers displayed by those questioned in Lisnaskea, County Fermanagh (part of Sands' constituency) and travelling by bus to his funeral in Belfast. 'Are we', muses the reporter Brian Walker (clearly surprised by the strength and conviction of grassroots nationalist feeling), 'breeding a new generation of militant Republicans?'

The continuing strength of the grassroots support for the hunger strikers was shown in three programmes broadcast during the second by-election in Fermanagh and South Tyrone in August 1981.

PANORAMA (17 AUGUST 1981)

In this edition – 'The H-Block Election' – Peter Taylor reports on the 'anger beneath the surface'. He first brings out the anger of the unionists – with their candidate Ken Maginnis saying that he was horrified by Sands' election, since this meant that his Catholic neighbours must have voted for him. The bulk of Taylor's report however is devoted to Owen Carron's campaign, to demonstrating the widespread support for the hunger strikers among Catholic voters, to explaining why the SDLP decided not to stand (an issue already examined at length by *Newsnight* on 3 August), and finally capturing a tough confrontation between Seamus

Close, the Alliance candidate, and Nora McElwee – whose brother had recently died on hunger strike. The support for the hunger strikers, concludes Taylor, has now achieved a momentum of its own.

NEWSNIGHT (20 AUGUST 1981)

This report deals briefly with the unionist view, but again is mostly concerned with the Carron campaign. There is 'almost universal sympathy for the hunger strikers' says the reporter Brian Walker, since 'loyalty transcends any moral reservations'. Nora McElwee is seen again, this time addressing a crowd in a village churchyard after Mass, and attention is drawn to the number of young people demonstrating in support of the prisoners in Coalisland. And, perhaps most significantly, Carron suggests that since 'democratic parties can't make an impact on the Catholic side', the PIRA might turn to politics – an early pointer to the subsequent policy combination of the armalite and the ballot-box.

NEWSNIGHT (21 AUGUST 1981)

This theme recurs in this report, on this occasion in an interview with Richard Macauley of *Sinn Féin*. It begins with the declaration of the poll and the predictable response of both sides, but is largely made up of an extremely acrimonious discussion between a very angry Harold McCusker of the Official Unionists and Seamus Mallon of the SDLP. McCusker says that apparently the SDLP would prefer to see a representative of the PIRA in Parliament than a Unionist; Mallon, who responds with impressive coolness to McCusker's anger, counters by saying that the SDLP is not in the business of electing Unionists, who had debased the democratic process in Northern Ireland; that his party is committed to a peaceful long-term solution; and that when the British Government, which has caused this problem, is prepared to move, the SDLP will be there to help pick up the pieces.

PANORAMA (21 SEPTEMBER 1981)

Whereas the *Panorama* of 27 April had been called 'The Politics of Suicide', and that of 20 July 'A Time to Compromise', the *Panorama* of 21 September – quoting Mrs Thatcher – was called 'The Provo's

Last Card'. As David Dimbleby said in his introduction to the programme, however, whilst the hunger strike might indeed be the Provisionals' *last* card 'it might also turn out to be a trump'. Peter Taylor's report emphasises the strength and depth of feeling which the whole issue had created in the Catholic, nationalist community, the increase in violence which had followed the British Government's refusal to compromise and the spur to PIRA recruitment which the hunger strike had provided. John Hume points out the high risk of a Government strategy which had alienated an entire community, and Bishop Daly talks of the moderate's resentment at the Government's intransigence, whilst Ian Paisley warns of the danger of a unionist backlash if the Government is not sufficiently 'resolute'. Once again, Ruari O'Bradaigh takes up the idea that *Sinn Féin* could now replace the SDLP as the largest political party in the nationalist community, and both he and Gerry Adams (seen here for the first time as a leading *Sinn Féin* spokesman) underline the view that the PIRA is engaged in legitimate resistance to an army of occupation and that Owen Carron is the true representative of nationalist feeling. The PIRA, concludes Peter Taylor, can carry on successfully for another ten years; but Mr Prior, the new Northern Ireland Secretary, has only two years to find a solution.

A final comment. There is little coverage in BBC current affairs programmes of the view, widely held in certain sections of the Conservative Party and the right-wing press, that the BBC's job was to give wholehearted support to the Government's position, and that any opportunity offered to spokesmen for the PIRA, *Sinn Féin* or even the hunger strikers was an abandonment of the Corporation's responsibilities as a public service broadcasting organisation. This was not the view taken by the BBC, as can be seen in the edition of *The Editors*, a regular programme about the media shown on 28 June 1981 and devoted to the BBC television coverage of Northern Ireland. This includes a long discussion between Jeremy Paxman (then a *Panorama* reporter) and Ann McHardy of the *Guardian* about the reporter's difficulties in Northern Ireland, and another between Richard Clutterbuck, a writer on military matters, Peregrine Worsthorne, editor of the *Sunday Telegraph*, Richard Francis, the BBC's Director of News and Current Affairs (and a former Controller, Northern Ireland) and Tony Clifton, the London bureau chief of *Newsweek*.

The climax of this spirited debate (whose extraordinary flavour it is unfortunately impossible to capture in a few words) is an exchange between Worsthorne and Francis, in which Worsthorne challenges Francis to say whether it is the BBC's job to help the Government defeat the PIRA, and Francis replies that it is the BBC's job to inform people of the problems, not to fight a propaganda war on the Government's behalf.

Any account of BBC television coverage of the hunger strike would be incomplete without the inclusion of a recent *Timewatch* called 'Hunger Strike – A Hidden History' (BBC2 13 October 1993). This includes some arresting first-hand testimony from hunger strikers who survived, and the inside story of Father Denis Faul's behind-the-scenes negotiations with their families. It also reveals that not only were there two quite separate sets of negotiations going on between the Government and *Sinn Féin* during 1981, but that both seem to have been conducted in ignorance of the other. It contains, finally, an acknowledgement from Lord Gowrie, one of the junior ministers in the Northern Ireland Office at the end of 1981, that only a few days after the end of the strike, the Government agreed to all the hunger strikers' demands.

NOTES

1. Liz Curtis, *Ireland: The Propaganda War* (London: Pluto, 1984), pp. 202 and 206.
2. The ICJP was established by Irish bishops in 1968 and had previously been active mainly in Third World issues. The five members of the Commission's Executive Committee were Bishop Dermot O'Mahony, Brian Gallagher, Father Oliver Crilly (a relative of both Tom McElwee and Francis Hughes), Jerome Connolly and Hugh Logue. Michael Allison was Minister of State at the Northern Ireland Office, with responsibility for The Maze.
3. John Tusa was one of the presenters of *Newsnight*, and later became Managing Director of BBC External Broadcasting.

12 From Hillsborough to Downing Street – and After

W. Harvey Cox

When the Downing Street Declaration was issued by Messrs Major and Reynolds on 15 December 1993, it was, to the day, eight years and one month since their predecessors had signed the Anglo-Irish Agreement at Hillsborough. The Agreement's proclaimed aims were those of 'promoting peace and stability in Northern Ireland; helping to reconcile the two major traditions in Ireland; creating a new climate of friendship and cooperation between the people of the two countries; and improving cooperation in combatting terrorism'.[1]

HILLSBOROUGH – UNIONISM SAYS NO

Any assessment at, for instance, the fifth anniversary of its signing would have had to conclude that it had largely been a failure. Its main achievement had simply been survival. It had proved, as its framers had intended, unsinkable by any unionist or republican opposition. It set up nothing internal to Northern Ireland, unlike in 1974, that anyone there could 'bring down'. But it had not, to that date, perceptibly advanced the cause of peace and stability, or reconciled the two traditions in Ireland. It may have furthered, somewhat, the lesser of the four initial objectives, but as for the major ones, in the short run at least it actually set those back. The statistics of violence told a story in themselves. In the three years to 31 December 1985 there were 195 deaths in Northern Ireland due to the political conflict; in the three years from 1 January 1986 there were 247. (In 1991, indeed, the annual toll reached 94, the highest since 1982.) The years after the Agreement saw the PIRA engage in some of its most spectacular offensive actions, such as the bombs at Enniskillen on 8 November 1987, at Deal on 22 September 1989, the murder of Ian Gow, MP and Thatcher confidant, on 30 July 1990, and a widening campaign on the European mainland, including the abortive would-be bombing at Gibraltar on 6 March 1988.

But the most important feature of the aftermath of the Agreement was its rejection by the unionist community. For the full flavour of unionist dismay at the Agreement, displaying a rhetorical efflorescence more associated with the Irish nationalist tradition, it is worth quoting Harold McCusker's reaction in the Commons on 27 November 1985:

> I stood outside Hillsborough, not waving a Union flag – I doubt whether I will ever wave one again – not singing hymns, saying prayers or protesting, but like a dog and asked the Government to put in my hand the document that sold my birthright. They told me that they would give it to me as soon as possible. Having never consulted me, never sought my opinion or asked my advice, they told the rest of the world what was in store for me . . . I felt desolate because as I stood in the cold outside Hillsborough castle everything that I held dear turned to ashes in my mouth.[2]

But, despite massive demonstrations, the unionist reaction was striking less for its intensity than its unanimity. Opinion polls showed Protestant support for the Agreement at about 8 per cent and opposition at 75–80 per cent (different polls). And on 17 December 1985 all fifteen Unionist MPs resigned their Westminster seats in order to force fifteen simultaneous by-elections, which would amount to a quasi referendum on the Agreement. These were held on 23 January 1986. The Unionist anti-Agreement vote was 418,230, representing 43.9 per cent of the total electorate. The Unionists succeeded in producing a higher total vote against the Agreement than the total Unionist vote at three of the four most recent province-wide polls, and it would have roughly equalled the 1983 General Election Unionist vote had it been swelled by the votes of Foyle and West Belfast. It was, in short, as impressive a demonstration of Unionist opposition to the Agreement as could realistically have been hoped for. More importantly, the 43.9 per cent Unionist 'no' vote passed the test set by Westminster itself in January 1978, when George Cunningham's amendment to the Scotland Bill (for devolution) inserted the requirement that the subsequent referendum show a 'yes' vote of 40 per cent of the electorate as a whole. In April 1979 the devolution scheme fell as the 'yes' vote, in Scotland, at 52 per cent of those voting on the day, fell well short of 40 per cent of the electorate. (It is possible that in some marginal constituencies the Unionist total may have been augmented by the votes of some pro-Agreement unionists; but such votes must have been very few.)

Table 12.1   The quasi-referendum of January 1986

i) By-elections January 1986; and some other recent Unionist polls

January 1986 By-elections Unionist anti-Unionist	Westminster 1979 Total Unionist vote	Assembly 1982 Total Unionist vote	Westminster 1983 Unionist vote	Euro-poll 1984 Total vote
AIA vote				
418,230	390,419	344,682	435,562	397,512

(N.B. 20,757 Unionist votes were cast in 1983 in Foyle and Belfast West, unconstested in January 1986.)

ii) Turnouts and outcomes (as % total electorate) of some recent referendums

	January 1986 15 By-elections	Border Poll March 1973	UK, EEC 1975	Scotland, devolution 1979
Turnout	62.2%	58.6%	64.5%	63.63%
Outcome as % of total electorate	43.9% Unionist No	57.4% Yes	43.0% Yes	32.85% Yes

	Wales, devolution 1979	Rep. of Ireland, 'abortion' Sept 1983	Rep. of Ireland, 'divorce' June 1986
Turnout	58.8%	54.6%	62.7%
Outcome as % of total electorate	46.9% No	37.79% Yes	39.5% No

Support for the Agreement amongst Catholics was not as strong as opposition to it clearly was amongst Protestants. One poll, for the BBC, showed 54 per cent Catholic approval, but as much as 35 per cent who didn't know or had no clear view. Clearly, Catholics had little reason actively to disapprove of something intended for their benefit, but would naturally want to wait and see whether it actually would be so. Meanwhile the obvious discomfiture of Protestants with the Agreement was its own incentive to Catholics to derive at least qualified satisfaction from the introduction of the Republic's Government into the governing process of Northern Ireland, in however limited a way. Some years on, the Northern Irish Catholic community had observably made great advances (as Fionnuala O'Connor documented in 1993 in her *In Search of a State*)[4] but, as with so much else to do with the Agreement, it would be impossible to quantify how much change to attribute to it; most would have happened anyway.

On the other hand, the Agreement, while advancing the cause of peace in Northern Ireland very little, did serve other key purposes of the two signatory governments. The Irish Government gained a foothold in the constitutional machinery of Northern Ireland for the first time, and ensured that it would be a player in any future negotiations, however distant these might be. It is arguable that the complex of negotiations of the 1990s could not have got off the ground without the inter-governmental framework laid down at Hillsborough. On a more immediate level, the Secretariat at Maryfield enabled the Irish Government to keep more closely in touch with the governing process in Northern Ireland, and to articulate, through the Inter-Governmental Conference, the preoccupations and needs of the nationalist community. The British gained a permanent collaborator in the management of Northern Ireland. Tensions between the two Governments were not absent in the post-1985 period (e.g. extradition, on which the Republic was slow to deliver, was one running sore) but the Conference, and Maryfield, did appear to be a means of speeding up the healing process when tensions arose. The British also secured a lessening of the international opprobrium which their handling of Northern Ireland had earned; especially, for some years, American opinion was more muted. Finally, there were improvements in cross-border security co-operation, showing itself in arms finds if not in shared intelligence.

Unionists were justified in discerning in the Agreement what Edna Longley later called a 'destabilising asymmetry where the United Kingdom Government appears to distance itself from its unionist clients while Dublin and the SDLP appear to share a common agenda.'[5] The Agreement nonetheless constituted, as John Hume insisted at the time of its signing, a framework for a solution, not a solution in itself. Granted, however, the determination of the two Governments to maintain it unless and until it would be transcended by a more comprehensive solution, the post-Agreement political process comprised the British Government, backed by its Irish counterpart, holding the line against the vain attacks of the unionists until such time as they would recognise that all their huffing and puffing could not blow the house down, and that their best interest would be better served by living within it. The role of the RUC, as agents of the state, in withstanding the pressures of loyalists in 1986 and 1987, especially during the marching seasons, and often at risk of personal attacks on their homes, was crucial.

The paradox of the Anglo-Irish Agreement was that for several years it appeared to have become in itself the most immediate obstacle to the achievement of its own proclaimed purposes. To a degree the implication of Hillsborough was the turning upside down of 1973–4, by starting at the inter-governmental level and then, in time, moving on to local power-sharing, with an 'Irish dimension' already in place. But this was no more palatable to unionists than Sunningdale had been in 1973–4. Now they were refusing to consider talks on power sharing or any other constitutional development until the Agreement was removed. This was a recipe for stalemate, unless and until the Unionists were to climb down and accept, *de facto*, the hated Agreement. In 1912–14 and again in 1974, the unionist community had been prepared to fight a government taking a route they detested. On this occasion the Agreement was not sufficiently tangible a threat, and 'fight' not a sufficiently plausible or effective response. Hence the main actual response: sullen impotence. By the late 1980s the indications were that the unionist community, though disliking the Agreement and its provisions as always, were prepared to live with it, especially as, self-evidently, the more lurid prophesies as to its meaning for the Union had not been realised, and it had changed little enough on the day-to-day level. The *Garda Siochana* was still not directing the traffic in Newry, let alone Donegall Square. In 1987 the unionist community showed signs of recovery from the shock of the Agreement; some of them were now thrashing around for ways forward either within or without it. The Ulster Defence Association produced its *Common Sense* report in January 1987, advocating a power-sharing devolved administration but without any Irish dimension; while in July 1987 a think tank of three younger Unionist leaders, McCusker, Robinson and Millar, came up with the *Task Force* report also advocating talks to produce a devolved power-sharing government. This was unacceptable to the two Unionist party leaders, though they did enter talks about talks with the Government, in which they continued to insist on the suspension of the Agreement as a prerequisite for political progress. Shortly after the failure of *Task Force* report one of its principal authors, Frank Millar, left politics altogether for journalism, a sign of the failure of unionism, under its then leadership and in its current predicament, to offer hope to newer generations within its ranks. (At the same time John Cushnahan, leader of the Alliance Party, resigned from Northern Irish politics for similar reasons, though he became a *Fine Gael* MEP for Munster in June 1989). In a similar vein of seeking a way out was the establishment of Conservative constituency associations in Northern Ireland in 1989. The

Conservatives had some initial success in North Down, capturing six council seats in May 1989, but secured a meagre 2.9 per cent in May 1990 in the Upper Bann by-election.

BROOKE'S INITIATIVE

We might date, crudely, the end of the post-Hillsborough phase and the beginning of a new one, leading to the Downing Street Declaration of December 1993, with the arrival of Peter Brooke as the new Secretary of State on 24 July 1989. Involved neither in the negotiation nor the selling of the Anglo-Irish Agreement, a new Secretary of State for a new decade was well placed to make a fresh attempt to move things on. Whether Peter Brooke as such was the best man to do this was a matter for conjecture; some of his initial utterances appeared alarmingly ill-judged, in particular a remark on 3 November 1989 which appeared to suggest an analogy between Northern Ireland and Cyprus, from which Britain of course withdrew after EOKA terrorist pressure.

Brooke observed at the same time that the Provisional IRA could not be defeated militarily, and that he would not rule out talks with *Sinn Féin* after violence had ended. The Government would be 'imaginative'. This was welcomed by the SDLP and by *Sinn Féin*, though not by Unionist politicians. For a time, Brooke was almost a figure of fun (in a thoroughly unfunny situation), a kind of elderly political Wooster. He was, reputedly, a clever man; if so, part of his cleverness lay in concealment of this behind a mask, almost, of well-meaning naivety.

Observers, already in a mood of puzzlement about Brooke, reacted with some surprise to his announcement, in a speech at Bangor on 9 January 1990, that he had found 'common ground' between the constitutional parties in Northern Ireland, such as to encourage him to believe there could be inter-party talks about 'workable and acceptable arrangements for the exercise of devolved powers'. Few observers believed Brooke was correct; most likely, he had misread the flurry of position papers and talks about talks, and taken up the accommodation-acknowledging elements within them (such as those about power-sharing) and ignored the sticking points (such as the existence of the Anglo-Irish Agreement). As 1990 progressed so too did scepticism as to whether the 'Brooke initiative' as it came to be called, was anything other than another in the Rees-Prior sequence whereby British governments did something mainly for fear of being accused of doing nothing. On 5 July 1990 Brooke had to announce to the Commons that he had not been able to achieve agreement on a formula for talks. Throughout the Brooke initiative, the basic formula for talks was that put forward persistently by John Hume throughout the 1980s – that there were three dimensions to the conflict in Northern Ireland which needed to be discussed and resolved, viz:

– that between the two communities in Northern Ireland
– that between North and South in Ireland
– that between Great Britain and Ireland

Unionists went along with this, if at all, with reluctance, some adding that an initial fourth dimension, Great Britain–Northern Ireland, was being ignored.

The problem the talks process faced was that the two main groups in Northern Ireland had agendas that were wider apart than ever. From October 1982, when he led the SDLP into boycotting Prior's Assembly, John Hume had pursued an 'Irish dimension' strategy, and the SDLP was not interested in any local Northern Ireland constitutional developments which sidelined it. The Anglo-Irish Agreement was the key success of this strategy to date. What was notable about the role of Dublin in the post-Agreement period, especially after the departure from office of Garret FitzGerald in March 1987, was the extent to which it not only *endorsed* John Hume's strategy but appeared virtually to have contracted out its Northern policy to him. In contrast, while Unionists *might* have contemplated some form of devolved administration with power sharing, the Ulster Unionist Party under James Molyneaux was now largely integrationist, as was 60 per cent of the unionist population, according to an opinion poll of July 1991.[6] And as far as unionists were concerned, they would not accept an Irish dimension that had any substance beyond the consultative and symbolic. On the contrary, one of their main objectives in the Brooke process remained that of finding a way of getting rid of the Agreement.

The 1990 phase of the pre-talks process failed to reach the talks start-line. Ostensibly the main problem was the involvement of Dublin in the process, Unionists insisting that Dublin be brought in on the talks only when substantial agreement had been reached on the proposed structure of government for Northern Ireland, whereas the SDLP and Dublin wanted talks on their agenda of 'sharing the island of Ireland,' at an early stage. The Unionists moreover insisted that they be included in the talks as part of the British delegation.

The Unionists' critics chose to view them as using procedural points purely as obstructive ploys. This may have been true; but it devalued to mere tactics the political consequences of the deep divide between the two traditions in Ireland, which the Agreement had done nothing to narrow. On the other hand, no party, including both the Unionist ones, was willing to accept the opprobrium of being held responsible for the failure of the process. The talks process would go on – but not for the time being.

1991 opened to one of the bloodiest and most despair-generating phases in the history of post-Agreement Northern Ireland. The PIRA killed eight Protestant workers at Teebane Cross, County Tyrone, on 17 January 1991, and the inevitable retaliation came at Graham's betting shop on the Lower Ormeau road on 5 February, with five Catholic deaths. (On 29 August 1991 came the 3000th death since 1969.) All these were occasions of public pressure for peace, and calls for the politicians to come to the negotiating table.

Brooke's explorations eventually bore fruit in an agreement to embody the three territorial dimensions in three 'strands' of talks, beginning with the internal Northern Irish dimension. The one concession, a meagre one, won by the Unionists, was that there would be a ten-week gap in the meetings of the Inter-Governmental Conference, within which the discussions could take place; and a start for the strand one talks was due to take place on 30 April 1991. However the parties did not actually sit down together till 17 June, owing to procedural difficulties which had not been dealt with before 30 April – chiefly the venue for the second strand of talks, when the Irish Government would be involved, and the identity of a chairman for these.

The British proposal of Lord Carrington was unacceptable to the Unionists, owing to his association with the Foreign Office, which they believed was out to wind down British commitments everywhere, and which they chiefly blamed for the Anglo-Irish Agreement. There were dark hints that perhaps Carrington's name had emerged as a deliberate attempt to wrong-foot the Unionists – not a difficult task at this time. But by the time this issue was resolved with the appointment, instead, of the Australian, Sir Ninian Stephen, 17 June left too little time before the next due meeting of the Inter-Governmental Conference. Unionist pleas for the seven lost weeks to be treated as 'injury time' were unavailing, and, with the next Inter-Governmental Conference due on 16 July, the inter-party talks broke down on 3 July.

What was notable about this episode was the clear evidence that the British Government valued its relationship with Dublin, and specifically the Agreement's legacy of the Inter-Governmental Conference, more highly than the sensibilities of their own citizens of the British tradition in Ireland. This might have offered proof, if proof were needed, that the Anglo-Irish Agreement was coming into its own as a permanent feature of the management of Northern Ireland.

In announcing the failure of the talks, Brooke promised to be listening out for 'rustlings in the undergrowth', for signs that they could resume at a later date but, although there was some fencing around the issues that autumn of 1991, they ran into the British election timetable and were not resumed again until Sir Patrick Mayhew, the new Secretary of State, reconvened them on 30 April 1992. On 1 July Mayhew announced the formal launch of strands two and three, though strand one had not been completed. The talks resumed in the autumn of 1992; on this occasion, the Unionists travelled to Dublin, for the first time since the foundation of the two Irish states. Dublin's failure to appreciate the significance of this gesture on the Unionists' part was notable. There was no sign of movement from Dublin on articles two and three of the Irish constitution. The talks came to a stalemated end on 10 November. The participants issued a statement saying that, while unable to find a basis for a settlement, nevertheless they had 'identified and discussed most, if not all, of the elements which would comprise an eventual settlement', had developed a clear understanding of each others' positions, and established 'constructive dialogue on the ways in which an accommodation might be reached on some of the key issues which divide them'. Sir Patrick Mayhew thought the objective of the talks process remained 'valid and achievable' and all participants 'had a duty to build on what had begun'.[7] Later, on 7 April 1993, John Major, visiting Northern Ireland, said 'I think many people underestimate the progress that has actually been made in the talks'.[8] This could do little to gloss over the essential fact of deadlock. On 24 January 1993 Jim Molyneaux said that the inter-party talks were actually *creating* instability.

There was bound to be some truth in this. 1993 opened to the prospect of yet another year of deadlock and instability. Dramatic moves were, in fact, afoot to break the deadlock, in a quite different quarter from the stumbling (and now indefinitely halted) three strands process. The public were not, however, to know of this until most of the year's leaves had fallen from the trees. It is remarkable how well kept a secret this was, considering how leak-prone the British governmental system in general has shown itself to be. The breakthrough was, of course, the re-opening of contact between the Government and the Provisionals, with a view to a cessation of the 'armed struggle'.

1992 – A UNIONIST OPPORTUNITY

If this opened up for the British Government one possible route out of its long Northern Irish entanglement and for the Provisionals an opportunity to move, with their agenda, closer to the centre stage, the Unionists, for their part, found themselves presented with an unexpected, if temporary, political resource with which to constrain any freedom of the Government to move too far in an anti-unionist direction. While the 1992 General Election failed to produce the change of government that had seemed, to the last minute, on the cards, it did produce a parliamentary situation in which the Northern Ireland MPs enjoyed a strategic position that had not obtained since the dying years of the Callaghan Government. John Major had a parliamentary majority of twenty-one, just above safety level but, given the early re-establishment (as at Newbury in May 1993) of the tendency for governments to lose most, if not all, by-elections, it was highly vulnerable to attrition. Moreover the Government faced a fractious Conservative Party. On Europe, in particular, it could not rely on total support. Unionist muscle was first shown in the great pit-closures fracas of October 1992, when the nine 'Official' Ulster Unionist MPs abstained; in November they joined Labour in voting against the Government over the Maastricht Treaty. On 22 July 1993 the nine Unionists helped secure the Government in the vote on Maastricht, when it otherwise risked defeat. This support, doubling the Conservatives' effective majority, was widely believed to have been part of a broader 'understanding' and there was much speculation as to what might be the *quid pro quo*. Certainly in December 1993, immediately after the Downing Street Declaration, the Unionists got confirmation of the earlier earnest of the Government's intention to deliver a Commons Select Committee on Northern Ireland, something of an integrationist symbol for which James Molyneaux had been pressing for a decade. While Labour spokesmen denounced the July 'deal' and deplored its effects on the inter-party talks process, it was simply part of a tradition, going back at least to 1886, that Irish parties of whatever kidney would naturally choose to exploit parliamentary mathematics to their own advantage whenever there arose an opportunity to do so. Moreover, Labour was in a particularly unfavourable position for calling 'foul' since, only a few days before the Maastricht showdown, Kevin McNamara, the Labour shadow Secretary of State, had been associated with a document advocating joint authority, a position that might have been calculated to drive the Ulster Unionists into the Conservatives' arms.

The Ulster Unionists had thus achieved a bankable accretion of strategic power. For the length of the 1992 parliament, they would be able to put a brake on any possible moves by the Major Government to go too far in the Dublin direction. But it was only a brake, and a temporary one at that. They were hardly going to put the Conservatives out to install a unificationist Labour government. Equally a putative Labour government, if it felt that Unionists had robbed Labour of an opportunity to put the Conservatives out before their 1992 term was up, would be quite likely to round on unionism with an even more unreservedly nationalist stance. So their little success over the Maastricht vote actually emphasised how boxed in even this asset was. By now James Molyneaux, hitherto the grey man of Ulster politics, was nonetheless beginning to win appreciation for playing a limited hand with some finesse. In 1994 he even won a Parliamentarian of the Year award.

THE PIRA – 'SICKENING THE BRITS'

The Anglo-Irish Agreement had had little evident effect in preventing the PIRA from pursuing its own strategy of 'sickening the Brits'.[9] In their armed campaign the Provisionals could frequently rely on the British themselves to turn even PIRA failure to good PIRA account. They could ensure that for the British, Northern Ireland would continue to embroil them in, as O'Leary and McGarry strikingly termed it, 'the politics of embarrassment'.[10]

If the classic illustration of this was the handling of the 1981 hunger strikes by a British administration which appeared never to have heard of Easter 1916, the post-Agreement years produced a fresh crop of their own. One was the Birmingham Six and the inter-related Guildford Four and Maguire Seven cases, with their blatant evidence of justice denied and the vindication of all republican and left-wing charges against the British police and judicial system. The Six were finally released on 14 March 1991. In the furore and embarrassment the Birmingham Twenty-One, murdered by the PIRA in November 1974, were forgotten. Even the unionist side had their cause for grievance, in the case of 'the UDR Four'.

Another public relations fiasco was the aftermath of Gibraltar shootings of 6 March 1988. The first reports of these to be given by British officials were simply untrue; in particular the first statement from the Ministry of Defence on the afternoon of the shooting spoke about the finding of a suspected bomb, and a later one said it had been dealt with. This remained the official line until the following afternoon, when Sir Geoffrey Howe said in the Commons that no bomb had been found and that the three PIRA members were unarmed. (The bomb was subsequently found, but at Marbella; it had not yet been moved to Gibraltar.) On 28 April Howe intervened to ask the IBA to postpone the Thames Television investigation *Death on the Rock*. They refused; the programme highlighted several crucial inconsistencies in the official version of events. Subsequently, the Windlesham report exonerated Thames in confirming the journalistic integrity of *Death on the Rock*, even if some of its evidence might still have been questionable. The furore over the programme, as well as the attempts by the *Sunday Times*, on 1 and 8 May 1988, to cast doubt on Thames' evidence, especially on the veracity of Carmen Proetta's eyewitness account, all added to the tally of 'embarrassments' stemming from the shootings of 6 March. So too did the proceedings at the Coroner's Inquest in September, the only official investigation undertaken by the British.

Another case, redolent of British policy made without apparent thinking through of longer-term implications, was the introduction of the broadcasting ban in the autumn of 1988. The immediate precipitating event was the killing, on 20 August 1988, of eight young soldiers in a bus at Aughnacloy. The 'ban' emerged out of an emergency meeting of Ministers held at Downing Street. Introduced by Douglas Hurd in the Commons on 19 October, it gave the impression of being something produced at short notice from a scraping of the bottom of a barrel (though it had been discussed by Ministers earlier in the year). At first the 'ban' appeared quite effective, in that it did keep *Sinn Féin* off the screens, since broadcasters tended to opt to avoid them in cases where circumstances did not *compel* them to cover *Sinn Féin*. *Sinn Féin* regarded the ban's chief effect as preventing them explaining themselves to their own supporters and potential sympathisers. There was a strong civil liberties case against the ban; but its fatal weakness as an instrument of broadcasting policy was also its vagueness. Broadcasters considered this unfair, in that it placed on them the onus for interpretation of the regulation, a task properly belonging to government but which the latter refused to shoulder itself. Ed Moloney commented that 'Mrs Thatcher's broadcasting restrictions have become the ultimate in censorship. It has made journalists, through intimidation, boredom or indolence, the instruments of the ban when they should be its principal victims and most vigorous opponents.'[11] Confusingly, spokespersons for banned groups could speak on non-constitutional or non-terrorist matters and at election times, which was not true of the much stricter ban in the Republic, in operation since 1976. By 1993 the broadcasters had wreaked their revenge by so refining the reportage of *Sinn Féin* spokesmen to the point where Gerry Adams was reported as saying that the best of the actors hired to speak his words played him better than he played himself. In vain did Government apologists argue there was no broadcasting 'ban' as such. The idea of a 'ban' had become firmly lodged in the public mind and the broadcasters' increasingly bold and evidently unchallenged interpretation of the scope it gave them had turned it into a farce; and the Government, by implication, was made to look ridiculous.

But undoubtedly the PIRA's biggest success was in their capacity to keep their campaign going regardless of whatever the British did. On 7 February 1991, they brought their war to the British Cabinet directly, for the second time, with their daring and ingeniously conceived mortar bomb attack on 10 Downing Street. But the most ominous development was their pair of bombs in the City of London on 10 April 1992 (the day after the General Election) and just over a year later on 24 April 1993. The first, at the Baltic Exchange, caused damage estimated at first at £750 million or more. Though later much reduced, it was still more than all the criminal damage claims in Northern Ireland since 1969. The second, at Bishopsgate, was even more costly, and extensively damaged the buildings of several prestigious international financial houses. Where bombs on Protestant towns in Northern Ireland, or assassinations of British military or diplomatic personnel on the continent, were part of a long war in which either side could square up for a test of endurance, the two city bombs, like the attack at Heathrow in March 1994, were aimed at a jugular vein of the British state. No government, least of all a Conservative one, could afford to have the PIRA destroy the one economic complex left in Britain which still has a world class role – the financial centre of the City of London. As for British public opinion, at the very least the message conveyed by this campaign was that the Government had failed to keep the conflict within Ireland, and would probably continue so to fail.

The PIRA was fond of using the image that the British were painfully slow learners, but *they* were wondrously patient teachers. The British were, in fact, learning quite a lot – about the need to go as far as possible, and to be as explicit as possible, in explaining to the Provisionals the terms on which they were still in Northern Ireland, and the scope and limits of any putative British negotiating position vis-à-vis Irish republicanism.

TOWARDS AN UNARMED STRATEGY

The Provisionals, for their part, had also been engaging in a far-reaching process of reappraisal of their position, their view of Britain, the Republic and the unionist community. This was going on throughout the period from Hillsborough to Downing Street, though it was never quite clear how far it would go, or how far it was the work of an *avant-garde* who might have much difficulty in bringing the whole movement along with the consequences of their analyses. The first signs of fresh thinking appeared in the 1987 document, *Scenario for Peace*. Subsequently, *Ard Fheis* reports and other *Sinn Féin* documents indicate that an 'unarmed strategy' was under active consideration from at least 1991. Not only had the 'ballot box', when allied to the armalite, reached the apparent limit of its scope in the May 1985 elections (when fifty-one *Sinn Féin* councillors were elected) but, more importantly, the Provisionals' 'Southern strategy' had failed miserably. Demonstrably lacking significant support in the Republic, and with the SDLP now enjoying wind assistance from the Anglo-Irish Agreement and pulling away from *Sinn Féin* in popular support, the movement was increasingly stalemated. *Sinn Féin* as a political party had shown itself as having several pockets of significant support, but it was manifestly ghettoised within those limits. As long as the armed struggle went on, so would it confine the scope for republican political influence.

To some degree, the very success of the ballot box strategy, limited though it was, fed back new perspectives into the *Sinn Féin* thought process.[12] Many of *Sinn Féin*'s councillors had deeply felt community serving objectives, which they could best pursue by some discreet distancing of themselves from the physical force element in their tradition. Importantly, violence came to be seen less as the 'cutting edge' of the struggle than simply a symptom of the conflict. As Fintan O'Toole put it in November 1993, the community had 'remade *Sinn Féin* in its own image, forcing it to move away from the assumed authority of violence and towards the earned authority of hard graft.'[13]

As for Britain, John Hume, in the abortive Hume–Adams talks of 1987–8, had tried to persuade *Sinn Féin* that Britain was effectively neutral (following Article 1c of the Anglo-Irish Agreement) on the constitutional future of Northern Ireland, and did not stand in the way of an Irish unity achieved by the persuasion of those who opposed it by those who supported it. From 1990 British official statements and speeches gave support to this view, especially Peter Brooke's November speech. *Sinn Féin*'s *Towards a Lasting Peace in Ireland*, launched at its February 1992 *Ard Fheis* in Ballyfermot set out how far they had now travelled in developing a new view of Britain's role in the conflict – not just as the original creators of the problem who should simply withdraw, but now as potential *facilitators* of 'a democratic resolution and a lasting peace'. It had to involve, 'within the context of accepting the national right of a majority of the Irish people, a British government joining the ranks of the persuaders in seeking to obtain the consent of a majority of people in the north to the constitutional, political and financial arrangements needed for a united Ireland'.[14]

Sinn Féin was thus turning on its head its traditional demand for precipitate British withdrawal leading to a united Ireland. The implication now was that Britain's role was to *remain* 'in' Northern Ireland for the time being in a new role as 'persuader' of the unionists. While the latter were not to be accorded the freedom to withhold consent to unification, since 'the British bestowed unionist veto needs to be removed', the specific arrangements for attaining unity did require a measure of unionist consent (referred to as 'a debate about national reconciliation') and Britain was to facilitate this. *Sinn Féin* writings, of course, continued to accuse Britain of political, economic and military repression, and of having a pro-unionist political agenda. Nonetheless, the roots of a possible 'unarmed strategy' can be seen in the new doctrine that saw Britain as a key member of the 'ranks of the persuaders' for a new, unified Irish dispensation.

In parallel with its reappraisal of the British the republican movement was reappraising its view of the Protestant community. As with its view of Britain, the reappraisal re-positioned the Protestants. Hitherto seen as political collaborators in imperialism, of little account in their own right, now the Protestants were appreciated as a group with real fears and insecurities – which were also attributed (with good reason) to the British connection. Unionists, argued Gerry Adams, have rarely had confidence in the British Government; they were victims of a history they had not made. Out of unionism's historical identity crisis arose an opportunity for 'national reconciliation'. Adams, and even more, Mitchel McLaughlin, who was emerging as an important contributor to the new approach, argued for an inclusive, broad Irishness, in a language which echoed more the republicanism of the 1790s than the Catholic–nationalist approach of the mid-twentieth century. *Sinn Féin*'s approach to unionism still nonetheless presumed that they had no right not to consent to unification, and that unification remained the inevitable end, pre-determined by demography and the certainty of sometime British withdrawal.

THE BRITISH RESPONSE – BROOKE AND MAYHEW

What is striking about *Sinn Féin*'s more advanced language in the early 1990s, and that publicly used by British politicians, is the extent to which they were beginning to converge. While the public politics of solution-seeking was focused upon Brooke's faltering talks process, vital developments were unfolding behind the scenes, namely the re-activation of contact between the British Government and the Provisionals. Channels through which such contacts might be made (churchmen, businessmen, politicians) had been available since the early days of the conflict. During the 1980s they had been largely unutilised, such was the distrust and dislike mutual to Margaret Thatcher and the Provisionals. According to Dillon's account it was, nonetheless, Mrs Thatcher who opened the lines of communication to the PIRA, per-haps, he conjectures, hoping to play the political heavyweight in de-livering a solution to the Irish question in parallel with efforts to solve the Palestinian one. Ironically, the first step in this was taken in the month before Thatcher's fall, October 1990.[15] A message had been sent to a *bona fide* intermediary, indicating a British wish for a meet-ing between him, a British Government representative, and Martin McGuinness, the foremost link between political *Sinn Féin* and the PIRA. The meeting took place in October 1990, McGuinness playing the role of silent observer (such was the Provisionals' scepticism). Within weeks came Peter Brooke's speech of November 9, one of the most significant speeches on Ireland made by any British politician since 1968 (if not long before). Although Brooke affirmed the majority con-sent principle once again, he portrayed the British as neutral on the Union, an honest broker between the two Irish aspirations:

> We acknowledge that there is another view, strongly held by the nationalist minority within Northern Ireland. That is the aspiration to a united Ireland, not simply to the Republic of Ireland which exists today, but to a 32-county state covering all the territory of the island, and worthy in their view of the support of all the Irish people. It is possible to take either view with integrity. It is accept-able to uphold the one or advocate the other by all legitimate peace-ful and democratic means. . . . An Irish republicanism seen to have finally renounced violence would be able, like other parties, to seek a role in the peaceful political life of the community. In Northern Ireland it is not the aspiration to a sovereign united Ireland against which we set our face, but its violent expression.

Brooke then pointed to the prospect of an inclusive political settlement, which would involve reconciliation 'between the communities in Northern Ireland; within Ireland; and between the peoples on both these islands'. He concluded, 'The British Government has no selfish strategic or economic interest in Northern Ireland: our role is to help, enable and encourage.'[16]

This speech went further than any British Minister had gone before to spell out that partition, and the British involvement in Ireland, was a product of Irish realities, not British interests or even preferences. The affirmation of 'no selfish strategic or economic interest' was to be repeated like a mantra over the next three years, and it re-emerged in the Downing Street Declaration. It was, at least in part, a public disavowal of the strategic British interest in retaining Northern Ireland, whose appearance as a memorandum to the post-war Attlee Government had so excited republicans when released in the 1970s under the thirty-year rule. Brooke's speech was not, of course, enough to satisfy the Provisionals, but they had received an advance copy of it and, Dillon reports, they debated it with great interest. Meanwhile, their campaign went on in 1991 unabated, including, early on, the mortar attack on the Cabinet in 10 Downing Street on 7 February.

Despite this, contact was maintained, with the PIRA continuing to be highly suspicious of British overtures. These continued after the 10 April 1992 Baltic Exchange bomb, indicating not only that the British were serious in wanting dialogue, but also that the message intended by the bombing was getting home. The British kept the Provisionals informed of the progress of the inter-party talks chaired by Sir Ninian Stephen. In October 1992 the British told the Provisionals of their scepticism about the future of the talks and indicated the possibility of a joint British-Irish 'imposed solution', in the framing of which the Provisionals would have an input.

Britain's next major public move in response to the Provisionals came in Mayhew's Coleraine speech of 16 December 1992, when, returning to Brooke's theme of two years earlier, he was even more explicit in spelling out what the British Government now offered to Irish nationalism in general, and, perhaps, the republicans in particular. He identified four dividing lines in Northern Ireland – those of national identities, major religious groupings, cultural traditions, and that deriving from the economic and social disadvantages experienced by the minority community. Problems required a solution that recognised those divisions. He recognised that the nationalist aspiration to a united Ireland was no less legitimate than the unionist one to maintain the Union. 'Provided it was advocated constitutionally, there can be no proper reason for excluding any political objective from discussion. Certainly not the objective of an Ireland united through broad agreement fairly and freely achieved.' Then came the heart of the speech, the reward awaiting republicans following a cessation of violence:

> In the event of a genuine and established cessation of violence, the whole range of responses that we have had to make to that violence could, and would, inevitably be looked at afresh. When terrorism is seen to have genuinely ended, there will indeed be profound consequences for the maintenance of law and order, and for the administration of justice.

The police could 'give fresh priority to the quality and accessibility of its service,' and the army could return to barracks. Similarly, the emergency legislation on which many of these responses were founded would have served its purpose and normality could return. It might be noted that Mayhew's scenario depended upon a permanent end to violence, not simply an extended ceasefire. As regards Irish culture, Mayhew said that, although 'we have not plans for a bilingual society' he went further than any of his predecessors to endorse the culture of Irishness as on a par with that of Britishness in Northern Ireland. 'What we are about', he said, 'is working to the agenda of the people of Northern Ireland, not pursuing any interests of our own.' The role of the British Government was:

> one of facilitating, not steering in a particular predetermined direction. As Britons we may seek to ensure fair play as best we can . . . But a real resolution of the division of society can be found, I suggest, only by those who have first hand experience of them, who know the hearts of their fellow countrymen and women, who know what they can and cannot accept. Only an accommodation hammered out on a *local* anvil, and with widespread local support, will survive the tests of time and practice.[17]

There was an element of disingenuousness in Mayhew's disavowal of pre-determinacy of British 'steering'. Integration with Britain, the Ulster Unionist preference, was pre-determined *out*, just as power-sharing local institutions, with an all-Ireland dimension, were just as surely predetermined *in*. As with Brooke's two years earlier, this speech spelled out to the republicans that Britain recognised the validity of their aspirations and their cultural identity; that Britain had 'no self interest leading it to pursue a separate agenda of its own', and held out the carrot of the consequences, on the security forces side, of a cessation of PIRA violence. But, in this, and in subsequent speeches (Belfast, 2 March, Liverpool, 23 April) Mayhew at no time pointed to a scenario of British withdrawal or explicit support for a reunification of Ireland. The Provisionals, if they were to take up Mayhew's offer, would have to settle for less than the goal to which twenty-three years of armed struggle had been aimed. On the other hand, the offer was not inconsiderable. A declaration of neutrality on the future of Northern Ireland, plus full recognition of Irish identities within it, including the pledge to remove as soon as practicable the legislation prohibiting street-names in any language other than English (in practice street-names were in Irish only in republican districts already, and Derry City Council had erected Irish names alongside the English ones, in the city centre); plus the removal of the security force presence from nationalist areas, could be claimed by the Provisionals specifically as an achievement of theirs rather than one won by the SDLP. It was not 'freedom' in the republican sense; but with their sense of Irish history the Provisionals would have been conscious of the possibility that, as Michael Collins said of the 1921 Treaty, it *could* mean the freedom to win freedom, as they would understand (and work for) it.

1993 – TOWARDS DOWNING STREET

The Provisionals' response to Mayhew's Coleraine message came at their *Ard Fheis* in February 1993, when in a speech by Martin McGuinness, *Sinn Féin* appeared to accept the concept of a talks process involving all sides in Ireland. 'We are quite prepared to be open and flexible to serious proposals which can lead to agreement,' he said.[18] A first meeting was held with an intermediary on 22 February. The British account of this meeting, released with yet another flurry of embarrassed confusion in November, had the Provisionals saying that 'The conflict is over, but we need your advice on how to bring it to a close.' The Provisionals themselves repudiated this wording, and certainly this would have been a remarkably grovelling message to have come from a body still to explode its two Warrington bombs and its Bishopsgate one. Dillon[19] attributes the British wording simply to a desire to create the impression in Britain that the exchanges of spring 1993 were entirely due to a PIRA decision to end its campaign.

Three days after the second, fatal, Warrington bomb (i.e. on 20 March) dialogue continued at a meeting between McGuinness and the British representative. The *Sinn Féin* internal report of this meeting, released in November 1993 and referred to subsequently in October 1994 by McGuinness, is crucial (if true and correct). It has the British representative saying that Mayhew was determined to have *Sinn Féin* play a part in political negotiations, his Coleraine speech being a significant pointer in this direction. Mayhew, said the British representative:

> wants Sinn Féin to play a part . . . because it cannot work without them. Any settlement not involving all of the people North and South won't work. A North/South settlement that won't frighten the Unionists. The final solution is Union. It is going to happen anyway. The historical train – Europe – determines that. We are committed to Europe. The Unionists will have to change. This island will be as one.[20]

Mayhew subsequently denied that any British representative was *authorised* to say that Government policy was aimed at unification. He did not, however, deny that the meeting did take place, with approval at the topmost level, or indicate precisely what the British representative *was* authorised to say.

Talks between *Sinn Féin* and John Hume of the SDLP recommenced on 10 April, and from this point on much of the dynamic of the moves towards a Provisional cessation of violence based upon a set of agreed declaratory principles about the parameters of a 'solution', lay in the Hume–Adams talks.

In all, the British and *Sinn Féin* exchanged sixteen written and four oral messages in the spring of 1993. According to Dillon's account, by mid-May 1993 John Major had decided he would talk to the Provisionals. However, he was dissuaded almost at once from this course by Cabinet colleagues who felt that, in the aftermath of Warrington and Bishopsgate, and with the Government's parliamentary position weak without Ulster Unionist support, the political risks were too high. Thereafter the Government was looking for a way out, or at least of avoiding serious commitment to the Provisionals. At the same time, the Government had to head off a risk that the latter would expose its secret exchanges with them. The logic of this pointed to seeking an accord with Dublin. This would override the Hume–Adams talks, drown out any Provisional revelations about the spring series of communications, and engage both Governments in the peace-seeking process. It would also put pressure on the Provisionals and test their real commitment to peace – exposing them if they failed it.[21]

Although the Hume–Adams agreed document was never published, to the intense frustration of many, it became Provisional policy to press for talks towards political settlement along its lines; and the two Governments, working through the autumn of 1993 towards what became the Downing Street Declaration, clearly had in mind the principle of reflecting in the joint declaration as much of 'Hume–Adams' as possible, while retaining the irreducible minimum of the British (and latterly also Irish) pledges of 1920, 1949, 1973 and 1985 to respect majority wishes in Northern Ireland as to remaining in or leaving the United Kingdom.

The Declaration committed Britain to the role, not of persuader for Irish unification, but of validating the concept of Irish self-determination, and it fitted unionists neatly into this concept by splitting it into two components, North and South, which were to endorse the proposed new settlement concurrently. This, plus the concession of the Commons Select Committee, was enough to keep the UUP though not the DUP, 'on side' for the Declaration. The Declaration, like the Anglo-Irish Agreement eight years and one month earlier, was presented as a balanced package, offering comfort and reassurance to both aspirations and traditions in Northern Ireland.

And so, in one sense, it was, in that it balanced acknowledgement of Irish republican aspirations with reiteration of the majority consent principle. But the Declaration was unmistakeably addressed to republican priorities. One commentator noted that there were twenty-seven references to Irish unity in the document, but only two to Northern Ireland within the United Kingdom.[22] As John Wilson Foster put it, the Declaration was constitutionally tilted towards only one settled condition, that of a united Ireland:

> Although there are references to the maintenance of the union, they are perfunctory and formulaic, and only a united Ireland is given the credence of elaboration. It is a statement of withdrawal in spirit from Northern Ireland by the British government, leaving only the provisional letter of its presence. Whereas the British concession that they have no selfish strategic or economic interest in Northern Ireland is meant to appear as generously neutral, even avuncular, it is in fact a shedding of the British population of Ulster, which some will welcome but others will regard as a deep insult.[23]

Another commentator, Feargal Cochrane, noted that although the message to nationalists was that unification had to be opted into by unionists, the message to the latter was that 'while they would not be thrown out of the British house against their wishes, theirs was the guest room.'[24]

1994: DOWNING STREET TO THE CEASEFIRES –
CONCLUSION

The wooing of *Sinn Féin* in the aftermath of the Downing Street Declaration indicated how far Britain had come from any supportive view
of the Union. On 23 February 1994, on the eve of the *Sinn Féin Ard
Fheis*, Sir Patrick Mayhew re-emphasised British neutrality on the long-
term future of Northern Ireland. He argued that the advocacy of the
Declaration by Albert Reynolds 'in no way departed from the classic
nationalist position that the partition of Ireland was wrong' though its
ending had to be worked for peacefully and achieved by consent. The
most striking and historic feature of the Declaration was 'its explicit
treatment of the principle of self-determination'. He repeated that Britain
had 'no economic or strategic concerns which would lead us selfishly
to stymie the people's exercise of their free political will'. And, in a
crucial phrase, he said that the North–South joint institutions which
were envisaged 'could take on an increasingly dynamic role'.[25]
    It took the Provisionals another eight months from the Declaration
before they declared their ceasefire on 31 August 1994. While an instan-
taneous response to the Declaration from them was not to be expected
(notwithstanding media expectation to the contrary) the length of time
was inordinate, punctuated as it was by two occasions on which an
answering cessation of operations might have been decided upon, but
was not. The Declaration clearly put the Provisional leaders on something of a spot, given that it went some considerable way to meet
what Hume and Adams had thrashed out, but fell well short of a full
endorsement of the republican position. The two Governments did not
require the Provisionals, before they came into the negotiating arena,
to accept the Declaration, but merely to cease their armed operations
permanently. The Provisionals' response was to do neither but to call
for 'clarification' of points in the Declaration, though they were often
irritatingly vague as to precisely what needed clarifying. The call for
clarification served several Provisional purposes. It might have prised
open some clear ground between the British and Irish Governments; it
served as a cover for the leadership while it played for time to convince its followers of the novel 'unarmed struggle' strategy; and it
helped to gain their acquiescence in an eventual ceasefire by showing
that the leaders had done their best to pull the meaning of the Declaration further over towards the Provisional position. (While a permanent ceasefire would have required a PIRA Army Convention, for which
the political ground would have needed much preparation, a provisional

one presented much less of a problem, but the above considerations still applied in delaying its arrival).

The Provisionals made much, at this point, of the need for Britain to go beyond endorsement of Irish unification as a 'valid objective', to 'joining the ranks of the persuaders'. While the Declaration clearly signalled British intention to remain, for the time being, in Northern Ireland, it equally clearly indicated the contingency of this upon majority wishes there. For Britain to join the ranks of the persuaders, therefore, would be tantamount to declaring an intention to withdraw. Even if this would not be until Britain had succeeded in its persuasion of the necessary proportion of unionists to produce 50-per-cent-plus-one for unification, a shrewd assumption would be that Britain 'joining the persuaders' would *in itself* lead to an erosion of the unionist majority, since the obvious next step for at least a section of the unionist population would be to seek terms as an Irish national minority, while for others the indication that Britain wished to leave would be a signal that anyone wishing to stay British should leave for Great Britain. The indications were that many Protestant school leavers were doing that in any case.

Although the incumbent British Government would not take the persuasion role, Provisionals could note that a Labour Party committed to Irish unification and which had plans for 'persuading' the unionists by tying them into a series of cross border arrangements creating unificationist facts, was well ahead in opinion surveys and stood a good chance of forming a British government before too long. The Government also resisted the Provisional call for clarification, interpreting it as an attempt at pre-emption of post-ceasefire negotiation. But this came in time to appear a barren and counterproductive attitude, and one which did open up, to British detriment, a division between London and a more complaisant Dublin. Eventually, on 19 May, Britain did supply a twenty-one page commentary on twenty questions about the Declaration submitted by *Sinn Féin*, and this put an end to the Provisional campaign on this, without their having elicited significant movement from London.

This left the ball back in the Provisional court, but now they stood to lose ground. John Hume came under criticism from within the SDLP. Adams' triumphant trip to the USA from 31 January to 2 February had a bill attached which had not yet been paid in terms of movement by the Provisionals. On 29 June they announced there would shortly be a delegate conference to discuss the Declaration. Comparisons were made with the 1970 conference which crystallised the split between the Official and Provisional IRAs.

Minds may have been concentrated by the continuing evidence of aroused loyalist militancy. On 18 June the UVF killed six Catholics in a bar at Loughinisland, County Down. In 1991 loyalists had virtually matched republicans in deaths caused; subsequently they outnumbered them. From February 1989 to the ceasefire loyalists shot dead twelve active *Sinn Féin* members and as many again of their close relatives and associates – whereas only seven *Sinn Féin* members had been killed in the previous twenty years. In 1994 alone, to 1 September, loyalists were to kill in all thirty-three Catholics, while twenty-four deaths were attributed to republican paramilitaries. The loyalist attack on the Widow Scallan's pub in Dublin on 21 May, using sixteen kilograms of Powergel, appeared to confirm the security forces' assessment that the loyalists were acquiring sophisticated bomb-making capability.

If *Sinn Féin* did not get much joy from Britain out of their campaign for further clarification (i.e. amendment) of the Downing Street Declaration, the British response on 19 May did hint at a possible acceptance of a trade-off of amendment of the Government of Ireland Act, 1920, for amendment of articles two and three of the Irish constitution. Hardly mentioned in Anglo-Irish discourse before 1994, the 1920 Act emerged during the year as an issue, its amendment being taken up by nationalists as a symbol of significant British movement towards recognition of the process of Irish self-determination. Virtually on the eve of the PIRA ceasefire, the Dublin press confirmed that among several draft documents exchanged between the two Governments were proposals by the British side for removing the clause in section seventy-five of the 1920 Act which stated: 'Notwithstanding. . . . anything contained in this Act, the supreme authority of the Parliament of the United Kingdom shall remain unaffected and undiminished over all persons, matters and things in Northern Ireland . . .'[26] and inserting the principle, already in the 1985 Agreement and the 1993 Declaration, that there could be a change to a united Ireland if a majority so wished. This was rightly seen as purporting to hand over sovereignty from Westminster to 'the people' of Northern Ireland. Virtually all the rest of the 1920 Act had been repealed by the Northern Ireland Constitution Act of 1973. Since Section 75 reiterated the 'truism' that 'the Westminster Parliament retained its power to trump anything that a regional parliament enacted',[27] its dropping would reverse the situation, for it would *subordinate* the United Kingdom legislature, in matters relating to Northern Ireland, to the wishes of the people of Northern Ireland, as, for example, expressed in an Assembly. A Westminster government would be unlikely to tolerate such a situation for long, except as a transition to a permanent abdication of responsibility for Northern Ireland. In contrast, any modification by Dublin of articles two and three (or possibly only of article three) was pretty insignificant stuff.

The Provisionals' convention to discuss the Declaration was held at Letterkenny, County Donegal, on 24 July. Once again, as at their February *Ard Fheis*, they came out with an equivocal, balanced statement, welcoming the Declaration in some respects as 'a further stage in the peace process', but not accepting it or suggesting the imminence of a ceasefire. This was interpreted by the media and most politicians and commentators as a rejection. (One of the few to see positive features in it, from the peace viewpoint, was Albert Reynolds.) The *Sinn Féin* leadership was reported as surprised and dismayed by this, and indeed on 3 August Adams confirmed that he *had* discussed the possibility of a ceasefire with PIRA leaders before Letterkenny. On 12 August Danny Morrison, *Sinn Féin* Publicity Director before his imprisonment, said Republicans were discussing the possibility of 'an unarmed strategy'. It became increasingly clear, as the month progressed, that a cessation of PIRA violence was likely within a short time; the once-canvassed possibility of a three-month stoppage having been ruled unacceptable by the two Governments, and especially on 22 July by Deputy Premier (and leader of the Irish Labour Party) Dick Spring. By now, the momentum had built up to the point where the PIRA and *Sinn Féin* stood to lose much of what they had been gaining since Downing Street if they failed to call a halt to armed operations.

Clearly the long delay of the Provisionals after Downing Street was testimony to the risk its leaders were taking that a ceasefire would be repudiated by part of their movement, especially in the rural sections of the PIRA, and that the resulting peace process would fail to deliver sufficient to satisfy republican aspirations. But the position was even more critical for unionists. Firstly, deny it though some of its component partners would, the years since Hillsborough had seen the forging of a *de facto* pan-nationalist alliance, with only the Conservative British Government and the unionists on the 'other' side. And Britain, for its part, had publicly declared itself no longer unionist, while the Provisionals, at least, believed they had privately gone significantly further. Ultimate Irish unification was, to a greater or less degree, on everyone's agenda except that of the unionists. Maintenance of the

Union, on the other hand, was only on theirs. The state of which Northern Ireland was part had, officially, no view at all on the matter. The disavowal of a selfish or strategic interest in the Union meant that, at the high constitutional level, what mattered to Britain was simply that the decision as to whether Northern Ireland should stay in the Union or leave it should be made in a procedurally correct way, ie peacefully and subject to periodic local head-counts until a majority for leaving should emerge. What the Declaration appeared to be saying, judging from its content, was that Britain had no particular views on how Northern Ireland might become a valued part of the United Kingdom family but only on under what circumstances it might leave. The Declaration did not say that this was what Britain would prefer, nonetheless, except for a small number of Conservative right wingers, the silences of the majority as well as the spoken views of a minority of British politicians indicated assent to the view that Britain's best interest lay in the dissolution of the Union, provided only that this should not too overtly be seen as a capitulation to terrorism. Hardly a single utterance by a British politician of weight, since the departure of Thatcher, indicated any valuing of or emotional attachment to Northern Ireland as part of the United Kingdom. (Compare, by contrast, the position of the Anglo-Scottish Union). This was a singular situation, little appreciated in Britain; for it meant that as long as violence continued, the state's agents, the Army and the RUC, as well as others, would continue to put their lives at risk in defence of a state which had proclaimed to the world that it did not care whether the territory remained in its jurisdiction or not. Moreover, even Britain's official neutrality could be expected to last only until the arrival of the next Labour government, unless it turned out to be one which needed to court the Westminster Unionists for reasons of parliamentary mathematics.

Labour's position was, in fact, remarkably similar to that now espoused, after its radical reappraisal, by the Provisionals. On 22 October 1993, for example, Kevin McNamara, the long-standing (since July 1987) Labour spokesman, reiterated in the Commons that no Labour government would 'allow its commitment to consent to be transformed into a veto on political progress towards seeking Irish unification by consent'.[28] Labour would, in essence, become one of the persuaders; and it would do so by creating such all-Ireland institutions as would erode away the issue of 'consent' to the point of meaninglessness.

Kevin Toolis, in his study of the PIRA, describes its ceasefire strategy succinctly thus: 'If the Provisionals can immerse the blatant desire of the Protestants of Ulster to remain separate from a united Ireland within the greater Catholic majority of Ireland's desire to be united, then the IRA will have dissolved partition . . .'. The aim of the pan-nationalist strategy is, he says, to achieve a 'historic handshake' with the Crown like that between Mandela and de Klerk. As in the South African case, there is to be no overnight transfer of authority, but 'similarly in Ireland, power would at first trickle, then flow, from the Crown into nationalist Ireland until the balance of power was so weighted in the nationalist/republicans' favour that a section of the unionist community would break away and strike a political deal with the ancient enemy'.[29]

The change in the British position on Ireland in the years between Hillsborough and Downing Street may be approached simply by contrasting the political thrust of the two documents. The Anglo-Irish Agreement was an attempt to contain and if possible reverse the rise of *Sinn Féin* by addressing the needs of the Catholics of Northern Ireland as interpreted by the SDLP to the Irish Government. In signing it the British 'bought in' to the SDLP's analysis and project, while maintaining its long-standing constitutional commitment to the majority. The unionists would have been wiser to accept the Agreement and then hold the two Governments to the letter of it. As it was, their rejection of the Agreement had profound consequences. While it stalled further constitutional development for some years, it did not succeed in wrecking the Agreement, and the main losers from their attitude were the unionists themselves. The language of the next major constitutional document, the Downing Street Declaration, indicated a degree of 'buying in' to the analysis and project of *Sinn Féin*, albeit courtesy of the brokerage skills of John Hume, even while remaining faithful once again, to the bare essential of the 73-year-old majority consent principle. Intriguingly, however, on the eight year journey from Hillsborough, *Sinn Féin*, for its part, had developed its analysis considerably, moving closer to a position with which the British, given a credible ceasefire, could do some business. At least some of the credit for this could be given to the Anglo-Irish Agreement, its consequences, and to British policy and politicians since 1985.

If Britain would not join the ranks of the persuaders, unionists would be foolish to rely passively upon their 'greater number'. For one thing, the pro-union plurality among the electorate was not overwhelmingly large, and it showed every sign of diminishing in future electoral tests. In the European elections of June 1994 the difference between those voting for pro-Union and anti-Union candidates was 105,875. In other words, only 52,998 voters, or 9.5 per cent, needed to be persuaded to change sides for an anti-partition majority to have emerged. Of course, what would determine this matter would be demography, not persuasion; though what matters politically may be more a question of what people believe future trends, and their implications, to be, than of what specialist analysts may make of them. More widely, the politics of solution seeking in Ireland, as it developed in the 1980s and 1990s, put all parties into the position of having to be persuaders. Ulster's Unionist parties were rather bad at this; often they didn't even seem to be trying.

The Economist greeted the PIRA ceasefire, when it came, with the observation that 'extraordinarily, it does seem to have given up its armed campaign without achieving any of its goals.'[30] Certainly, the PIRA and *Sinn Féin* were obliged to forego the satisfaction of being seen to have brought about a sudden, Eastern European style collapse of the British state in Northern Ireland. Nonetheless, a reasonable view was that, as Martin Dillon put it, British policy was 'moving inexorably towards disengagement. No writer about the conflict, myself included, would deny that PIRA violence, particularly in mainland Britain, has changed the political landscape more than any series of events in the last twenty-five years.'[31]

Indeed, and yet the paradox of PIRA military operations was that, deep and genuine though British loathing of the PIRA and its apologists might be, the language of the Downing Street Declaration testified amply to their success in driving home the point that republicans and their campaign were *not* the essence of Britain's Irish problem. Rather, it is the persistence of the majority in Northern Ireland's desire to stay in the United Kingdom which is the basic reason why the British cannot get out of their costly Irish imbroglio. The logic of that was and is ineluctable.

On 31 August 1994 the PIRA announced that at midnight there would be 'a complete cessation of military operations'. They did not accept the Downing Street Declaration, but noted instead that it 'is not a solution, nor was it presented as such by its authors. A solution will only be found as a result of inclusive negotiations'. Gerry Adams chose to mark the occasion by praising the PIRA leadership and 'a generation of men and women who have fought the British for 25 years and are undefeated by the British'.[32] He did not claim victory. To most in Northern Ireland, relief was genuine, celebration premature. An opinion poll in the *Belfast Telegraph* indicated a majority (comprised of 75 per cent of the Protestants and 25 per cent of the Catholics) disbelieving in the permanence of the ceasefire. Overall, 31 per cent believed

Sinn Féin had done a 'secret deal' with the Government. The word 'permanent' would not be uttered by the Provisionals, pending the calling of an Army Convention which alone could make an authoritative decision to that effect. Nonetheless, by the time the loyalist paramilitaries followed suit with their ceasefire declaration on 13 October, the British Government was on the brink of accepting as a 'working assumption' the permanence of a cessation of military operations. So were the people of Northern Ireland: at least provisionally. There was, however, no consensus on what it all meant – except maybe a consensus for caution, whether optimistic or pessimistic. Military writers, referring to the inevitable confusions of the battlefield, have a useful phrase – 'the fog of war'. Northern Ireland now peered into a fog of peace. 'It's over', proclaimed the *Belfast Telegraph* on 31 August. Perhaps.

NOTES

1. Anglo-Irish Summit Meeting 15 November 1985. Joint communiqué.
2. *House of Commons Debates*, 6th ser. vol. 87, col. 912, 27 November 1985.
3. W. Harvey Cox, 'Public Opinion and the Anglo-Irish Agreement', *Government and Opposition*, vol. 22, No. 3, Summer 1987, p. 342.
4. Fionnuala O'Connor, *In Search of a State: Catholics in Northern Ireland* (Belfast: Blackstaff, 1993).
5. Edna Longley 'Submission to the Opsahl Commission', *Fortnight*, March 1993, pp. 20–23.
6. *Fortnight*, September 1991, pp. 18–19.
7. *Irish Times*, 11 November 1992.
8. *Ibid.* 8 April 1993.
9. See Brendan O'Brien, *The Long War* (Dublin, O'Brien Press, 1993), Ch. 8.
10. B. O'Leary and J McGarry, *The Politics of Antagonism* (London: Athlone Press, 1993), p. 171.
11. Ed Moloney, 'Closing Down the Airwaves: The Story of the Broadcasting Ban', in B. Rolston (ed.), *The Media and Northern Ireland* (Basingstoke: Macmillan, 1991), p. 48.
12. This section draws on discussion in Kevin Bean, *The New Departure: Recent Developments in Irish Republican Ideology and Strategy*, Occasional Papers in Irish Studies, No. 6 (University of Liverpool, Institute of Irish Studies, 1994).
13. *Irish Times*, 24 November 1993.
14. See Bean, *op. cit.* Ch. 3.
15. Martin Dillon, *The Enemy Within* (London: Doubleday, 1994), p. 228.

16. Quoted in O'Brien, *op. cit.*, pp. 209–11.
17. 'Culture and Identity', text of speech by Sir Patrick Mayhew at University of Ulster, Coleraine, 16 December 1992 (Northern Ireland Information Service).
18. Quoted in Dillon, *op. cit.*, pp. 235.
19. *Ibid.*, p. 236.
20. *Ibid.*, p. 238.
21. *Ibid.*, p. 243.
22. Gregory Campbell, *Ulster's Verdict on the Joint Declaration* (Democratic Unionist Party, 1994).
23. John Wilson Foster, 'Processed Peace', *Fortnight*, March 1994, pp. 35–6.
24. Feargal Cochrane, 'Ourselves Alone', *Fortnight*, March 1994, pp. 16–19.
25. *Independent*, 24 February 1994.
26. Government of Ireland Act, 1920, 10 & 11, Geo. V.
27. Rula Law, 'Excuse Me I'm a Lawyer', *Fortnight*, September 1994, p. 27.
28. *House of Commons Debates*, 6th ser., vol. 230, col. 495, 22 October 1993.
29. *Guardian*, 18 November 1994.
30. *Economist*, 3–9 September 1994.
31. Dillon, *op. cit.*, p. 262.
32. *Irish Times*, 1 September 1994.

13 The Northern Ireland Question and European Politics[1]

James Goodman

INTRODUCTION

European Union (EU) integration is focused on socio-economic issues rather than cultural or political concerns. Partly due to the weakness of a pan-European political identity it has been riven with conflicts between 'national', usually state-centred political orientations, and 'regional' orientations at the sub-state or supra-state levels. Across the EU this translates into an ideological division between issues ostensibly related to 'national' sovereignties and regional, EU-related issues.

This dichotomy is particularly sharply defined in Northern Ireland, where politics is dominated by a conflict over national jurisdiction. While not transforming or superseding these national conflicts, the process of regional integration into the EU has challenged existing political orientations. As politicians have been forced to reconcile a commitment to state-centred 'national' sovereignty with policy positions on European integration they have been faced with deep ideological dilemmas and have been forced into significant political realignments.

For many political observers, Britain's role in Ireland has been transformed by the process of integration into the EU, primarily because of its impacts on British and Irish state sovereignty. The EU was seen as superseding exclusivist concepts of sovereignty, disposing of the British-Irish 'sovereignty-identity obsession'. As the EU offers the 'possibility of emancipation for the . . . nations and cultures' of Britain and Ireland, in a Europe of weakened state sovereignties, it was expected that the conflict would be 'repositioned', in a new regional context allowing political reconciliation in Ireland as a whole.[2] Regional integration in the EU has, indeed, offered a basis for common agreement between Britain and the Republic of Ireland, permitting a relative 'unbundling' of their roles, mostly on North–South economic issues.[3] But there has been little regionalisation as, in the context of continued unresolved conflicts between the United Kingdom and the Republic over the national question, the two states have adapted to minimise the impacts of EU institutions, in some cases strengthening their respective roles in managing the conflict.[4]

EUROPEAN POLITICS AND POLICIES

In 1975 the issue of whether Northern Ireland should remain a member of the European Community (EC) split both political blocs in Northern Ireland: constitutional Nationalists and 'Official' Unionists favoured membership while republicans and loyalists opposed it. Subsequently this cross-community support for EC integration grew at a remarkable rate. In the referendum, Northern Ireland cast 47.7 per cent of its votes against membership, and was the most anti-EC region in the United Kingdom. By 1991 it had become one of the most 'Europhile' of these regions, with 5.2 per cent favouring withdrawal compared with 19.3 per cent in the United Kingdom overall.[5]

This reflected a strengthened, shared regional identity of Northern Ireland, as part of the EU, which both Nationalist and Unionist politicians could claim to represent.[6] Politicians competed to define themselves as regional ambassadors, defending regional interests and maximising the flow of EU funds to the region, a type of 'pork barrel regionalism' that conflicted with the logic of national conflict – disrupting ideological positions, forcing policy realignments along regionalist lines, and potentially recasting 'national' constituencies.[7]

European Elections

Although attitudes to the EU cut across political and communal divisions in Northern Ireland, in the first European elections political parties mobilised on traditional nationalist versus unionist lines. Due to what the British Government called 'special circumstances' in Northern Ireland, the region was defined as a single Euro-constituency, with its three Members of the European Parliament (MEPs) selected under the proportional representation system.[8] Partly because of this, elections were treated as a contest for political leadership in Northern Ireland and as a vote for or against the dilution of British sovereignty. Perhaps also reflecting the power of personalities over policies in elections which sent representatives to a largely powerless European Parliament, there were very few transfers across the communal divide and cross-community parties – such as the Alliance or the Workers Party (WP) – fared worse than in either Westminster or local government elections.[9]

This favoured the Democratic Unionist Party (DUP) which tripled its share of the votes cast – from 10.2 per cent in the 1979 Westminster election to 29.8 per cent in the European election of that year – claiming 170,688 first preference votes, compared with the successful Ulster Unionist Party (UUP) candidate who polled 127,169. It also favoured the Social Democratic and Labour Party (SDLP), which claimed 24.6 per cent of the vote – 4.7 per cent more than in the 1979 Westminster and 7.1 per cent more than in the 1981 local government elections. In contrast, the UUP, which fielded two candidates in the 1979 elections, saw its share fall by 14.7 per cent to 21.9 per cent of the vote.

Although the DUP continued to top the poll after 1979, there was a slight movement away from the anti-Maastricht DUP and *Sinn Féin*, towards the less anti-EU UUP and, more significantly, towards the pro-EU SDLP. Reflecting the growing acceptance, even enthusiasm, for European integration from the mid-1980s, voters began to favour political parties with a positive programme for European integration. As illustrated in Table 13.1 below, there was a slight movement away from anti-integration parties in European elections after 1984: both the DUP and *Sinn Féin* saw their share of the vote fall by 3.4 per cent between 1984 and 1994 while the less negative UUP saw their vote increase by 2.4 per cent and the SDLP by 6.4 per cent, both over the same ten-year period.

At the same time party representatives were forced to collaborate in 'getting the best deal' for Northern Ireland at the EU level. The three MEPs, representing loyalist, unionist and nationalist communities, worked together on joint regional concerns.[10] Cross-party voting on regional issues was commonplace and the three MEPs often made joint representations to the EU and to the British Government.[11] As early as 1980 the MEPs visited Brussels with the Mayor of Belfast to call for more EU funds for Northern Ireland and in 1989 they were united in their condemnation of the Northern Ireland Office after the Northern Ireland attracted half as much regional funding, *per capita*, as the Republic.[12] In 1993 they again acted together in opposing the exclusion of Northern Ireland from access to Cohesion funds and following a meeting with the British Prime Minister, they returned to Northern Ireland with the promise that the Treasury would top-up Northern Ireland public expenditure levels.[13]

Such *ad hoc* joint action was not seen as conflicting with the pol-

James Goodman 215

Table 13.1 Percentage of votes cast in Northern Ireland European Elections, 1979–94

	UUP	DUP	SDLP	SF	All	WP	Other	Turnout
1979	21.9	29.8	24.6	–	6.8	0.8	16.1	57
1984	21.5	33.6	22.1	13.3	5.0	1.3	3.2	65
1989	22.2	29.9	25.5	9.2	5.2	1.0	7.1	44
1994	23.8	29.2	28.9	9.9	4.1	1.0	3.1	49

Source: B. O'Leary, 'Party support in Northern Ireland 1969–1989', in B. O'Leary and J. McGarry (eds), *The Future of Northern Ireland* (London: Clarendon, 1990), pp. 342–57; *Irish Times*, 14 June 1994.

iticians' positions in the national conflict, as John Hume and the Reverend Paisley pointed out in 1988, it was their 'duty' to get the 'best' for Northern Ireland.[14] Nonetheless, politicians were becoming increasingly willing to bury their differences on EU-related issues – when it came to competing to represent the Northern Ireland region at the EU level, 'cash was thicker than blood'.[15]

Party Policies

During the 1980s and especially in the early 1990s this increased articulation of political concerns in an EU political framework was having direct impacts on party policies, including policies on the national conflict. Despite some politicians' assurances to the contrary, EU-related shifts in party policy can be detected across the political spectrum in Northern Ireland, from republicans and nationalists to unionists and loyalists. These can be illustrated using party policy papers and statements, beginning with the most 'Europhile' (the SDLP), and ending with the most 'Europhobe' (the DUP).

In the 1980s the SDLP substantially re-cast its nationalist agenda in the EU context. In 1975 the Party campaigned for continued EC membership and at Westminster supported both the Single European Act (1987) and the Maastricht legislation (1993). In 1977 at its seventh annual conference the Party focused on the socio-economic impacts of EU membership and in 1984 it argued that these constituted an alternative agenda, separate from the sectarian politicking of rival candidates.

Ten years later, in the 1994 European Parliamentary (EP) elections, the Party had developed these campaigning themes into an ideological formulation that expressed the nationalist aspiration to greater unity in

Ireland within a wider 'Europe of the Regions'. The election literature spoke of 'the ever closer Union' between the peoples of Europe, pointing to the 'breaking down of old conflicts and barriers' in the EU as a 'major source of assistance in tackling our own problems'.

This theme had been elaborated in the 1990 party position paper – the SDLP analysis of the nature of the problem – which argued that the 'pooling of sovereignty' in the EU would enable people to 'work their common ground together at their own speeds towards a unity that respects diversity', founded on sub-state regionalisation and democratic EU institutions; what the Party leader described as a 'dilation of democracy'.[16] Reflecting this EU-related political agenda, the Party presented proposals for a six member 'Commission' for Northern Ireland at the Brooke talks in 1992, composed of three representatives from the North, a representative for each of the two Governments and a European Commission representative, that would exercise executive powers in tandem with a North–South Parliamentary Assembly and an Anglo-Irish inter-governmental body, mirroring institutional arrangements at the EU level.[17]

Sinn Féin also reorientated itself to a more positive engagement with EU politics. The Party programme, *Éire Nua*, published in 1971, favoured a strong Irish national state which would distance itself from the 'rich men's club of former colonial powers in the EC'. In 1984 the Party argued in its manifesto – *One Ireland, One People, The Only Alternative* – that the EU had 'subjugated' Ireland to the interests of larger EU states. It called for a 'negotiated withdrawal', substituting trade agreements for EU membership and in 1992 during the Maastricht Treaty referendum in the Republic it campaigned for a 'no' vote, publishing an anti-Maastricht pamphlet – *Democracy or Dependency: The Case against Maastricht.*

Soon after the referendum campaign *Sinn Féin* began to adapt its position, building closer links between republicanism and EU integration. In 1992 the Party President argued that 'the involvement of the British government in Ireland is a European issue' and in 1993 *Sinn Féin* representatives visited the Belgian EU Presidency, calling for an enhanced EU role in the conflict and soon after, the Party announced it would be setting up an office in Brussels.[18]

The Party was convinced that post-Maastricht EU integration would encourage British withdrawal from Ireland and at the same time would increase pressures for North-South economic and social integration.[19] This integration was seen as having direct political impacts in Ireland. Concepts of EU-encouraged all-Ireland democratic economic management formed a central theme in the *Sinn Féin Submission to the Opsahl Commission* of November 1992 and were detailed in its policy document – *The Economics of a United Ireland* – published in February 1994, which argued that 'a united economy could increase wealth creation but without economic democracy it will create less wealth and in fewer hands'.

Its 1994 manifesto – *Peace in Ireland, A European Issue* – also highlighted this theme and argued that without democratic North–South institutions EU integration would create an 'undemocratic island economy'. The Party argued that it was possible to construct 'an alternative to the undemocratic, anti-worker EU' and did not reject EU integration; on the contrary, it was seen as a key site of political engagement and the manifesto came close to praising the Commission for its use of funds 'to promote the image of "the island of Ireland" as one unified economy', regretting that this was not sufficiently reflected in the policy priorities of either the Republic or Northern Ireland.

Other non-unionist parties also moved towards accepting the logic of EU regional integration in Ireland. The Workers Party – historically linked to the Official Irish Republican Army – had been opposed to EC membership in 1975. But by 1989 the Party had become more positive about EU developments and the possibilities for political intervention to improve Northern Ireland's position within it. They argued for improved representation for Northern Ireland at the EU level and saw the EU framework as a means of superseding the 'medieval quagmire' of sectarianism in Northern Ireland. In its 1994 manifesto – *Peace, Work, Democracy, Class Politics* – it focused on the 400,000 unemployed in Ireland – North and South – and on the need to construct a pan-EU 'Left unity' to challenge neo-liberal policy agendas at the EU level.[20]

This increasing articulation of nationalist and republican aspirations in a regionalising, EU context shifted the framework for ideological conflict in Northern Ireland, forcing unionists also to abandon rejection of European integration and to compete to define themselves as the more capable ambassadors at the EU level. In 1975 many unionist politicians had opposed EC membership – seeing it as a 'Trojan horse'.[21] As powers were exercised jointly with other states, including the Republic, and through common institutions, the EC was seen as undermining British sovereignty, potentially damaging the Union with Northern Ireland.

Of the main unionist parties, the small cross-community Alliance Party was the least hostile to EU integration. It argued that EU regionalisation offered a means of overcoming divisions in Northern Ireland, suggesting in its 1989 manifesto – *Show Europe a New Face* – that there should be coordinated EU action on regional development in Ireland, North and South. The 1994 manifesto – *Our Future Together in Europe* – called for regional government for Northern Ireland to improve representation of the region at the EU level and to 'provide . . . a political structure which all sections of this community could support'. EU regionalism was seen as defining a pluralist, anti-nationalist political agenda that had the potential to supersede national conflict in Ireland and the Party argued that such regional integration was desirable, but only within the United Kingdom state framework, as, regrettably, 'national' states remained key actors in the EU, despite increased regionalisation.

Unlike the Alliance Party, the Ulster Unionist Party was ideologically opposed to the concept of European regionalism, although it too became relatively positive on EU issues in the 1990s. In the 1975 referendum the Party was undecided, with some politicians favouring membership while others argued that European integration undermined Northern Ireland's constitutional position – including Jim Molyneaux, who participated in the 'get Britain out' campaign.[22]

In the 1980s this initial indecision developed into a position of conditional support. In the 1989 manifesto – *Europe in the '90s* – the Party welcomed measures to liberalise trade in the EU, introduced under the Single European Act, and in a paragraph on 'relations with the Republic of Ireland', the Party clarified that it was 'not opposed to co-operation where there are no political or constitutional implications'. The UUP saw itself as presenting a positive vision of European integration that preserved and expressed national state sovereignties and in 1989 praised the Thatcher Government for having 'aligned itself with Unionists' in her 1988 Bruges speech. It committed its candidate to 'safeguarding the integrity of the UK' and, underlining this, its 1990 policy document – *Signposts to the Future* – committed the Party to oppose any attempts to 'further erode the role of our national parliament at Westminster'.

The Party's position paper – *Blueprint for Stability* – of February of 1994 and the 1994 EP manifesto – *Europe: Making it Work for Ulster* – deepened this approach, linking it to the Party's political position in the national conflict. In the *Blueprint* for instance, arguments for the removal of articles two and three of the Republic's constitution were phrased in terms of the need to learn from 'European co-operation, namely, recognition of existing frontiers, abandonment of territorial ambition and mutual co-operation', suggesting a closer engagement with EU-related issues. This hesitant pro-Europeanism was most explicitly combined with the Party's political agenda in the national conflict when, in 1993 – as stressed by the UUP leader in the Party's 1994 EP campaign material – the Party's backing for the Maastricht Treaty at Westminster brought an end to legislation in Northern Ireland by Orders in Council, and was followed by the creation of a Select Committee for Northern Ireland at Westminster.

Some Party representatives went beyond this hesitant approach to argue that EU integration was restoring the pre-1921 Union, bringing Ireland 'back under the predominant influence of the British Isles from which it had been separated for only seventy years'.[23] In 1992 this was formulated into a proposal for a 'Council of the British Isles', that would allow the creation of a British-Irish parliamentary body and an inter-Irish relations committee, conditional upon removal of the Republic's constitutional claim to jurisdiction in Northern Ireland. Such a 'Council' was seen as the logical consequence of British-Irish convergence in the EU and was presented at the 1992 Party Conference and by Party representatives at the Brooke talks in the same year, and constituted the Party's main response to the SDLP's proposals for an all-Ireland Council or 'Commission'.[24]

The DUP was more hostile to the process of EU integration – seeing the EU as eroding national sovereignty and undermining the border between North and South in Ireland – although it too began to revise its position in the early 1990s. In 1975 the Party campaigned against membership and in 1979, according to its election material, the Party leader stood for the EP as a 'free and fearless Protestant and Loyalist voice' against EC interference in Northern Ireland affairs. These concerns were combined with a sectarian branding of the EU as a Catholic institution; in 1984 the Party argued that Northern Ireland was 'the last bastion of Protestantism in Europe and stands between the Vatican and her goal of a united Roman Catholic state of Europe' and in 1988 its MEP – the Reverend Paisley – attempted to disrupt the Papal address during an EP session, culminating in his being ordered out of the Chamber.[25]

The Party fought the 1984 election with the slogan 'the EC puts your pound in Dublin's pocket' – which ironically reflected the British Government's reluctance to distribute EC agricultural funding to Northern Ireland on the same basis as in the Republic. The Party was 'opposed not merely to our terms of membership but to the very principle of membership itself' and the 1989 election was treated as a vote against Tom King – the Secretary of State responsible for the Anglo-Irish Agreement.[26] In 1992 the Party was 'implacably opposed' to the Maastricht Treaty and remained committed to 'milking the cow of the EU, before slitting its throat'.[27] These themes were again confirmed in the Party's 1994 campaign which was treated as a 'crusade' against the Downing Street Declaration and against 'the creation of a European super-state or anything which strikes at the sovereignty of the UK'. This opposition to EU integration was set against the Party's increasing and substantial commitment to EU structures that went well beyond 'milking' the EU cow and certainly did not imply any attempt at 'slitting its throat'. In 1992, for instance, the Party had begun to argue for 'cooperation in Europe without incorporation', a position similar to the UUP.[28] In 1994 its manifesto called for EU action on unemployment, proposing a new Commissioner to 'channel the resources of the community into reducing unemployment'. The Party favoured EU action on working conditions, supporting the EU Social Charter, and called for an EU-defined 'family policy' under which an income would be provided for 'full time mothers equivalent at least to the minimum wage in many EC states'. Meanwhile, on North–South regional issues, the Party had in practice adopted a very similar position to the UUP in its policy paper – *Breaking the Logjam* – which did not oppose North–South institutions on principle, instead favouring a new North–South rapprochement and possibly the creation of all-Ireland bodies once Articles 2 and 3 of the Irish constitution had been removed.[29]

POLITICAL DILEMMAS

The increasing consensus on questions of EU integration contrasted with party political conflict over the national question, raising a series of dilemmas for Northern Ireland politicians and forcing limited policy realignments. These are explored here using interview material gathered in the early 1990s from each of the five main political parties.[30]

The SDLP – 'Euro-Nationalism'?

For the SDLP the EU delinked people from 'national' state jurisdictions, allowing a move away from the certainties of sovereignty, towards a more fluid politics in a multiplicity of local regional units 'below', 'national' units 'in between', trans-national units 'across' and EU units 'above' the pre-existing sovereign states. Within this fluidity the recognition and constitution of Ireland as a unified 'national' region was seen as the most hopeful, peaceful approach to resolving the conflict. As a Party representative argued, 'this piece of earth is already united – it is the people who are divided'. Thus reconciliation must be aimed at bringing together the people of Ireland, North and South, in a joint sharing of interests at the regional and local level.

This binding-together of nationalism and regionalism imbued SDLP rhetoric with a dual, often competing ideological logic. Northern Ireland would be redefined as part of the regional 'island of Ireland' in the EU, rather than as a region of the United Kingdom. But it would not necessarily be part of a single all-Ireland, 'national' jurisdiction. Hence the Party moved away from a commitment to Irish unity in the formal sense of national state sovereignty, instead arguing that regional integration would deliver national reconciliation between the two parts of Ireland.

Sinn Féin – 'Tactical Republicanism'?

Sinn Féin representatives were also caught in something of a dilemma. The Party was formally committed to the creation of a sovereign independent all-Ireland state which would define its own relationship with the EU, in accordance with the expressed wishes of its populace. In the early 1990s the Party had begun to argue that the EU opened up new political opportunities as well as threats, suggesting that the EU had much to offer, both in terms of defining the socio-economic context for Irish unity and in terms of offering a source of political legitimacy for the republican cause.

Given the Party's reluctance to forego its commitment to an independent sovereign all-Ireland state, Party representatives began to have difficulties in overcoming what was becoming a sharp ideological tension as the role of EU institutions and the Party's proactive orientation towards them intensified. In the first instance this was avoided through a temporary, tactical endorsement of some aspects of EU integration. In the future this tension was likely to stimulate broader policy changes, leading to a possible adaptation of the assumed linkages between national self-determination and state sovereignty.

The Workers' Party and the Alliance – 'Reluctant Statism'?

Both the Workers' Party and the Alliance Party advocated an 'internal' solution to Ireland's national conflict, based on political agreement in

Northern Ireland. At the same time both adopted a positive political stance on the process of regional integration in the EU.

The Alliance Party, as an active member of the 'European Liberal, Democrat and Reform Party', pursued a Euro-regionalist agenda on EU political issues, with a 'Europe of the Regions' as its ultimate goal. But the Party failed to advocate this approach for Northern Ireland as it would have forced it to favour a stronger political role for EU institutions, undermining its support base in a unionist community hostile to non-UK political involvement in the conflict. The Alliance then, wavered between its liberal unionist position on the possible solution to the national conflict and its liberal Euro-regionalist perspective on the issue of EU integration – a tension that was resolved by arguing that the EU had not progressed sufficiently down the regionalist road for it to merit having a greater political role in the Northern Ireland conflict.

The Workers' Party found itself in a similar position. The Party stressed the need for an internal Northern Ireland agreement in the first instance – as a Party representative argued – 'it is here that the division exists and it is here that the solution must be found'. Like Alliance, it favoured European integration but played down the role of the EU in shifting the framework for economic or political development, North and South, thereby undermining the Party's ultimate political objective of politically re-unifying the island.

The UUP – 'Statist Integrationism'?

The UUP was also caught on the horns of an ideological dilemma. Reflecting its British nationalist, integrationist position in the national conflict, the Party favoured state-led EU integration, in which the state would retain its powers and in which EU institutions would remain accountable to 'national' Parliaments. Any suggestion that Northern Ireland could become an autonomous region or would join with the Republic of Ireland as an 'island region' in the EU – rather than as a region of the United Kingdom – was condemned. At the same time, Party representatives pragmatically accepted a role for EU institutions as long as they dealt with issues not related to the politics of the national conflict and as long as their role was determined and mediated by the British state.

These definitions of acceptable EU jurisdictions and acceptable EU lines of authority were difficult to sustain and led to seemingly contradictory policy positions. Aspects of EU integration would be condemned, apparently arbitrarily, as they seemed 'political' or would come to be seen as 'political'. A prominent business person, for instance, was condemned for proposing the creation of institutions to manage the North–South all-Ireland economy in the Single European Market, as 'when he makes his proposals they seem political, no matter how unpolitical he may try to make them'.

The DUP – 'Loyal Statism'?

The DUP was more actively hostile not only to federalist aspirations but, more fundamentally, to the concept of EU integration as a whole. But like the UUP, the Party was forced to become involved in the development and formulation of EU policies and was actively involved in and quite often claimed the credit for maximising the benefits of EU membership for Northern Ireland.

To avoid the resulting tensions, representatives were also forced to construct a false distinction between the economic or social impacts of EU membership which were accepted as necessary, and its political consequences, which were opposed. Like the UUP this forced representatives into seemingly arbitrary and irrational policy positions. As the Party became increasingly involved in EU-related issues its slogan of wanting to milk the EU 'cow' before 'slitting its throat' became increasingly ironic – as the Alliance leader pointed out, if you own a cow and become dependent on its milk, you do not kill it, you feed it.

CONCLUSIONS

Tensions or contradictions between positions in the national conflict and policies on the process of EU integration reflected wider ideological struggles over the definition of EU integration being fought out across the EU. In Northern Ireland these had significant effects as they shifted the context for political conflict, thus altering the terms of the national question – although not answering it as suggested by the more enthusiastic Euro-regionalists.

The emergence of largely positive public attitudes to EU integration and of ostensibly *ad hoc*, 'non political' joint political action by Northern Ireland politicians on EU-related issues, combined with the increasing significance of the EU dimension to Northern Ireland politics, forced parties to adapt their political positions. Given these shifts in party policy, to some degree reflected in voting patterns, there are grounds for arguing that the process of EU integration led to a degree of convergence towards a shared acceptance of the process of EU integration and towards a common policy agenda on EU-related issues.

After the Maastricht Treaty all but one of the 'reserved powers' that had been retained by Westminster under the 1920 Government of Ireland Act were subject to EU regulations or were at least partially exercised through joint inter-governmental, if not supranational EU institutions rather than directly by the British Government. These included foreign affairs, external defence, nationality, corporation and income tax, customs and excise duties, trade marks and patents, external trade and currency regulation.[31]

In the 1990s politicians in Northern Ireland began to compete in designing the regional agenda for these issues, and to some extent shifted ideological conflict out of the 'national' state framework and into the regional EU framework. As such issues were articulated in a common, EU frame of reference, it was possible to conceive of a redefinition of social interests, leading to a positive sum, 'synergy of positive collaboration' between the regions of the EU – including between North and South in Ireland – generating a politics of regionalism to replace the 'tired slogans' of national sovereignty.[32]

This optimistic assessment underemphasises on-going ideological conflict over sovereignty-related issues. Indeed, the one remaining 'reserved' power under the 1920 Act, namely the absolute power of the Crown in Parliament, remained central to the claim to state sovereignty in the United Kingdom and was at least as symbolically central to political affiliations in Northern Ireland as it was prior to EU membership in 1972. Regardless of the explicitly political dimensions of EU integration, for instance involving citizenship rights, these claims to sovereignty remained firmly in place, both in practical and in symbolic terms.[33]

Nonetheless, the 'spilling-over' of EU issues into the national conflict was generating deep policy dilemmas and was forcing limited, but significant changes in party political positions on the national question. While EU issues were often treated as a 'stake' in the national conflict to be supported or opposed according to their impact on the British presence in Ireland, they were also perceptibly altering its context. The European dimension was certainly being 'nationalised' and in some instances sectarianised by Northern Ireland politicians, but at the same time the national conflict was being Europeanised, with potentially far reaching consequences.

Limited Europeanisation of political relations in Northern Ireland was paralleled by increased regionalisation of British policies in Northern Ireland. During the 1980s EC institutions had defined the conflict as a European issue and had encouraged the emergence of an 'EC-engendered trust' between the British and Irish Governments, providing the practical basis for Anglo-Irish inter-governmental dialogue on Northern Ireland. The British Government was forced to take 'international opinion' into account, leading it to recognise that the conflict was an international issue involving the two states and the two parts of Ireland, as much as the two communities in Northern Ireland – that was later reflected in the 'three-strand' negotiating framework of the Brooke and Mayhew talks of 1991–3 and in the Downing Street Declaration of December 1993.

This provided the framework for British Government proposals to increase North–South economic integration in the context of accelerated EU integration in the early 1990s. These initiatives reflected a growing awareness of all-Ireland regional interests as Northern business leaders began to argue that if it was to survive in the Single Market, Northern Ireland had to formulate a new, all-Ireland framework for economic development – a dramatic shift in business orientation that was paralleled in the Republic – although to a lesser degree.[36]

From 1989 the Anglo-Irish Conference provided the mandate for civil servants to work together on EU-funded cross border projects and in September 1992, more substantive British proposals for North–South institutions to manage the regional economy were put to 'strand two' of the inter-party talks process. These were explicitly aimed at 'optimising the benefits of the EC framework for the two parts of Ireland' and reflecting this, in the following year, a joint North–South Chapter for the 1993–9 EU structural funds programme was drawn up by the two Governments aimed at integrating and coordinating spending plans in the two jurisdictions.[37] Subsequently the Downing Street Declaration stated that, regardless of the wider national question, 'the development of Europe will of itself require new approaches to serve interests common to both parts of Ireland' and in 1995 it was correctly anticipated that the British Government's 'framework document' for inter-party talks on the conflict would include proposals for North–South economic institutions to manage the process of Ireland's integration into the Single European Market.[38]

In general terms, then, the process of EU integration had a significant impact on political relations in Northern Ireland. The policies of political parties were, to a degree, shifting towards a common agenda on EU-related issues. Similarly, the policies of the two states – especially of the United Kingdom – were moving towards a common concern to jointly manage the conflict and to improve North–South economic links. It was likely that these political shifts would intensify in the mid-1990s, particularly in the context of the 1996 review of EU institutional structures and in the context of deepened integration into the Single European Market.

NOTES

1. I would like to thank those who gave comments and criticisms on an earlier draft of this paper, especially James Anderson.
2. R. Kearney, *Irish Times*, 5 May 1993; see also R. Kearney (ed.), *Beyond the Frontiers* (Dublin: Wolfhound, 1988); K. Boyle, 'Northern Ireland – Allegiances and Identities', in B. Crick (ed.), *National Identities* (*Political Quarterly* special edition, 1991), p. 69; R. Kearney and R. Wilson, *Northern Ireland's Future as a European Region* (Submission to the Opsahl Commission, 1993).
3. J. Anderson and J. Goodman, 'Euroregionalism and National Conflict: The EU, the UK, Ireland North and South', in P. Shirlow (ed.), *Development Ireland* (London: Pluto, 1995). For a broader treatment of the 'unbundling' process, see J. Anderson and J. Goodman, 'Regions, States and the European Union: Modernist Reaction or Postmodern Adaptation?', *Review of International Political Economy*, Vol, 2, No. 2 (Summer 1995).
4. A. Aughey, 'Community Ideals and Northern Ireland', in A. Aughey *et al.* (eds), *Northern Ireland in the EC* (Belfast: Policy Research Unit, University of Ulster and Queens University, 1989), pp. 5–28; A. Aughey, 'Cross-sectarian Support for a European Role in Northern Ireland', in H. Skar and B. Lydersen (eds), *Northern Ireland: A Crucial Test for a Europe of Peaceful Regions?* (Oslo: Norwegian Institute of International Affairs, 1993), pp. 54–65.
5. In the 1975 referendum there was a 47.4 per cent turnout in Northern Ireland and 47.9 per cent voting against membership, while in the United Kingdom overall there was a 64.5 per cent turnout with 32.8 per cent voting against. In 1991 the regular Euro-barometer survey found that 5.2 per cent out of a sample of 300 people interviwed in Northern Ireland favoured withdrawal compared with 19.2 per cent in the United Kingdom overall, out of a poll of 1300. See J. Derby 'Regionalisation, New Allegiances and Identification in Northern Ireland and Europe', in H. Skar and B. Lydersen (eds), *op.cit.*, pp. 40–50; Euro-barometer, 1992.
6. P. Hainsworth, 'Business as Usual: The European Election in Northern Ireland', in P. Hainsworth (ed.), *Breaking and Preserving the Mould: The Third Direct Elections to the European Parliament (1989) – The Irish Republic and Northern Ireland* (Belfast: Policy Research Institute, 1992), pp. 143–61.

7. P. Murray, 'The European Parliament and the Irish Dimension', in P. Hainsworth (ed.), *op.cit.*, pp. 342–7.
8. This was designed to ensure that the nationalist community would have a representative in the European Parliament: House of Commons, *Direct Elections to the European Parliament* (Command Report 6768, April 1977); S. Elliott, *Northern Ireland: The First Elections to the European Parliament* (Belfast: Queens University, 1980).
9. B. O'Leary, 'Party Support in Northern Ireland 1969–1989', in B. O'Leary and J. McGarry (eds), *The Future of Northern Ireland* (Oxford: Clarendon, 1990), pp. 342–57; A. Guelke, *Northern Ireland: The International Perspective* (Dublin: Gill & Macmillan, 1988), p. 156.
10. Since 1979 the Reverend Ian Paisley has represented the DUP in the European Parliament, the SDLP has been represented by John Hume and the UUP has been represented by John Taylor (from 1979 to 1989) and by Jim Nicholson (from 1989).
11. S. Elliott, 'The 1989 election to the European Parliament in Northern Ireland', *Irish Political Studies*, Vol. 5 (1990), pp. 93–100.
12. *Irish Independent*, 14 October 1980; *Belfast Telegraph*, 29 January 1989.
13. *Irish News*, 29 January 1992.
14. See 'John and Ian Unite in Amity', *Belfast Telegraph*, 20 February 1988.
15. *Irish News*, 29 January 1992. Opinions diverged on the question of whether the EU should be funding cross-border projects – for instance under the INTERREG programme, which was in place from 1991.
16. John Hume, *Subsidiarity and the Role of the Regions*, 9 December 1992, Edinburgh University.
17. *Irish Times*, 26 January 1993 and 13 May 1992.
18. *Irish Times*, 24 February 1992; *Irish Times*, 14 October 1993; *Guardian*, 7 December 1993; *The Times*, 29 February 1994.
19. Mitchell McLaughlin, Northern Chair of *Sinn Féin*, *Guardian*, 5 April 1993.
20. *Belfast Telegraph*, 2 June 1989.
21. P. Hainsworth, 'Northern Ireland: A European Role?', *Journal of Common Market Studies*, Vol. 20, No. 1 (September 1981), pp. 1–15.
22. *Irish Times*, 19 April 1975.
23. John Taylor, UUP MP and former MEP, *Irish Times*, 16 June 1992.
24. *Irish Times*, 12 October 1992; *Irish News*, 20 October 1992; *Irish Times*, 2 February and 24 May 1993.
25. *Irish Times*, 13 July 1984; *Agence Europe*, 11 October 1988; *Belfast Telegraph*, 12 October 1988.
26. DUP election material 1984; *Irish News*, 31 April 1984.
27. Peter Robinson, DUP MP, *Financial Times*, 1 January 1992.
28. *Belfast Newsletter*, 4 June 1992.
29. *Belfast Newsletter*, 12 November 1993.
30. These interviews are discussed in greater depth in J. Anderson and J. Goodman, 'European Integration and Irish Integration: Contradictions of Regionalism and Nationalism', *Journal of European Urban and Regional Studies*, Vol. 1, No. 1 (1994), pp. 49–62.
31. The Reserved powers are detailed in A. Quekett, *The Constitution of Northern Ireland, Part 2: The Government of Ireland Act and Subsequent*

Enactments (Belfast: HMSO, 1933), pp. 7–15. This was predicted in 1972 by Garret FitzGerald, later leader of *Fine Gael* and *Taoiseach*: see G. FitzGerald, *Towards a New Ireland* (London: Charles Knight, 1972), p. 109.

32. H. Logue, Submission to the Opsahl Commission (1992); B. Conlon, 'Integrating: Europe, Ireland', *Fortnight*, May 1990, pp. 8–9.

33. K. Boyle and T. Hadden, *Northern Ireland: The Choice* (Harmondsworth: Penguin, 1994), p. 146.

34. *Irish Times*, 17 October 1988; *Financial Times*, 17 August 1986 and 16 November 1990; *Agence Europe*, 4206, 18 November 1985; P. Loughlin 'The Anglo-Irish Agreement: Federal Arrangement or Affirmation of the Nation-State?', *Federalisme*, Vol. 3 (1991), pp. 183–97.

35. R. Rolston, 'Containment and its Failure: The British State and the Control of Conflict in Northern Ireland', in A. George (ed.), *Western State Terrorism* (New York: Routledge, 1991), pp. 155–80.

36. J. Anderson, 'Problems of Interstate Economic Integration: Northern Ireland and the Irish Republic in the Single European Market', *Political Geography*, Vol. 13, No. 1 (1994), pp. 53–73; for a Northern perspective see a speech delivered by George Quigley, Chair of the Ulster Bank and President of the Institute of Directors Ireland: 'An Island Economy' (1992); for perspectives in the Republic see *Ireland in Europe: A Shared Challenge, Economic Cooperation on the Island of Ireland in an Integrated Europe*, (Dublin: DSO, 1992).

37. *Irish Times*, 15 September 1992 and 28 October 1992; *Northern Ireland Structural Funds Plan 1994–1999* (Belfast: HMSO, 1993).

38. *Ulster Newsletter*, 25 January 1993; *Financial Times*, 16 December 1993.

39. *The Times*, 1 February 1995.

Index

Belfast *cont.*
  poverty in, 52
  Trades Council, 72–3
Belfast Newsletter, 32–3
Belfast Telegraph, 33, 38, 94, 150,
    153–5, 209–10
Bell, Martin, 175
Bell, Ronald, 142
Belleek, 23
Bennett Inquiry, 115
Beresford, David, 170
Beveridge Report, 52
Bevin, Ernest, 50, 89
Bew, Paul, 89, 95
Biggs-Davidson, John, 133, 142
Bing, Geoffrey, 79
Birkenhead, Lord, 28
Birmingham bombing, 113
Birmingham Six, 192
Bishopsgate bombing, 121, 194,
    200–1
Black and Tans, 19
Blackmore, Charles, 36
Blacksmiths' Union, 76
blanket protest, 115, 163, 175
Bleakley, David, 126
Bloody Sunday, 107, 176, 178
Boland v. An Taioseach, 109
Bonar Law, Andrew, 13, 16–18, 20,
    23
border campaign, 1956–62, 131
boundary commission, 25, 31, 36
Boyce, D. George, 31
Boyle, Kevin, 143
Boyson, Rhodes, 157–8
Brabourne, Lady, 116
Braine, Bernard, 142
Brett, Sir Charles, 96–7
Brighton bombing, 120
Bristol bombing, 115
Britain, 9
  constitution, 11
  deaths from terrorism in, 113,
    115–16, 119–21, 182, 200
  devolution in, 6, 43, 183
  and Europe, 111, 139, 224
  idea of federal reorganisation of,
    4, 13, 16
  Irish citizens' rights in, 66

and Irish Free State, 23–4
and Irish Home Rule, 2, 15–25,
    28
and Irish Republic, 7–8, 35, 65,
    80, 88–9, 92, 117–18, 121,
    123, 185, 189–90, 201
  miscarriages of justice in, 192
  neutrality towards Northern
    Ireland, 8, 22, 24, 66, 124,
    143, 197, 199–203, 206–7
  as persuader of the unionists,
    123, 185, 196, 201–2, 204,
    207–8
  relative unimportance of Northern
    Ireland to, 2–3, 10, 23–4, 98,
    110–11, 118, 139, 144–5,
    150–5, 160
  reluctance to intervene in
    Northern Ireland, 4, 6, 26,
    31, 62, 67, 74, 91, 96–8, 100,
    103–6, 112, 124, 129, 138, 171
  and Second World War, 47–8,
    50–2
  impact of Second World War on
    attitudes to Northern Ireland,
    61–2, 65–6
  security co-operation with the
    Irish Republic, 118, 120, 185
  role of SDLP in shaping policy,
    188, 195, 208
  strategic interests in Northern
    Ireland, 5–6, 22, 60–2, 65, 89,
    122, 143, 198, 202, 207
  impact of terrorism on policy, 2,
    102–3, 107–8, 113, 123–4,
    132, 135–6, 209
  and unionists, 2, 4–5, 8, 16, 26,
    63, 65–6, 88–9, 93, 96, 98–9,
    103–4, 141, 154, 183, 185, 209
British Army, 135, 207
  casualties, 105
  casualties inflicted by, 106–7
  deployed 'in aide of the civil
    power', 99, 105–6, 131
  and internment, 107, 126
  relations with the RUC, 105, 114
  reluctance to defend Northern
    Ireland, 19, 23–4
  and UWC strike, 110, 127

Wilson *cont.*
  and sending of troops to
    Northern Ireland, 99, 105
Wilson, Sir Henry, 19
Windlesham Report, 193
Winterton, Nicholas, 135, 142
Wood, Sir Kingsley, 52

Woodhouse, C.M., 142
Woolwich bombing, 113
Workers Party, 152, 214–15,
    217, 221–2
Worsthorne, Peregrine,
    180–1
Wright, Sir Oliver, 92–93